The Art of TRAVELING ITALY

AN INSIDER'S GUIDE TO TRAVELING FEARLESSLY AND WISELY™

by Sandy Serio Gregory

THE ART OF TRAVELING ITALY

AN INSIDER'S GUIDE TO TRAVELING FEARLESSLY AND WISELY™

Library of Congress Control Number: TXu 2- 285-349

Printed in the United States of America

First Edition

First Printing, 2021

ISBN: 978-0-578-32497-5

Imprint: Independently published

Che Bella Tours

chebellatours.com

A journey of a thousand miles begins with a single step.

- Lau Tzu

Above *Piazalle Michelangelo is the perfect place to enjoy a panoramic view of Florence.*

Photo by Janette Tepas Images

AN INSIDER'S GUIDE TO TRAVELING FEARLESSLY AND WISELY™

Why I wrote this book. *The Art of Traveling Italy* is written for Americans traveling to Italy. Traveling well is an art form in itself: in the harmonious cadence of a trip; in the delight of the senses through art, music and food; in the connection with people and cultures. Many, however, become so overwhelmed by the process and planning of travel that they set their dreams of exploration and experience aside in frustration or fear.

This book will open your heart and mind to all that Italy has to offer. It is full of tips, tricks and insights gained from my lifetime of travel and my long career as a tour director and tour operator. Use it as a framework from which to plan and prepare for your own trip and to empower you to travel fearlessly and wisely.

Each chapter begins with a musing about my own travel life, which has inspired me, challenged me and healed me.

You will also find:

- Important websites, in-country emergency contacts and phone numbers
- To-do lists, packing checklists, language cheat sheets and my favorite travel products
- Photos and recipes to inspire and excite
- Pages where you can jot down notes and memories from your own trip

As a bonus for purchasing this printed book, I would like to include a **free pdf version** to put on your phone or tablet to reference while you travel. Email me at sandy@chebellatours.com, attach your proof of purchase to recieve the pdf file..

Throughout the book, you will be introduced to my tour company, Che Bella Tours. We warmly invite you to travel with us to share our experience, knowledge and resources as we move through bella Italia.

I hope you enjoy my book. And, as I always say on tour,

Andiamo! Let's go!

Sandy Gregory

Founder, Che Bella Tours

chebellatours.com

sandy@chebellatours.com

Scan this code to go to the Che Bella Tours Marketplace for direct links to products, books and films listed in this book.

THIS BOOK IS DEDICATED
TO ALL OF THE TRAVELERS
WHO SEEK NEW LANDSCAPES.

CONTENTS

Andiamo!

WANDERLUST AND WISDOM 8-13

HOW I BECAME A ROAD WARRIOR AND TRAVELED THE WORLD

- *My Favorite Things to do in Italy* 12

TRAVELING IN ITALY 14- 45

DANCING IN THE MOMENT

- *Sandy, Your Tour Director* 18
- *Che Bella Tours* 19
- *Che Bella Tours' Suggested Itineraries* 23
  - *Italian Dreams* 24
  - *A Taste of Italy's North* 26
  - *Italy's Northern Lakes and Veneto Wine Road* 28
  - *A Romantic Winter Getaway* 30
  - *Piedmont and Lake Maggiore* 32
  - *Tuscany and the Wine Country* 34
  - *Tuscany and Siena's Palio* 36
  - *Le Marche and Umbria* 38
  - *Puglia, Naples and the Amalfi Coast* 40
  - *Bella Sicily* 42

PREPARING FOR YOUR TRIP... 46-89

CLOUDLESS SKIES, CLEAR VISION AND HAPPY TRAVELS

- *Planning Your Trip is Half the Fun* 48
- *Mindful and Responsible Travel* 52
- *Safety and Security* 54
- *Passports and Travel Docs* 56
- *Trip Insurance* 60
- *Planes* 62
- *Trains* 66
- *Automobiles* 70
- *La Bella Figura* 72
- *The Anatomy of a Well-Packed Suitcase* 74
- *Hotels, Villas and Views* 76
- *Out and About* 82
- *My Favorite Books* 84
- *My Favorite Films* 86

EATING IN ITALY 90-137

PARLA COME MANGI = SPEAK THE LANGUAGE OF YOUR FOOD

- *The Italian Restaurant Experience* 92
- *The Italian Menu* 94
- *Il Conto* 104
- *Eating Seasonally* 106
- *Coffee* 108
- *Pizza* 110
- *Pasta* 112
- *Formaggio* 116
- *Tagliere* 118
- *Olive Oil* 120
- *Balsamico* 122
- *Gelato* 124
- *Cooking Lessons* 126
- *Wine Tastings* 128
  - *Noteworthy Italian Wines* 132

SHOPPING IN ITALY 135-155

ITALIAN SHOES AND OTHER DELICIOUS THINGS

- *Planning What You Can Bring Home* 140
- *My Favorite Things: What to Buy, Where and How* 143
  - *Artisan Shops* 144
  - *Local Markets* 150
  - *The Grocery* 152

HOW TO VIEW ART AND MAKE IT FUN.............................. 156-197

RESTLESS NOMAD. CREATIVE SPIRIT.

- *Art is Everywhere* 158
- *Painting* 160
- *Sculpture* 164
- *Architecture* 170
- *Antiquities* 176
- *Iconic Italian Design* 182
- *Music* 184
- *Taking Great Travel Photos* 186

MAKE IT WITH LOVE.......... 198-263

RECIPES FROM MY ITALIAN TRAVELS FOR THE AMERICAN KITCHEN

MAKING MEMORIES 264

TRAVEL CHEAT SHEETS 270-281

- *Important Contacts* 271
- *Packing Checklists* 272
- *Learn a Little Italian* 274

WANDERLUST AND WISDOM

HOW I BECAME A ROAD WARRIOR AND TRAVELED THE WORLD

Midday Rome is when I take refuge from the crushing tourists and scorching sun. My hotel room overlooks the Pantheon. Its massive dome and giant columns tower over Piazza Rotunda. It is spring. The crowds are in full bloom. A conga line of tourists smile for their selfies as they push onto the portico. People watchers sip their spritzes. The rhapsody of a violin fills the piazza. I pinpoint a woman in the crowd and watch her as she scans her guidebook, then gazes up at the dome. I think to myself, "Who are you? And how did you find yourself in this piazza?"

How did I find myself in this piazza?

For many of us, the thirst to travel cannot be quenched. Is it nurture? Or nature? According to some scientists, it might be a gene — DRD4 7R — dubbed "the wanderlust gene," which makes us feel creative, curious, restless and alive.

I think I was born with this travel gene. My first taste of wanderlust came very early in life from my Aunt Dorothy. I was nine years old in 1969 when I watched her head out from our home in Chicago. Her butter yellow VW bug was stuffed with everything she owned. She pointed west, waved goodbye and took off to adventures unknown. The next few years took her to Tahiti, Hawaii, Alaska and Europe. She even was a crew member on a Windjammer Cruise. Her summers of love were in San Francisco, where she lived for 17 years.

During that time, Aunt Dorothy gave me my first love beads, a Chinese kite, a yogurt maker, a sprout farm and 150 sets of chopsticks. She taught me how to stir-fry, practice yoga and put cool patches on my jeans. For my college graduation, she gave me ... the VW bug!

However, the most important gift she gave me was inspiration. Our family outings often involved going to Customs Viewing at O'Hare airport (remember when we could do that?). We eagerly waited to spot Aunt Dorothy as she connected back through Chicago to San Francisco from her latest international adventure. I stood nose against the glass, anxiously searching the lines of weary travelers until I found her floppy hat. She would look up, smile and wave. I scoured the maps and guidebooks she sent me to follow her routes, plastered my walls with her postcards and dreamed of the day I would be boarding a plane. I was destined to be an adventuress.

She stood in the storm, and when the wind did not blow her way, she adjusted her sails.

Elizabeth Edwards

Above *The long and winding road*

Photo by Mark Rangell

Next page *The view of the Pantheon in Piazza della Rotunda in Rome*

Photo by Janette Tepas Images

M·AGRIPPA·L·F·COS·TERTIVM·FECIT

I was the oldest of four in a slightly crazy tight-knit Italian/Polish family. My parents were each the firstborn in their families. Perhaps being the first of two firsts explains my determination and perseverance. Add to that, I'm a Leo, which explains the rest. To me, life always has been a great adventure. I can't help but get involved. My tendency to be at life's center also meant I grew up to a chorus from my siblings of that famous 70s line from Jan Brady, "Marcia, Marcia, Marcia."

A born nomad. I thankfully and intentionally took advantage of the opportunities available to me and tripped the "light fantastic" through high school and college. As a high school junior, I was a foreign exchange student in Oaxaca, Mexico, with AFS Intercultural Programs. Today, this amazing organization brings students and families together in 113 countries around the globe. There are over 500,000 alumni like myself and over 50,000 volunteers who make it possible for almost 12,000 students a year to study, live and learn about another country. The goal remains to help develop knowledge, skills and understanding that we need to create a more just and peaceful world.

I studied graphic design, advertising and creative writing at the University of Illinois. My junior year was spent studying in Florence and traveling throughout Europe.

I married in my late 20s. My husband and I were YUPPIES, then DINKS. He quickly scaled the corporate ladder, while I grew a busy graphic design business. We raised two boys, Jackson and Joseph. In 1997, we put down roots in Denver.

Then the wave crashed. When the planes hit the towers and the economy went bust, it was the beginning of the end of my marriage. A corporate commute that lasted two years, a reluctant stint in the car business, financial failure and eventual divorce forced me to re-evaluate my life.

The 50,000-mile tune up. It didn't take five years in the car business to quickly realize I needed a few minor repairs. My first decision, "Have less so I can do more." When I listed our home, I ordered an 8' x 8' x 8' storage pod. What fit into that pod went with me to my next life. The rest was left to history.

Above *Aunt Dorothy 1969*

I scoured the maps and guidebooks she sent me to follow her routes; plastered my walls with her postcards; and dreamed of the day it would be me boarding that plane. I knew then I who was going to be: an adventuress.

Sandy Serio Gregory

Above *Aunt Dorothy on tour with me in 2011, tossing coins into the Trevi Fountain to assure our return.*

A whole new world, a new fantastic point of view. I posed the questions I needed to help figure out what was next. Spreadsheets have always been key to making my big decisions, and as my "What-To-Do-With-My-Life" spreadsheet evolved, travel became a recurrent theme.

"I'm a traveler. I'm a nomad! I'm an adventuress!" In reality, I just wanted to run away from home. Whatever the reason, it was time to get back on the road. I've always been the go-to-gal when it's time to plan a trip. My happiest memories have included a suitcase and a plane ticket. But, I was broke and needed to be *paid to travel.*

So I Googled, "Be paid to travel." Teaching English as a foreign language? Not for me. Importing or exporting? Maybe. Hopping over to Italy to see about George Clooney? That ship had passed.

Tour Director. Well, now we're talking! Ironically and fortuitously, two associates from my ex's corporate days gave me the advice I needed. Scott and Jen both worked for Globus, one of the largest tour operators in the world. "Travel. Art. History. Cuisine. Comedy. You're built for this! Go get certified," they said, and promptly directed me to three places in the world you could get certified as an International Tour Director — The Netherlands, San Francisco and Denver. The *International Guide Academy* web address, *bepaidtotravel.com,* cinched my decision. The Academy was right down the street from where I lived. My stars aligned. I completed my certification, got a job as a Tour Captain with a local start-up and set my course.

The end and the beginning. The gavel fell to end 23 years of marriage at the same time I was preparing to leave for my first tours in Italy. What I thought was going to be the lowest point of my life was actually a rebirth. All I could say was, "I gotta go." Just like that, I drove away from that courthouse, from that man who was so much of my history and hopped a plane to Rome.

Since 2009, I have lead tours throughout the world. Many of my guests have traveled with me again and again.

Photos by Sandy Gregory and guests

Good times. Great friends. Making memories that last a lifetime.

My Favorite Things to do in Italy

When on tour, my guests always ask: "Where is your favorite place?" My answer: "My favorite place is where I am at that moment."

Traveling still makes my heart skip. No matter how many times I have been somewhere, I always learn something new. Seeing a city through the eyes of my guests — who often are seeing it for the first time — is something I never take for granted.

I have traveled to more than 39 countries, but I will tell you, my heart belongs to Italy. I am of Italian heritage, I lived in Italy and I have had the wonderful opportunity to bring guests there over and over. I developed wonderful friendships and an excellent in-country team. Seeing the sights and souls of this magical country brings me back again and again. Here are some of my personal favorite things to do. Perhaps they will inspire you too.

MILAN

- The roof of the Duomo
- La Scala Opera House: six tiers of red velvet and gold with hundreds of years of history
- Shopping in the Brera
- Risotto Milanese served in a parmesan crust

THE LAKE DISTRICT

- Cruising on Lake Como to a long lunch on Isola Comacina
- The walk from Portofino to St. Margherita en Ligure
- Taking in the waters on Lake Garda

PIEDMONT

- A day on the Borromeo Islands
- The boat ride and meditative walk on Orta San Giulio
- Being a foodie in Alba, especially in the autumn when the white truffles are hunted and served

VENICE

- The early morning, walking through the quiet, empty streets to the Rialto Market
- The evening, in the Piazza San Marco, listening to the orchestras
- The view of the Grand Canal from the Accademia Bridge
- The Bovolo spiral staircase
- Concerts in the Chiesa Santo Stefano
- Getting lost

VERONA

- Writing my letter to Juliet
- Seeing a concert in the Arena

PORTOFINO

- A lazy seafood lunch at the port
- Hiking up to San Fruttuoso

BOLOGNA

- Sharing a tagliere at the market
- Modena balsamico
- The Ferrari Museum with my kids

THE CINQUE TERRE

- Hiking from Monterosso al Mare to Vernazza

LUCCA

- Biking the city wall

FLORENCE

- Watching the sunset over Florence from Piazelle Michelangelo
- Michelangelo's slaves
- Shopping, shopping, shopping!
- The artisans of the Oltrarno
- Having an Aperol spritz on the Luccese rooftop — what a view!

CHIANTI

- Wine tastings and long lunches
- Sampling wines from all over Italy at my favorite Greve Enoteca
- Solociccia at Dario in Panzano

SAN GIMIGNANO

- Chocolate gelato from Dondoli
- My olive wood "superstore"
- Morning hikes through the vineyard

SIENA

- The Palio horserace
- Men in tights on parade
- The striped marble interior of St. Catherine's Cathedral
- Rooftop evenings above the Campo
- Mushroom hunting and cooking with Chef Gina Stipo

CERTALDO

- Cooking with Giuseppina while looking over the landscape
- Driving a vintage Fiat Cinquecento

CORTONA

- Hiking to the convent
- Passeggiatta (the evening walk)
- The Etruscan Museum
- Paola's ribollita

AREZZO

- Piero de la Francesca frescos as explained by my friend and associate, Dr. Susanna Buricchi
- Lunch under the arcades of Piazza Grande with Genevre's homemade pasta
- Scouring the antique market to add to my linen collection

PERUGIA

- Eurochocolate Festival

ASSISI

- Placing a candle at the tomb of St. Francis and making time to quietly reflect

THE APENNINES

- The drive up to the La Verna Franciscan Sanctuary through the mountain forest to see the della Robbia ceramic reliefs

ORVIETO

- The nautical details of the Duomo facade

MONTEPULCIANO

- Boscarelli Vino Nobile

MONTALCINO

- Brunello and Mozart

PIENZA

- The panorama of the Val d'Orcia
- Pecorino cheese
- Flower boxes

PESARO

- The Pomodoro orb on the beach

ROME

- Opening my hotel window to a view of the Pantheon
- The Fountain of the Four Rivers at night
- The Aventine Keyhole to see St. Peter's Dome
- Early morning entrance into St. Peter's to spend quiet time enjoying Michelangelo's Pieta and then hiking up the cupola
- Bernini's Apollo Chasing Daphne at the Borghese Gallery
- The Borghese Gardens, an oasis of green from the crowded city

NAPLES

- Absorbing the passion of my friend, Luigi, as he describes his city, which is also part of my own Italian heritage
- The Gabinetto Segreto in the Archeological Museum. Oh my!
- Pizza Margharita - simple and perfect

SORRENTO

- Lunch with a view on the Amalfi Coast drive
- Seeing the night lights twinkling in Naples at the foot of Mt. Vesuvius from my balcony
- The drive to Donna Sofia

POSITANO

- Linguini with clam sauce on the beach
- Splurging on a cocktail at Le Sireneus
- Lemon granita
- White linen

CAPRI

- A private driver
- A fresh, warm sfogliatella before heading up the chairlift to Ana Capri
- Hiking Monte Solaro
- Swimming in the Green Grotto

SICILY

- The Passion Play during Easter
- Watching the fishermongers fillet the catch of the day
- Hiking Mt. Etna
- Taormina views

FRANCIS: THE PEOPLE'S POPE

It was a crisp October morning when I traveled to Assisi with my last group of the season. This itinerary was planned to the minute. I had done it a hundred times. But that day, I welcomed an exciting deviation to the schedule: The Feast of St. Francis, 2013.

Although Pope for only eight months, Francis was already leading a kind of revolution, one taking place in people's hearts and not merely behind the walls of the Vatican. Like his chosen namesake, the 13th century St. Francis of Assisi, his agenda was clear: to reform and rebuild the church in a time of turmoil. He saw the church taking focus on environmentalism. A lapsed Catholic, I was encouraged and curious to see The Papa.

Tourists and pilgrims irreverently jostled each other in the massive crowds. Jumbotrons were placed around the city for all to see. Larger than life, Pope Francis seemed perfectly at home in the birthplace of his saintly namesake. His simple white robes were designed to set the tone of simplicity and pastoral humility. He stepped out of the Popemobile, walked slowly through the town and stopped often. The crowd reached out to him, many clasped his hand and leaned in close to share their thoughts and feelings. He bent down and greeted the children. He hugged a disabled man.

When he arrived at the entrance to the Basilica, he took to the pulpit. I caught bits and pieces of his message, as my language skills are always a work in progress. The Papa spoke of the challenges of today's society and shared homespun wisdom. A main theme was, "focusing on the family rather than individual rights and privileges." "Marriage is a real vocation," the Pope explained, "Just like the priesthood and religious life."

He paused for a moment in quiet contemplation. From the silence of the crowd, one woman shouted out to him, "Papa, what can I do to encourage my 40-year-old son to get married?" Without missing a beat, he looked out into the crowd, and with a devilish grin replied, "Stop ironing his shirts!"

TRAVELING IN ITALY

DANCING IN THE MOMENT

Over the years, my guests have touched me in many ways. My world has become an odd, magical adventure. I am doing what I was built to do ... take people on vacation.

March 15, 2010: I didn't cry at all this week.

Morning light never streamed into my brother's basement, where I had been sleeping since my 2009 divorce. But today, a spring ray peaked through the tiny corner window and the warmth on my face woke me up. The Ariel comforter on my niece's Little Mermaid big girl bed twisted around my feet. I stared up at the low ceiling as I did every morning, rearranging my covers and checking in with my surroundings: gym equipment and ski boots in the corner, tangled Wii cords and VCR tapes on the brown couch, a beanbag chair slumped on the carpet that smelled of old dog.

My family gave me a soft landing after my separation, but the basement was still hard. The cold winter months underground had trapped me on a dark hamster wheel of mental chatter about my ex, as well as the obvious dip in my standard of living. But on the flip side, these months also provided a cocoon from which to prepare for my future.

My first job begins. Going to the office. "World Headquarters" of our small start-up tour company was strewn throughout the owner's house. Every horizontal surface was a workstation. The fax machine rattled on the washing machine. Our meetings took place at the kitchen table, complete with a noisy toddler and the sweet smell of chocolate chip cookies baking. There we began to build a company offering small group tours to Europe.

Back in my own basement, amidst the discarded décor, I prepared for my new life. My commentary and trip notes were lined up and neatly organized. My passport sat atop a pile of crisp Euros. My suitcase sat upright, carefully packed and at the ready. This "travel still life" made me smile, representing a year of preparation, certification and validation.

I emerged from the basement into the sunlight, stunned and blinking, armed with everything I thought I needed from those kitchen table meetings. I was ready to travel as a Certified International Tour Director. Or was I?

I headed to Italy to start a new chapter in my life ... and become part of a much bigger story.

I was ready to travel as a Certified International Tour Director. Or was I?

Sandy Gregory

***Above** Where will I be going next time?*

Photo by Susan LaBrie

My first tour was a whirlwind of dealing with everything from Caravaggio to coffee, confirmations to counseling, navigating motor coaches, lugging suitcases, doing stand-up comedy and a lot of, "I'll be happy to take care of that for you." The tour finished on the Amalfi Coast. Looking over the Bay of Naples, I raised a glass of prosecco to myself. Exhausted but happy, I looked forward to hopping a train to meet my second group in Milan. But my plans soon erupted.

An ash cloud shut down Europe.

In late March, a volcano in Iceland began to quietly sputter. On April 14, it blew. More than 300 airports and their corresponding airspace were cleared. Over 100,000 flights were cancelled, affecting seven million travelers in what was, at that time, the largest air-traffic shutdown since WWII. Thousands were stranded all over Europe. I was in the thick of it.

My job was clear — get from Sorrento to Milan with the hope that by the time I got there, the ash cloud would clear, flights would resume and I would be there to meet my guests to start our tour. I would need experience I did not yet have and training which I did not yet get, to follow procedures that were not yet created to pick up people I did not yet know. It was only my second tour. I was now on the Volcano Express.

I had a lot of lessons to learn.

I boarded the train to Milan. Before I could find my seat, the train was cancelled. Struggling with my suitcase, I disembarked and was caught up in a sea of people, moving like a school of fish toward the growing lines at the ticket counters. Everyone was trying to rebook, but nobody knew where to go. The departure board showed that while all of the express trains were shut down, the regional trains were still running. I knew I needed to keep moving north.

It was time to *faccia una mafia*. The term "*mafia*" means "acting as a protector against the arrogance of the powerful" and is equated, of course, with organized crime. In everyday Italian-American families like mine, however, *faccia una mafia* means "to do the workaround." "You do for me. I do for you. No one else needs to know. *Basta*." I'll explain it like this: My father was an obstetrician in our town, and would always say, "Get your car insurance from Jack. I delivered all of his kids." Or, "Have Billy work on your car. I delivered three of his kids." Our family never used the Yellow Pages.

I called our company driver, Luigi, who was more than happy to take me through the back door of his cousin's travel agency. I bought a stack of regional and intercity general seating tickets to get me on any train I needed.

Traveler Lesson #1: Learn to think on your feet ... and *faccia una mafia*.

Like a freight-hopping hobo, I didn't stop moving for two days. At the small stations that became part of my ever-changing route, I made split-second decisions to board the few trains that were still running. Naples to Formia. Formia to Rome. Rome to Arezzo. Arezzo to Florence. Rolling hills of spring vines flashed and faded past my window as we creaked and crawled northward, but there was no sign of the ash we were supposed to be running away from.

While part of my job was to romanticize train travel on our tours, right now it was just a blur. People were wedged in, filling every available seat, standing in the aisle and sitting on their suitcases. Some could nap, their heads bobbing. Others clung wide-eyed to anything that would stabilize them from the shifting and rocking. Florence to Reggio Emilia. Reggio Emilia to Parma, where my journey stalled. The Italian train system was completely shut down.

Traveler Lesson #2: Travel with a smaller suitcase.

People had set up camp all over the Parma train station. Panicked tourists were negotiating with taxi drivers who were proposing pricing somewhere between "more than the trip is worth" and "a lot more than the trip was worth." Locals became instant entrepreneurs, offering their personal cars, scooters, motorcycles, bicycles, boats, barns, rooms and homes to the highest bidder. The finger purse, the prayer clasp, the chin flick, the forearm curl – the Italian body language was flying – and I wanted no part of it.

My flip phone was blowing up with text updates from my boss. Two of my guests out of the original 16 scheduled would actually make it. I had only a few hours before they would land. I quickly hit the ATM. Cash in hand, I ducked into a side street and hunted for a driver to take me to Milan. You guessed it, within a few hundred steps, "Ciao bella, do you need a ride? Come with me, *cara*, and I can take you wherever you want to go." I hustled quickly away from Romeo and followed my gut right back to the station.

Traveler Lesson #3: Make good choices.

Back amidst the crowd, I began to eavesdrop on conversations. It didn't take long to find what I was looking for ... a couple trying to figure out how to get to Milan. With any luck, they would be safe traveling companions and split the hefty fare. I approached them with my plan and the three of us walked right past Romeo to find an older gentleman named Lucca, a few blocks up, eager to take us for a mere 750 Euro. Italians have a generosity and sweetness about them, but also are very complex and direct. Lucca wanted that money. In turn, he provided delightful conversation and bottles of water. When we arrived at my hotel, my new friend, Lucca, not only lugged my heavy suitcase into the lobby, but also took me to Malpensa airport at no extra charge. I was ready to meet my guests who were — hopefully — showing up.

Traveler Lesson #4: Appreciate acts of kindness and generosity, but mind your dollars and sense.

With minutes to spare, I gathered myself and waited at baggage claim with a smile and a sign for my two guests, Tena and Richard. "Where is the group?" they asked. I answered, "Well, you're it."

The next afternoon, our reluctant pre-booked, pre-paid driver transferred us from Milan to our Varenna hotel, nestled high above the shores of Lake Como. The driver's speed gave us all a strong sense he would have much preferred to be on the entrepreneurial highway, hoping to pick up a stranded tourist and making some big money before his day was over. The road narrowed and wound tightly through the mountains. We peered into the void of the cliff face, glancing wide-eyed at each other and relieved when we arrived at the hotel.

The crisp, blue view of the lake was breathtaking as we entered through the expansive veranda. Guests were gathered around tables, the hum of their conversation interrupted often by bursts of laughter. The smell of cigarettes, garlic and sizzling lake trout wasn't offensive, but rather warm and welcoming. We joined the crowd of diners. Over a long, luxurious meal, Richard and Tena shared their story of how they came to be at this table. It was a story of two 69-year-olds celebrating health and life.

In 2009, Tena was diagnosed with a condition called FMD, a narrowing of the arteries that led to a stroke. At the same time, Richard was diagnosed with prostate cancer. For a year, the two of them took the 30-minute drive daily from their home in Baytown, Texas, to a radiation treatment center in Houston. They were tense and frightened, but instead of focusing solely on weighty medical procedures, they turned those days into an adventure. Their appointments were scheduled early, freeing them up to explore other activities. One day was yoga class, another was for shopping and a movie while the rest of the week was for ballroom dancing classes.

The hum stopped, and the diners turned to watch, enchanted by this couple floating across the dance floor as one, with a passion and physicality that were beyond anything I could have imagined for two people who spent the last year battling illness.

"Dancing is in the moment," Tena explained. "You get swept away by the music and have to concentrate on the choreography. Our emotions were all over the place, and the different dance styles we learned allowed us to put those emotions into movement. It gave us something to look forward to and we did it together." Within a year, their medical treatments were a speck in their rear view mirror.

Richard and Tena continued to take that 30-minute ride to Houston; however, this time it was to join their team in gowns and tuxes as competitive ballroom dancers. In April of 2010, healthy and ready to travel, they were ready to celebrate life. With that came my group tour to Milan, Lake Como, the Cinque Terre, and the South of France.

After dinner, we walked to the end of the veranda to watch the sunset and compare our odysseys to Milan. Richard rerouted his flights, considering options through South America, Morocco, Turkey and Portugal. There were stops and starts, quick connections and uncertainty, but sure enough, two days later, they made it, assured by my boss that his "experienced Tour Captain" would be ready to go and waiting at the airport. With that fortitude, it was no surprise these two got to Italy in spite of an ash cloud.

Traveler Lesson #5: Go with the flow and be ready to pivot.

After dinner, Richard said to me, "Get your computer and Google 'Shall We Dance' on YouTube. *Shall We Dance* is a romantic comedy about a bored, overworked lawyer who, upon first sight of a beautiful instructor, signs up for ballroom dancing lessons. That night Jennifer Lopez, Richard Gere and Richard Hallum taught me the tango. We cleared a small area in the corner of the veranda. Richard cupped my hand, and as the beautiful dance instructor in the movie challenged her student, we also began.

"Don't say anything. Don't think. Don't move unless you feel it." Left foot forward, right sweeps to the side, two quick steps back, leaving left crossing right, right foot back, left sweeps across and both feet together. Repeat.

Our dance ended, and Richard held out his hand to his bride, pulled her close and wrapped his arm around her waist. The hum stopped and the diners turned to watch, enchanted by this couple floating across the dance floor as one, with a passion and physicality that were beyond anything I could have imagined for two people who spent the last year battling illness.

We arrived back at the hotel from dinner the next night, surprised to find the entire veranda cleared of furniture. An effervescent woman named Susanna blew in and pulled me over to the stereo, where some of the hotel guests gathered with smiles of anticipation. "I guess you better go get your computer," Richard shrugged. Of course, the country was still shut down! No one was going anywhere. So that night, and the next and the next, people from all over the world, with no place to go, shared the international language of dance.

Richard and Tena demonstrated the basic steps as we formed a line behind them, mimicking their movements and sweeping counter clockwise across the veranda. "First, the embrace. Follow your partner like a mirror," he explained. Some couples struggled over who was going to lead, doing their own thing, stepping on each other's feet, bumping shoulders and eventually settling into the familiar noodle arm "clutch and sway." Others were totally in the zone.

Richard continued, "Let go and let the man lead. The tango is not a dance – it's a feeling. Embrace the music and the melodrama." Smouldering looks of passion and desire gave way to uncontrollable giggles in a multitude of languages. Each couple was in their own intimate moment, while at the same time connected to a group of strangers moving to the music. Stranded. Vulnerable. Embracing this beautiful and unexpected experience together. "That," Richard said, "is tango."

Traveler Lesson #6: Sometimes you've got to make space for the dance, so clear the furniture.

This wonderful man was like a gladiator conquering prostate cancer, at the same time his courageous wife recovered from a stroke. They learned how to ballroom dance, got to Italy during a continent-wide shutdown and taught an entire hotel full of stranded internationals to tango.

As we moved on to the Cinque Terre and France, more of my guests were able to fly in, join the tour and swing into our dance. We embraced the challenging hike over the seaside mountains of the Cinque Terre. In Nice, I did another *faccia una mafia* and had my guests' rooms changed so they had balconies overlooking the park and the Mediterranean. We passed through Monaco and on to a lovely little town called Vence, one of the most beautiful towns in the French Riviera. We stopped at an inn Richard and Tena had enjoyed 14 years earlier. They had such fond memories of the chef's roast chicken and lavender crème brûlée, I surprised them by returning there for dinner that evening. The tour went great, I found my footing and knew I really was doing what I was built to do.

Traveler lesson #7: Life is full of situations outside of our control. Follow the itinerary, but leave room for happy surprises.

Richard's 70th birthday was to fall on the night of our tour's Farewell Dinner. I wanted to make it special. This wonderful man was like a gladiator conquering prostate cancer, at the same time his courageous wife recovered from a stroke. They learned how to ballroom dance, got to Italy during a continent-wide shutdown and taught an entire hotel full of stranded internationals to tango.

The perfect birthday gift waited for me at the market. In Italy, you can find pasta in just about any shape you can imagine. You also find the male organ just about everywhere: carvings in the front of homes, graffiti, mosaics, frescoes and statues. A few of my guests raised their eyebrows when Richard opened his present — a big bag of penis pasta. He took a double take, roared with laughter and read my card out loud, "You've certainly got balls, Dick. It's been a joy to travel with you. Learn from you. And dance with you. Think of me when you serve these up. But remember what I taught you: cook pasta to *al dente* only. You don't want these to be limp!"

Traveler Lesson #8: One of the important lessons in dancing is learning the art of leading and following. Lead your group, learn from them, and most of all, keep dancing.

Sandy, Your Tour Director

Che Bella is hatched. After seven years working as a Tour Captain, leading tours all over the world, schlepping our guests' suitcases (which led to three bulging hernias), and what was becoming too many moving parts, I decided it was time to move on. I was more than ready to focus my energies on my own tour company, and created Che Bella Tours.

Follow the itinerary! My family teases me that I always want everyone to "follow the itinerary!" Whether on paper or metaphorically, my itineraries show me the way. I use them as a framework to not only create trips of a lifetime, but also to keep me moving forward and focused. This focus has allowed Che Bella Tours to thrive, with partners all over the world, each individual bringing a deep wealth of knowledge, skills and resources.

Above left *Giving an introduction to the day on the motor coach. I'm always honing my commentary.*

Above right *Dancing in the moment during the aqua alta in Venice. "Aqua alta" literally means "high water." During the autumn and winter, thanks to a combination of the tides, a strong south wind and the periodic movement of sea waters, the sea often bubbles up into the city. The area around St. Mark's Square is the lowest on the island ... and therefore, the first to get flooded.*

Left *The Loggia dei Lanzi in the Piazza della Signoria is filled with sculptures and stories.*

Photos by assorted guests.

Che Bella (kay BEHL-lah) in Italian means "how beautiful."

The beauty of travel is not only about museums, hotels and restaurants, but also about the unforgettable feelings you experience and the memories you create. It's about being adventurous and open minded. At Che Bella Tours, we craft tours rich in what we are passionate about — good-life experiences for culture seekers to savor and treasure. We like to think of ourselves as travel mixologists. Our goal is to create the perfect blend of personal passions, cultural encounters, famous landmarks, secret hideaways, art, cuisine, literature and wellness. We add a spicy dash of the unexpected and provide plenty of time to savor the flavors. How beautiful is that?

I hope you enjoy this chapter, which outlines my favorite itineraries.

Traveling in Italy with Che Bella Tours

Above *Arriving in Venice by private boat with Che Bella Tours*

Photo by Sandy Gregory

SMALL GROUP TOURS AND CONCIERGE TRAVEL SERVICES

CHEBELLATOURS.COM

Previous page *The Tuscan countryside is a magical place where time seems to stand still. Dark green rows of Cyprus trees line the fields of olive groves and grapevines. Patches of sunflowers stand at attention as they march tidily down the side of a slope.*

Below *The hills of San Gimignano. Centuries of history weave into one of the world's most beautiful landscapes.*

Right *Stunning contemporary sculptures contrast with old-world charm at one of our favorite villas just outside of Florence.*

Photos by Sandy Gregory

ITALY
Bolzano
TRENTINO-ALTO ADIGE
Belluno
FRIULI-VENEZIA GIULIA
Tarviso
Udine
Trento
Pordenone
VENETO
Vicenza
Treviso
Trieste
Verona
Padova
Venice
Rovigo
Sondrio
Verbania
Lecco
Bergamo
VALLE D'AOSTA
Aosta
Varese
Como
Biela
Novara
LOMBARDY
Brescia
Vercelli
Milan
PIEDMONT
Pavia
Lodi
Cremona
Turin
Piacenza
Mantova
Asli
Alessandria
Parma
Ferrara
Modena
Reggio nell'Emilia
Bologna
Cuneo
Genoa
Savona
LIGURIA
EMILIA-ROMAGNA
Ravenna
Imperia
La Spezia
Massa
Forlì
Rimini
Pistoia
Prato
Lucca
Pesaro
Pisa
Florence
Livorno
Arezzo
Ancona
TUSCANY
Perugia
MARCHE
UMBRIA
Ascoli Piceno
Elba
Grosseto
Terni
Teramo
Pescara
Viterbo
Rieti
Chieti
L'Aquila
LAZIO
ABRUZZO
VATICAN CITY
ROME
Isernia
MOLISE
Latina
Frosinone
Campobasso
Foggia
Barletta
Benevento
Bari
Caserta
CAMPANIA
PUGLIA
Avellino
Potenza
Naples
Matera
Taranto
Brindisi
Salerno
BASILICATA
Lecce
Otranto
Olbia
Tempio Pausania
Sassari
Nuoro
Sardinia
SARDEGNA
Oristano
Lanusei
Sanluri
Carbonia
Cagliari
CALABRIA
Cosenza
Crotone
Catanzaro
ISOLE EOLIE
Vibo Valentia
Messina
Reggio di Calabria
Palermo
Trapani
SICILIA
Enna
Caltanissetta
Catania
Agrigento
Gela
Siracusa
Ragusa
Sicily
Pantelleria (ITALY)

Suggested Italy Itineraries

Above *Few places in this world are as photogenic as Venice. It is pure magic as the sun is setting in this colorful city, making it the perfect time to take a gondola ride.*

Photo by Sandy Gregory

My job is to move my guests from place to place; however, the more I move around, the more I have come to appreciate staying put. Traveling too quickly and trying to see too much in a short time wears you out both mentally and physically. That's why at Che Bella Tours we prioritize consistency and contentment over stop-offs and drive-bys. The gift of soaking it all in brings a healthy view of the world so you return home rested and refreshed, rather than travel-weary.

Traveling can be a costly investment. Minimize the risk when you call on us to create the perfect guided or independent travel itinerary. We work closely with groups who want a personalized, private experience. Che Bella Tours is creative travel and the partner you want when planning your trip of a lifetime.

chebellatours.com

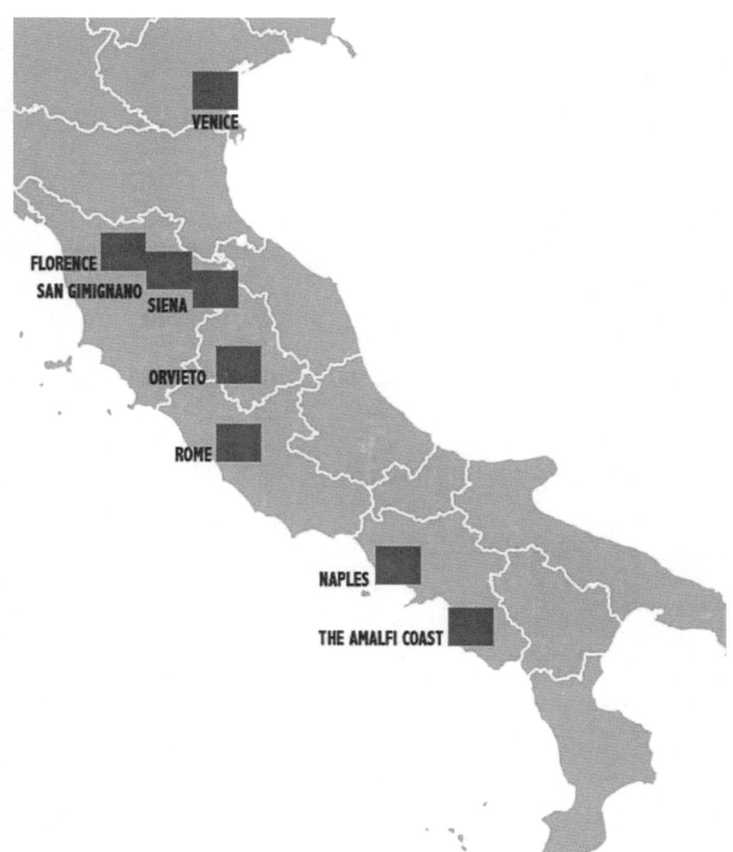

Italian Dreams

Travel to Italy's great cities for the perfect mixture of everything this country has to offer. This itinerary is perfect for the first-time traveler to Italy.

VENICE

FLORENCE

A TUSCAN VILLA

SAN GIMIGNANO

SIENA

ORVIETO

ROME

NAPLES

THE AMALFI COAST

Previous page, top
Santa Maria del Fiore, the Duomo, lights up Florence at night.

Previous page, bottom
At the peak of power in the 13th century, San Gimignano had 72 towers. Today there are 15 still standing. Le Torre Grossa of San Gimignano is the tallest and offers breathtaking views of the Tuscan countryside.

Left *Santa Maria della Salute in Venice rises from the water prominently at the entrance of the Grand Canal.*

Photos by Sandy Gregory

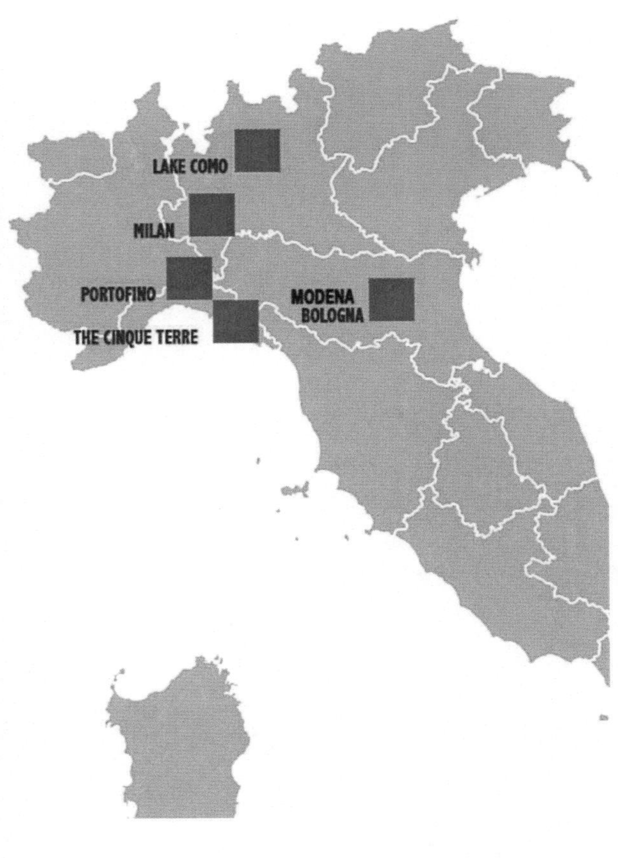

A Taste of Italy's North

Enjoy this delicious cultural journey through Lombardy, Liguria and the Emilia-Romagna. You will begin in the sophisticated city of Milan, relax along the shores of Lake Como, and hike the hills of the Cinque Terre to get ready for the culinary delights of Bologna.

MILAN

LAKE COMO

PORTOFINO

THE CINQUE TERRE

BOLOGNA

MODENA

Previous page, top *The fishing boats of Vernazza in the Cinque Terre.*

Photo by Janette Tepas Images

Previous page, bottom *The sun sets behind the Italian Alps on Lake Como.*

Above *Piccolo Marina in Varenna on Lake Como.*

Left *After the cruisers and day-trippers have left, the Cinque Terre becomes a wonderful place to spend the evening. Stroll the boardwalk in Monterosso al Mare and stop at one of the wonderful wine bars before dinner.*

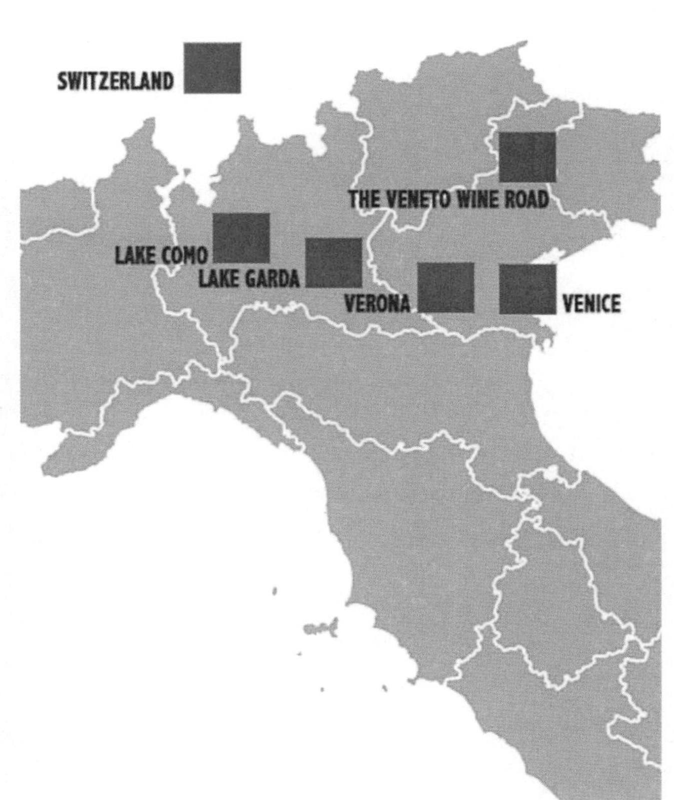

Italy's Northern Lakes and Veneto Wine Road

Immerse yourself in the views and vintners of Northern Italy: Lombardy, the Veneto and Fruili-Venezia Giulia.

SWITZERLAND PRE-TOUR

LAKE COMO

LAKE GARDA

VERONA

THE VENETO WINE ROAD

VENICE

Previous page, top *The city of Venice is made up of 118 small islands and 150 canals connected by 409 bridges and over 3000 alleyways. Every time you cross a bridge you are walking onto another island. Enjoying a meal right on the canal is one of the most romantic things to do in this magical city.*

Previous page, bottom *The red sunset on Lake Garda signals it is time to stop and savour the moment.*

Left *On the lakeshore in Bellagio, the Gardens of Villa Melzi display sculptures beautifully placed amidst walking paths, terraces, and botanical gardens of azaleas and rhododendrons.*

Photos by Sandy Gregory

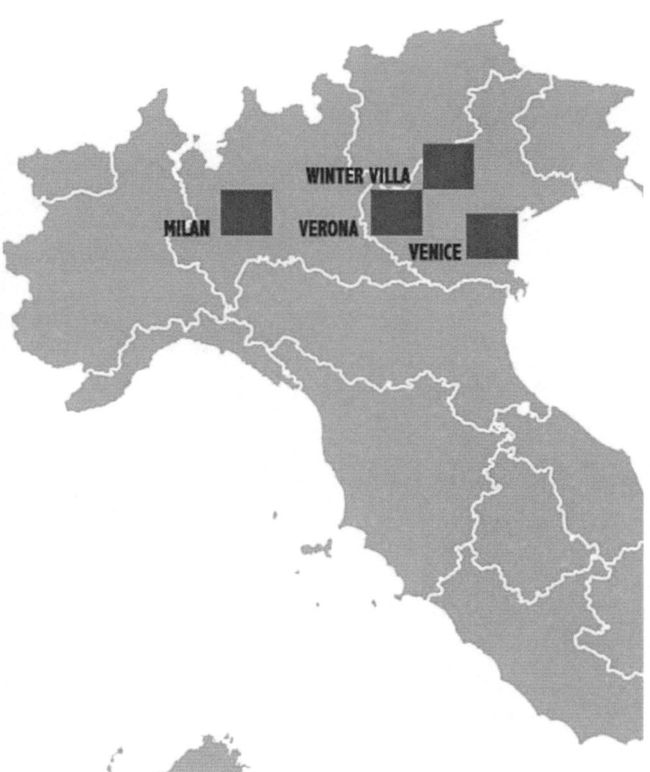

A Romantic Winter Getaway

Get a few couples together and celebrate Valentine's Day a la Romeo and Juliet. Enjoy crisp mountain air from a hot spring or perhaps do a little skiing. Finish with the colorful spectacle of the Venice Carnivale.

MILAN

VERONA

A WARM WINTER VILLA

VENICE

Previous page, top *The dark interior of Milan's Duomo is a sharp contrast to its light marble exterior. Stained glass windows, with stories from the Old and New Testament, filter light into the church. Five naves, 52 pillars carved in dark stone, and an intricate floor of black, pink and white marble add to the imposing ambiance.*

Previous page, bottom *Carnivale masks of every shape and size can be found in Venice.*

Left *Monumento a Vittorio Emanuele II in the Piazza del Duomo, Milan. Victor Emmanuel III was the last king of Italy from 1900 until 1946, when Italy became a Republic.*

Photos by Sandy Gregory

Piedmont and Lake Maggiore

Travel through Italy's Western Alps. From its fog-shrouded hills to the shores of Lake Maggiore, this itinerary allows plenty of time for relaxation and reflection. Italy's most culinary progressive region is rich in eggy pastas, truffles and hearty red wines.

TURINO

ALBA

THE PIEDMONT WINE ROAD

ORTA SAN GIULIO

STRESA ON LAKE MAGGIORE

THE BORROMEAN ISLANDS

MILAN

Previous page, top *Piedmont is home of the noble wines: barbaresco and barolo.*

Previous page, bottom *Mornings are for truffle hunting in the foggy forest.*

Above, top *The Isola Bella palace is owned by the Borromeo Family. It is filled with many family treasures and equally beautiful gardens.*

Above *The Orta San Giulio ferry boat takes you to Isola San Giulio, a small island where silence is treasured. It is the home of a Benedictine Abbey where 70 nuns dedicate themselves to silent contemplation and prayer. In that spirit, visitors enjoy a cobble-stoned, meditative walk that curves around the island. You encircle the island twice, reading the ornamental signs that appear along the way. The clockwise walk is The Way of Silence. The signs offer inspirations such as: Listen to the water, the wind, your steps. Silence is music and harmony. The counter clockwise walk is The Way of Meditation. These signs offer inspirations such as: The moment is present, here and now. When you are aware, the journey is over.*

Photos by Sandy Gregory

Tuscany and the Wine Country

Relax and unwind at a luxury villa and experience the gems of Tuscany, including cooking lessons, wine tastings and exciting day trips to the nearby hill towns.

FLORENCE

A LUXURY VILLA IN SAN GIMIGNANO

PIENZA

MONTALCINO

MONTEPULCIANO

CHIANTI

AREZZO

CORTONA

SIENA

Previous page, top The tiny streets of Pienza are lined with colorful flower boxes.

Previous page, bottom *It's always a treat to enjoy a quiet, rainy morning in the Piazza Cisterna, San Gimignano.*

Above *A view of the Palazzo Vecchio (old palace) from Piazelle Michelangelo. The palace was the seat of the Signoria, the government of the medieval and Renaissance Republic of Florence, until Cosimo I de Medici moved the residence to the Palazzo Pitti.*

Left *A panoramic view of one of our favorite Tuscan villas takes your breath away.*

Photos by Sandy Gregory

Tuscany and Siena's Palio

Enjoy race week and everything the Tuscan countryside has to offer. A luxury villa. Medieval hill towns. Cooking lessons and wine tastings. A pre-race dinner with a contrada. And VIP reserved seating at the Palio horserace.

FLORENCE

A LUXURY VILLA IN SIENA

THE SIENA PALIO

SAN GIMIGNANO

AREZZO

CORTONA

CHIANTI

PIENZA

MONTALCINO

MONTEPULCIANO

Previous page, top *There are 17 "contrade," or neighborhoods, in Siena. These are the fabric of life in this medieval town. Each has its own family history, church, community center, museum, flag and colors. They prepare all year for the Palio, often parading in their medieval finery.*

Previous page, bottom *The Palio is a horse race that takes place every year on July 2 and August 16. Its beginnings date to the 13th century. Ten horses, three laps and 90-seconds of no-holds-barred horse race take place in the Campo, or main square. The winner is awarded a banner of painted silk, or palio, which is hand-painted by a different artist for each race.*

Left *In Siena, flag throwing is a serious business. Flag throwers practice all year for the famous Corteo Storico, the elaborate costume parade that precedes the horse race.*

Above *Guests of Che Bella Tours can enjoy an al fresco dinner high above Siena's Campo.*

Palio photos by Ales Cecchi

Siena photo by Sandy Gregory

Le Marche and Umbria

Take the road less traveled and enjoy autumn harvest season in one of the most beautiful regions of Italy. Hill towns and mountainous vistas lead down to long stretches of sandy beaches along the Aegean Sea. October is time for the Perugia Chocolate Festival — always a good time to stop and reflect at the Basilica of St. Francis of Assisi.

URBINO

GUBBIO

ASSISI

PERUGIA

MONTE CORNERO

CORINALDO

FANO

Previous page, top The Basilica of St. Francis in Assisi, where Saint Francis was born and died. This is one of the most important places of Christian pilgrimage in Italy.

Previous page, bottom Make sure your itinerary offers plenty of time for strolling and shopping.

Left The statue of St. Francis returning home after the war is located in front of the facade of the Basilica of St. Francis in Assisi.

Photos by Sandy Gregory

Above Perugia, the capitol of Umbria, is also the chocolate capitol of Italy. It's a lively university town that mixes the old with the new. Perugia also boasts a flourishing bar and restaurant scene.

Puglia, Naples and The Amalfi Coast

Age-old cultural and gastronomic traditions, fascinating history and ancient architecture make this colorful region of Italy a charming, authentic and relaxing destination. Over 750 years old, The Amalfi Coast Drive is a masterpiece of engineering.

MATERA

ALBEROBELLO

LOCOROTONDO

CISTERNINO

OSTUNI

LECCE

BARI

NAPLES

HERCULANEUM

SORRENTO

POSITANO

CAPRI

Previous page top *Naples Galleria Umberto is filled with designer shops and high-end cafes.*

Previous page bottom *Climb down to the water in Ana Capri for this secluded view.*

Above left *Start your day with a breathtaking view of the Piccolo Marina on the Bay of Naples in Sorrento.*

Left *Herculaneum is one of the best preserved archaeological sites in the world. Many of the buildings, with their beautiful mosaics and murals, look virtually the same as they would have before the eruption of Mt. Vesuvius in 79 AD.*

Photos by Sandy Gregory

Above right *Trulli, the beehive-style structures you see throughout the Itria Valley in Puglia, have likely been there since the 1500s. The word "trullo" means cupola or dome. Trulli were traditional homes made of readily available limestone, which provided good insulation in the winter, while the whitewash kept the structures cool in the summer. The conical roof design not only kept the structure airtight, it had a gutter system that collected rainwater. Today, many trulli have been transformed into hotels, restaurants and shops.*

Photo by Janette Tepas Images

Bella Sicily

Arab, Greek and Spanish influences run deep in this local culture. Sicily's spirited people welcome visitors with amazing wines, beautiful beaches and archaeological treasures. Winding alleys lead to fantastic views of the Ionic Sea and Mount Etna, the highest and most active volcano in Europe.

ORTIGIA IN SIRACUSA

NOTO

RAGUSA

CATANIA

MT. ETNA

TAORMINA

Previous page top *The old town of Ortigia in Siracusa is a colorful maze of tiny alleyways.*

Previous page bottom *A picture of pretty pups in Catania.*

Photo by Janette Tepas Images

Left *Taormina has wonderful shopping and breathtaking views.*

NOTES

PREPARING FOR YOUR TRIP

CLOUDLESS SKIES, CLEAR VISION AND HAPPY TRAVELS

CAVU is an acronym used in aviation meaning "Ceiling And Visibility Unlimited." My husband and son are both pilots and they tend to speak in acronyms. I especially like CAVU because it is used to describe an excellent day for flying.

Travel brings the opportunity for adventure, lessons about life, a better understanding of ourselves and the sheer anticipation of something new. You can have all the experiences the world has to offer but sharing them makes it so much better. Leading small group tours has brought so many new and interesting people into my life. On tour, my guests step out of their comfort zone, their senses are heightened and lives examined. Their relationships are strengthened while new friendships are formed. We certainly remember the breathtaking sunsets, the exquisite meals and the sights we see, but what endures are the memories of the people who share these moments.

What we learn when we travel. Being a professional traveler, tour operator, tour director and travel writer, I feel strongly about the value of incorporating world travel into one's life experience. If we want a new generation of leaders and innovators, traveling with our family and sending our children to study overseas is not a luxury, but a necessity. Yes, there's a lot of uncertainty in our world today, but we must celebrate, not fear, other cultures and customs if we hope to contribute to a better world.

My challenge to you:

- Travel as much as you can as a family. Soak it all in.
- Get out of your comfort zone.
- While you're abroad, take a good look at your own country from the outside-in. Be grateful for what you have. It's good for you. It's good for the world. It's super fun. So, as you prepare for your trip to Italy, I wish you CAVU: cloudless skies, clear vision and great travels.

Preparing for Your Trip. Now that you have some itinerary choices, this chapter focuses on planning and preparing for your trip; traveling and packing; and lots of tips and tricks I've learned along the way. Travel uncertainty, transportation and being unfamiliar with the location all add stress to your vacation. Check out my travel cheat sheets at the end of this book. Good planning allows you to travel at your own pace so you can return home rested, refreshed and ready to get back to "real life."

"IL DOLCE FAR NIENTE"

This is a wonderful Italian expression which translates as "the sweetness of doing nothing."

The art of doing nothing — and doing it well — is what vacation is all about. Take time to relax. Sketch. Wander. Hike a vineyard. Grab a bike. Sit at a cafe and watch the world go by. Enjoy.

***Next page** Sketching at the villa*

Photo by Sandy Gregory

Planning Your Trip ...

The beauty of travel is not really about cities, museums, hotels and restaurants, but rather the unforgettable feelings you experience and the memories you create.

More and more, my clients want itineraries that make precious travel time more personal and meaningful. Multi-generational adventures that create treasured memories. Heritage travel to the ancestral homeland. Deep dives into literature, art, architecture or cuisine. A sisters' getaway. A graduation trip. A milestone birthday.

I started writing this guide while quarantined in 2020, praying for a vaccine to eradicate COVID-19 and compelled to finish by the time we would all start traveling again. The world shut down, but my hope did not. During this time, my clients also kept their travel dreams alive. Here are some of their requests:

- Propose to my girlfriend in a hot air balloon floating over a lavender field in Provence. (Wicked romantic!)
- Get married in Greece.
- Honeymoon in Italy.
- Have our family reunion at a Celtic castle in the Scottish Highlands. Fish, golf and wear our tartans for a family portrait.
- Celebrate Holy Week with my children where I was born in Marsala, Sicily. We'll walk the streets in the Processione dei Misteri di Trapani on Good Friday, as I show them the beautifully maintained doors I remember from my childhood.
- Take our sons sport fishing in Panama before they head to college.
- Cook, eat, drink wine, hike, spa and do yoga with my girlfriends ... anywhere!

We're all hungry to travel, and the anticipation of something new is why planning for your trip is half the fun. I hope this guide helps you plan a trip to somewhere you have always dreamed of in the company of the people you love.

Above *Australians Scott and Paula got married on Santorini and then traveled with Che Bella Tours on their Italian honeymoon.*

Photos by Sandy Gregory

... is Half the Fun!

Above *Whether it's Italy, Australia, New Zealand, Croatia, Montenegro, Boznia-Herzegovina, France, Spain, Portugal or Morocco, these families from San Antonio know how to travel with Che Bella Tours!*

Photos by Sandy Gregory

If you have no interest in going to churches, art galleries or museums in your hometown, why would you suddenly enjoy doing it abroad?

Planning a Group Trip. You would think a trip of a lifetime would bring you together, but sometimes, it can be challenging. Here are a few tips to consider when planning a group vacation:

- Don't assume everyone's finances are the same. Make your choices with all income levels in mind so that the reunion is affordable for all.
- Do you need to travel at a certain time of year to accommodate work and school schedules? Pick a date and stick to it.
- The more organized you can make your trip, the better. Plan well ahead of time. Work with a professional. Establish firm deadlines so you can manage itineraries, reservations and payments.

You be you. First you must decide where to travel. Will it have historical significance to your group? What attractions are nearby? Will you be mobile and travel from city to city, or prefer to center at one villa and spoke out from there? Should you visit a certain city, site, villa or hotel just because your friend or neighbor found it wonderful? You may have similar tastes, but you might want something that better suits your group.

Be there, don't just see there. Don't over plan. Rather than try to force a single itinerary, plan a few activities for everyone that will involve all ages and passions. For some, spending time meandering the streets and poking around antique shops is the perfect day. For others, a long hike followed by a luxurious lunch is heaven. Some people are prolific shoppers. Others are foodies. Some want to share precious moments with their children and grandchildren. Others are on a pilgrimage to understand their religious history. You do you. If you have no interest in going to churches, art galleries or museums in your hometown, why would you suddenly enjoy doing it abroad?

Some travelers are on a mission, "I'll sleep when I'm dead!" To others, "amazing" just comes. No matter your group's travel style, don't forget to include time to just sit, talk, reminisce and be together.

TRAVEL DURING THE OFF-SEASON AND ADD A FEW OFF-THE-BEATEN-PATH EXPERIENCES

If you have the flexibility, traveling in the off-season can offer relief from the scorching summer heat and heavy crowds, as well as save you money on airfare and hotels. April/May and October/November offer a very pleasant Mediterranean climate, and the cities and towns become more like places where people actually live. Many villas and restaurants turn damp and cold from November to April and close down for the winter. There are places, however, that are magical in winter. **Venice** is divinely quiet, romantically misty and everything stays open — especially during February Carnival. Nearby **Verona** lights up during Valentine's Day week. **Lake Como** never freezes and is not too far away from the ski towns. **Cortina D'Ampezzo** offers some of the most beautiful Alpine landscapes — and skiing — in Europe. **Piedmont** and **Bologna** are all about the food — and offer the perfect place for an intensive cooking holiday. A visit to **Rome** means having the Vatican, Colosseum and vast museums virtually all to yourself. Since it's a major international city, hotels and restaurants are always open. Head south to **Puglia**, **Naples** and **Sicily,** where tourist crowds in winter are non-existent. The weather is temperate so you can visit, sweat free, **Pompeii**, **Herculaneum** or even climb **Mount Etna**.

Check out our website at ***chebellatours.com*** to see our suggested itineraries, complete with alternative suggestions to cities, small towns and the countryside. Avoid the tourist crowds, and dig a little deeper in places that will surprise and delight.

Above *A quiet breakfast at the foot at the Pantheon.*

Above right *Biking along the city wall of Lucca.*

Opposite page *Check out the flags. I am always herding these turtles.*

Photos by Sandy Gregory

CITY HOTELS VS. VACATION RENTAL PROPERTIES

When traveling with Che Bella Tours, you stay in hotels located in the heart of the cities. After enjoying breakfast, which is included in your tour, you walk right out the front door to begin your day. There is a comfort and security knowing that someone is always at the front desk to help answer questions, give recommendations, manage lost luggage delivery and, most of all, watch over your comings and goings.

We don't use vacation rental services because we cannot guarantee the quality and safety of each individual property. The AirB&B/VRBO market has added to the rising problem of overtourism, city congestion and rising housing costs for locals. Neighborhoods are transformed from familial communities to transient complexes. Property owners who switch from long-term tenancies to these short-term rentals certainly make more money, but they are not on site to supervise their clientele. Noisy tourists come in and out at all hours; many park on old town streets, which adds to the congestion in residential areas. Many European cities now restrict the amount of rental days they allow, and have even stopped issuing new tourism housing licenses to help manage this growing issue.

A TOUR OPERATOR HAS ALL THE TOOLS TO PLAN YOUR TRIP

The decision to spend your valuable time and money traveling can be a costly investment. Tour operators work closely with groups to craft personalized, high-quality travel experiences. We have a large network of in-country partners to set your itinerary, make all the arrangements, manage all the details, and make sure you feel safe and cared for the entire way. The goal of Che Bella Tours is to create the perfect blend of personal passions, cultural encounters, famous landmarks, secret hideaways, art, cuisine, literature and wellness.

A TOUR DIRECTOR TO MANAGE YOUR GROUP? PRICELESS!

Tour Directors travel with you, making travel worry free for everyone. A Tour Director's job is a whirlwind of attending to guests, maneuvering motor coaches, confirming hotels and guides, herding turtles, in-depth commentary, stand up comedy and a lot of "I'll be happy to take care of that for you." Typical days have included 32,000 steps, great wine, bad airports, unexpected treats and keeping all the balls in the air ... without missing a beat.

Experienced travel professionals can make the difference in the success of your trip. Let Che Bella Tours be with you every step of the way. You'll avoid family drama and having to answer a lot of these questions:

"Where are we going? What time are we leaving? Where do we meet? Do I have to go? How do I get there? Where's my luggage? Where's my room? How do I turn on the room lights? Where's my husband? What's the weather like outside? What do I order? What's that? Do I have to eat that? How much is my part of the bill? Where's the restroom? Where are we? How old is that? What does this mean? When will we be there? How do I find it? What do you recommend? How do I buy this? Where is everybody? Where are we going again?"

Mindful and Responsible Travel

How can we be more mindful travelers as we prepare to travel wisely? How do we, as citizens of the world, refocus on what traveling is meant to be? How can we, planning our next vacation, be part of the overtourism solution, not part of the problem?

The world is being loved to death. The combination of affordable air travel, large group tours and massive cruise ships, as well as every tour operator, blogger and influencer promoting "must-see" destinations, has resulted in more people traveling than ever before. Once a privilege, travel is now considered a basic right, often pursued without a sense of responsibility for how it affects the places we love. This has caused a crisis of overtourism. The earth has been pushed to its limits over the last few years. While the 2020 ban on worldwide travel due to the COVID-19 pandemic was devastating for the travel industry, our earth did get a much-needed rest.

Large ships and large groups. The "strategy of gigantism" combines the features of a resort with the entertainment of a theme park, all jammed on to an enormous boat. Thousands of passengers and crew members dine, shower and defecate — leaving a lot of damage in their wake. According to the U.S. Environmental Protection Agency, in the course of one day, the average cruise ship produces: 21,000 gallons of human sewage; one ton of solid waste garbage; 170,000 gallons of wastewater from showers, sinks and laundry; 6,400 gallons of oily bilge water from the massive engines; 25 pounds of batteries, fluorescent lights, medical wastes and expired chemicals; and 8,500 plastic bottles. Every day, a tsunami of passengers pours into the ports. The pollution from diesel engines that continue to run while the ships are in port equate to tens of thousands of idling cars. Multiply this by 400 ships cruising year-round on fixed routes.

On shore, large group excursions cause damage to fragile ruins and sites, as well as create noise pollution, traffic jams and congestion in the streets. Daytrippers are shuttled in large buses and herded into museum lines that stretch around the block. Their job is to keep in sight of the distant flag of their tour guide, who is walking and talking into her microphone. She leads them through a museum and past the highlights. A pre-fixed lunch follows, and then back to the bus. This leaves little time for tourists to explore at their leisure, shop with an artisan, stay at a local hotel or enjoy the authentic regional cuisine. The cruise lines take up to 50 percent of the local guide fees, while local merchants get little compensation from day-trippers, who are not staying at the hotels or spending at the stores and restaurants. Post-pandemic travelers are thinking twice these days about cruising with 3,000+ of their closest friends. As we have learned, all it takes is for one person with a virus to infect and quarantine an entire ship.

Tourism is the world's biggest industry and plays an important role in bringing jobs and opportunities to people all over the world. Communities, businesses and governments, as well as the travel industry and travel media, are sorting out what they want — and don't want — from future tourism and travel. Keeping tourism at the top of its game without hollowing out a country's culture, character and natural resources is the challenge.

Consider small group travel. Savvy travelers don't arrive in huge motor coaches, or need flags, hats or buttons to keep together. Small groups move at their own pace, navigate easily around town and stay "under the radar." Small groups are accommodated easily at the local, authentic restaurants and hotels. Small groups stay put for a few days, enjoy the local ambiance and bring dollars into the local economy. My guests become a community and a family as we travel. We learn from each other, embrace new experiences, keep open minds and maintain our collective sense of humor — most of the time.

Think about:

- Enjoying the freedom of slow travel, to explore and learn, rest and rejuvenate.
- Doing things that scare us like talking to strangers, trying new cuisines, striking off the beaten path and adapting to change.
- Opening our minds to new cultures and different ways of thinking and, in turn, digging deeper into our own selves.
- Enhancing our creativity.
- Seeing our own world from the outside in.

My hope is that:

- We all gain a better understanding for those who are frightened every day because of the color of their skin, what religion they practice or where they were born.
- Travel becomes what it was meant to be: Returning home not just with great souvenirs and photos, but also with cherished memories and a kinder, more tolerant worldview.

WHAT IS UNESCO?

The United Nations Educational, Scientific and Cultural Organization (UNESCO) is a worldwide organization that promotes collaboration through education, science, culture and communication. As part of its mission, the organization identifies, protects and preserves places that are of outstanding value to humanity. There are currently over 1300 natural and cultural places inscribed on the World Heritage List with 55 in Italy. UNESCO helps maintain the health of these sites, including an increased focus on sustainable tourism. UNESCO sights around the world are struggling to keep a balance between the economic benefits created by tourism and maintaining the cultural significance that originally put them on the list in the first place.

Small group travel with Che Bella Tours is a respectful and responsible style of travel that will help sustain over 50 precious UNESCO sites in Italy, including:

- The historic centers of Verona, Vicenza, Genoa, Venice and its lagoon, Florence, San Gimignano, Siena, Pienza, Urbino, Assisi, Naples, Rome, Mantua and Sabbioneta, Modena, Ferrara, Val di Noto and Palermo
- The archaeological sites of Pompeii, Herculaneum Torre Annunziata, Paestum and Velia, the Certosa di Padula, Etruscan Necropolises of Cerveteri and Tarquinia, Ravenna and Valcamonica
- The cathedrals and basilicas of San Francesco, Modena and Santa Maria Delle Grazie
- The properties of the Holy See, the Royal House of Savoy, the Medicis and other great families
- The Amalfi Coast, Portovenere, Cinque Terre, and the Aeolian Islands, Monte San Giorgio, Mount Etna, Sacri Monti of Piedmont and Lombardy, Syracuse, Pantalica and the Dolomites

In 2017, the Naples art of pizza making was added to the UNESCO list.

Safety and Security

Know the environment. Prepare accordingly and try to stay vigilant and alert, making sure you are not caught off guard or wind up in a place you shouldn't be.

Do we stay or do we go? Part of the travel experience is dealing with curve balls and unpredictability. Random things can happen. Based on the current situation in the world, it's no wonder people are skittish about booking international travel. However, if we love to travel we need to travel wisely.

Focus on fact rather than opinion. The media tends to focus on the bad news, but they rarely report on the millions of trips that run smoothly and go off without a hitch. So, do your research, be realistic and stay true to your own comfort level.

Trust your gut. Terrorists do not damage most people by what they do, but rather by the reaction to what they do. They want one thing — for you to be afraid. It is important to not allow fear to cloud your ability to assess risk. I will not be so cavalier as to say I don't carry some fear and nervousness when traveling. I do. But, I cannot and will not allow evil to paralyze me. Travel where you'll be comfortable. Let people know where you are and stay in touch.

Before you travel

- Check with the World Health Organization (WHO) and the Centers for Disease Control and Prevention (CDC) for relevant, up-to-date and country-specific health risk information.
- Register with STEP, the Smart Traveler Enrollment Program. This is a free service provided by the U.S. Government to U.S. citizens traveling abroad. Enrollment allows you to submit information about your upcoming trip. In case of emergency, such as being a victim of a crime, accident, illness, natural disaster, terrorism or civil unrest, the Department of State can more easily assess, locate and assist you. They also can communicate with your family or emergency contacts back home.

  step.state.gov/step/

Book your flight so you arrive during the day. Most international flights from the U.S. arrive in the morning, but confirm this before you book. It will be easier to manage your arrival and transfer to the hotel before dark.

Book a reputable global chauffeur service. Guests traveling with Che Bella Tours will be booked with one of our trusted transfer companies. If you are traveling on your own, however, think about hiring a transportation company that is fully vetted, rather than a local taxi or Uber driver.

Travel with multiple copies of important documents. Leave one set at home with a trusted friend or family member, another tucked in your carry-on, separate from your passport. Keep another copy on your smartphone.

Must-have documents:

- Your passport
- The front and back sides of your credit and debit cards, with phone numbers to your banks
- Your driver's license
- Travel insurance paperwork
- Medical prescriptions and the generic names
- An alert bracelet if you suffer from allergies or a chronic illness such as diabetes
- Flight details
- Contact information for your local embassy or consulate
- Extra passport photos. Getting a passport photo taken in a foreign country can be difficult, and will delay the process of replacing your passport in a timely manner if your passport is lost or stolen.
- Your Che Bella Tours itinerary and your copy of this book.

LA FARMACIA

My Italian associates are quick to offer a plethora of recommendations on jams, jellies, pills and potions that will take care of anything that ails you. So it's no surprise that neon green crosses illuminate almost every street in Italy. Italian pharmacies are more like mini-clinics with cosmetics counters.

If you lose your medication while traveling, most pharmacies will honor your prescription and give you enough medication to get you through your trip and home. You will have to provide a copy of the prescription and the generic name, as well as your passport and flight information.

MOBILE PHONES

Before your trip. Contact your mobile carrier to extend your telephone account to Europe. T-Mobile, Sprint, Verizon and AT&T all offer add-ons to existing plans (e.g., an extra $10/day while you are traveling), or dedicated international calling, text and/or data plans. Be sure to confirm the exact voice- and data-roaming fees, as they can add up quickly. You don't want to return to find a hefty cell phone bill.

Other data options. If your phone is unlocked, you can purchase a pay-as-you-go SIM card. Providers in Italy include Vodafone, Orange and Tim. You can top off a SIM at the airport, money exchange or *tabbacci* (tobacco stores). You also can purchase an inexpensive cell phone in Europe with a pay-as-you-go SIM card.

Update your software. You want your cyber security to be as strong as possible. Adjust your phone's settings to ensure that things like automatic backups to the cloud only happen over WiFi.

Turn off roaming. Put your phone in airplane mode or turn off cellular data. You will need to save your data for emergency phone calls, a quick Google search or using apps such as WhatsApp, Google Maps or Vivino.

Invest in a smart phone wrist strap. While you're engrossed in beautiful panoramas or leaning over a bridge to get the shot, having your phone secured to your wrist is key in case it slips or you get bumped.

PUBLIC WIFI

Any shared WiFi network is a risk, so make sure your data and information are kept safe. Banking, paying bills, credit card accounts or anything that requires a password can be at the mercy of a hacker, so be careful accessing personal information online. Clear your browsing history and any sensitive digital information on your devices before traveling.

Use two-step authentication. Facebook, email and your financial accounts will be more secure.

Don't use unencrypted sites. Sites with https at the beginning of the URL encode your information so are less interesting to hackers. You might want to install an extension like **HTTPS Everywhere** to make sure you are directed to the https site whenever possible.

Disconnect your device from the WiFi when you are done. This prevents hackers from accessing your connection and data.

VPN – Virtual Private Network – is an extra layer of security to protect your documents and data. A VPN is essentially a private network that only you can access. It protects all of your internet traffic, including emails, voice calls, videos, and music. The added bonus is that you can watch streaming services and continue binging your favorite shows while abroad. **Express VPN** has various pricing plans and will cover all of your devices. Simply download and install it on your phone, laptop or tablet. Connect to the internet, then start up your VPN. Choose the server and voilà! Your data is encrypted and your location remains a mystery.

Refrain from posting information about your travel on social media. Turn off your geo-location settings on your social media apps and do not "check-in" to locations in real time while you are traveling.

ELECTRONICS

Keep your electronics and cords organized. I use the **BAGSMART Electronic Travel Cable Organizer** to make my life on the road a lot easier. Buy cords and plugs in bright colors so you can find them easily, and of course, bring a few extra chargers. There is nothing worse than realizing you left a plug or charger at the last hotel.

Buy a converter/adaptor before your travel. An adapter changes the configuration of your U.S. power plugs to fit into wall sockets in the country you are visiting. A converter changes the electricity so dual voltage appliances work.

European voltage is 220. Look for the voltage rating on your appliances. If your hairdryer and curling iron from home are dual voltage (like 100V~240V), you'll only need a plug adapter suitable to fit European outlets. However, if your appliance reads 110V or 120V, it is single voltage and will require both an adapter and a converter.

Most laptops and tablets are dual voltage. I play it safe with a converter so as not to overheat and fry the motherboard. Converter/adaptors are not readily available to buy in Europe, so buy one or two before you travel.

I also carry a small **portable charger** and a **mini power strip** in my day pack in case I need to charge my device on the go. European hotel rooms are notoriously light on outlets.

SMART MONEY

Credit and debit cards. Don't bring every card you own. Two cards will suffice. Visa® and Mastercard® are widely accepted, while American Express® is taken in some places. No one has ever heard of Discover® in Europe.

Consider two different numbers linked to one card account. Keep one card in the hotel safe and carry the other one with you. If that card becomes compromised and is blocked, the other one still works and you don't have to freeze your card.

Travel alerts. Before you travel, have your bank and credit card providers put your cards on a travel alert with the dates and amounts you might spend. You will need a pin number attached to your debit card. Do a test withdrawal before you travel.

Italian ATMs allow you to withdraw between 250 to 500 Euros a day. Many banks and credit cards charge an *exchange fee*, as well as a *transaction fee* for each withdrawal. If your provider won't waive these fees, consider finding one of the many providers who will.

How much money should you bring? It's truly up to you. You know your habits and preferences. You can order Euros from your bank at home to get you started. I recommend having 200-300 Euro cash. During your travels, you can pull more cash as you need from the ATM. If you would like to see the latest exchange rates, go to *xe.com/currencyconverter/*

Currency conversion. When making a credit card transaction at a restaurant, hotel or shop, DO NOT CHOOSE TO BE BILLED IN U.S. DOLLARS. Dynamic currency conversion is a scheme that banks use to charge you an inflated interest rate when you use U.S. dollars to pay in a different country. You will be paying an overly inflated rate as well as a foreign exchange fee. So, in Europe, pay in Euros.

GETTING CASH

ATMs provide the best exchange rates available. Do not exchange at the kiosks that say ***CAMBIO*** at the airport or on the main plazas. Do not bring cash dollars to exchange for Euros. The exchange rates and transaction fees are steep. An international bank, or ***Bancomat*** ATM, are the best ways connect with your bank.

Beware of non-bank ATMs and take a close look at the card reader before you make a transaction. If it seems loose, crooked or damaged, don't swipe. A skimmer is an illegal device that is either positioned over the keypad or placed inside the card reader to collect card information.

After you enter your PIN, you will have the option to continue in English. When you are finished with your transaction, the screen will read, "Take your card within 30 seconds." Grab that card, because on the 29th second it will be sucked back into the slot and shredded.

Make a credit card and a debit card transaction as soon as you land in Europe. This way you can confirm your travel alert has been processed. If the transaction doesn't go through, you can call your bank and have them fix their error before you are deep into your trip.

Use a debit card for cash at the ATM and a credit card for all other transactions. If you put all purchases and meals on a credit card, it will be easier to dispute fraudulent transactions with your financial institution. It's also a good idea to call your bank and credit card company when you return from your trip, so that they know any foreign transaction past that date is unlikely to be legitimate.

A STOLEN CARD?

1. File a police report immediately.
2. Check to see if your Social Security number has been used fraudulently. **Lifelock Identity Alert System** is a great service to put on all of your devices. It alerts you if your Social Security number, name, address, or date of birth are being used in applications for credit or services.
3. Call your bank and credit card providers. You probably will need to close your accounts and open new ones. Make sure to use completely different PIN codes and passwords. Most providers will overnight new cards to your hotel.
4. Closely review your account statements for any fraudulent charges so that you can have them reversed.
5. Check your credit.

PROTECT YOUR VALUABLES

Don't bring the good stuff. While you are being a naive, trusting tourist, spending your energy absorbing the beauty around you, a scammer is absorbing you. The flirty man, the helpful local, the fake petition they ask you to sign ... all are watching to see how quickly they can separate you from your bag ... and your bling.

If you are carrying valuables, consider carrying a Pacsafe Portable Safe. This steel wire mesh bag can be cabled to hotel furniture, a beach or restaurant chair, scooter or anywhere items need to be left unattended for awhile. Use it with a combination lock so you don't have to worry about losing the key.

Passports and Travel Docs

Your passport must remain valid for six months after your return to the United States to get through passport control. Check the expiration date well before you travel.

YOUR PASSPORT BELONGS TO YOUR GOVERNMENT

Before you travel, make sure your legal house is in order. If you are delinquent on your taxes, owe child support or alimony, or are involved in a government lawsuit, the U.S. government can deny or cancel your existing passport at any time. No questions asked. No recourse.

PASSPORTS

If you are planning travel outside the U.S., check the expiration date on your passport well ahead of time. At the time of your trip, your passport must be valid for six months and have three to six blank visa pages to get through passport control upon your return to the United States. The U.S. passport office advises travelers to renew their passports nine months in advance of expiration.

travel.state.gov/content/travel/en/passports.html

To apply or renew your passport, you will need:

- An application form
- If you changed your name, a certified copy of your marriage certificate
- Two passport photos taken within six months of the application
- Payment via credit card
- Your existing passport if renewing

It is possible to expedite the processing of your passport. In some cases, applying by mail may be the best solution, and one that is recommended by the U.S. Department of State. Expect delays. Use only USPS when applying by mail, and track your package.

The good news is the U.S. is now issuing new e-passports with biometric processing which securely identifies the traveler as you. The encryption provides protection against identity theft, protects your privacy and makes it difficult to alter your passport.

Some people feel more comfortable having their passport with them at all times, but I prefer to keep it, and any cash I don't need that day, in the hotel safe. I have my passport scanned into my phone in case I need identification.

If your passport is lost or stolen:

1. File a police report immediately. You will need that documentation to file for a replacement passport, make a claim on a travel insurance policy, replace a credit or debit card, or receive any kind of assistance from your embassy.
2. Download this Lost or Stolen Passport Report before you travel just in case you need it.

   consfiladelfia.esteri.it/resource/2016/02/79725_f_cons57DENUNCIA2.pdf
3. Contact your nearest embassy or consulate. Ask to speak to the Consular Section to report your passport as lost or stolen. Once you report a U.S. passport lost or stolen, it is invalid and cannot be used for international travel.
4. You will need to appear in person to get a replacement. If your situation is urgent, the embassy may be able to expedite next-day processing.

Bring with you to the embassy:

- A copy of your stolen passport with the passport number
- Your driver's license as a second proof of identity
- Two passport photos
- The Lost or Stolen Passport Report

SPEED THROUGH SECURITY

Global Entry. Breeze by those excruciating lines when you return back to the U.S. after an international trip. When you land at your first U.S. airport from abroad, Global Entry allows you to quickly bypass the long lines at Passport Control, saving hours of time and providing you peace of mind, especially if you are catching a connecting flight. Global Entry also includes immediate access to TSA PreCheck benefits. To enroll, submit an online application. You can expect to receive a rigorous background check. Once you pass this check, you will schedule an interview and get fingerprinted. The cost for Global Entry is $100 and the pass is good for five years.

cbp.gov/travel/trusted-traveler-programs/global-entry

TSA PreCheck. Skip those long, standard security lines by enrolling in TSA PreCheck, which verifies you are low risk to flight security and allows you to pass more quickly through security checkpoints. Shoes stay on, laptop and liquids stay in your bag, you avoid the "nude-o-scope" and are on your way to your gate. To enroll, you submit an online application and schedule an in-person appointment that includes a background check and fingerprinting at an enrollment center.

tsa.gov/precheck/

CLEAR. Those with TSA PreCheck also can enroll in CLEAR, a private company that verifies your identity through your biometric information — fingerprints, eyes and face — to speed you even faster through the full airport security and screening process.

clearme.com/

WHAT IS SCHENGEN?

The Schengen territory is comprised of 26 states within the European Union (EU) that allow free and unrestricted travel: Austria, Belgium, Czechia, Denmark, Estonia, Finland, France, Germany, Greece, Hungary, Iceland, Italy, Latvia, Liechtenstein, Lithuania, Luxembourg, Malta, Netherlands, Norway, Poland, Portugal, Slovakia, Slovenia, Spain, Sweden and Switzerland. Once in, you will not have to present your passport when traveling from country to country.

Currently, U.S. citizens are allowed unlimited travel within these countries for up to 90 days within a 6-month period, starting from the date of your first entry into a Schengen country.

Passport Control, Immigration and Customs in Italy. When you make your first landing from the U.S. and enter the EU/SCHENGEN Zone, you will go through Immigration and Passport Control. You will see the signs "EU Passport" and "All Other Passports." American citizens follow the signs that say "All Other Passports." You approach the Customs Agent as an individual or a family traveling together. Have your passport open to the information page and be ready to answer questions about your travel dates and locations. You'll be funnelled out to Baggage Claim to retrieve your suitcases and leave the airport. You go through this Immigration/ Passport Control only when you enter Schengen this first time. When you leave Schengen, you will go through Immigration/Passport Control as well as Customs. You receive a customs form that you present to the U.S. Passport agent when you stamp back in to the U.S.

Electronic System Travel Authorization (ETIAS). U.S. citizens traveling to Europe will soon be required to undergo the ETIAS screening before traveling. You will be checked against a series of databases to verify your identity, confirm your documents have not been stolen and that you are not wanted for arrest. This screening will tighten border security and help flag any issues with illegal migration and terrorism. Europeans coming in to the U.S. have had a similar program for years.

Trip Insurance

Protect your travel investment. Che Bella Tours can help you search, compare and purchase the best travel insurance policy for your needs.

When traveling with Che Bella Tours, we strongly recommend trip insurance. No one is immune to travel mishaps. The right type of travel insurance can save you a lot of aggravation before, during and after your trip.

Let us help you find the right plan. Che Bella Tours has resources that can help you search, compare and purchase the best travel insurance policy for your needs. Travel insurance packages can include trip cancellation and interruption, medical, evacuation, baggage and flight insurance. Trip cancellation covers you if you have to cancel your trip before you leave. Trip interruption covers you for the portion of the trip you don't complete if something unforeseen gets in the way, such as:

- A complicated itinerary causes you to miss a flight, train or hotel reservation
- Illness or injury of you and/or your traveling companion causes you to miss planned excursions or activities
- The hospitalization or death of a non-traveling family member cuts your trip short
- Unforeseen natural disasters at home or in-country causes your trip to be delayed, cancelled or cut short
- A legal obligation, such as being called for jury duty or to appear as a witness in court causes you to cancel your trip

Check with your credit card company. You might already be covered for some emergencies abroad such as lost or damaged luggage. Check to see of items such as jewelry, camera equipment and computers are also covered.

Check with your medical insurer. You also might already be covered for some emergencies abroad, especially if you have a pre-existing condition. If you do need to extend your coverage, consider at least $50,000 in emergency medical coverage and $100,000 in medical evacuation coverage.

Look closely at each provider's clauses and conditions. Keep in mind that insurance policies don't cover fear-based decisions, they cover travel plans that are disrupted because you physically cannot take the trip or have to cancel due to unforeseen circumstances. Check each plan's coverage for baggage, trip delays and cancellations, as well as coverage for medical expenses and emergency medical evacuation. Your best bet is to choose a plan where you can cancel for any reason.

- Check the deductible. Most companies will not cover 100% of costs and you'll probably have to pay some fees directly on sight.
- Read the fine print. Carefully read what your policy does NOT include, such as war or terrorist acts. Each policy will define these differently.

- Check to see if the plan covers the losses associated with pandemic or epidemic conditions.
- Check to see if pre-existing medical conditions are covered.
- Be honest. When applying for travel insurance with pre-existing medical conditions, don't lie. Travel and medical insurance companies do check and if they find out you've lied, they might cancel your entire policy — just when you need it.
- Most providers of health insurance for overseas travel won't cover you if what happened is your fault. If you hopped on a Segway after cocktails and crash, you probably won't be covered. Make good choices.

FLIGHT CANCELLATION RIGHTS

In the U.S., no federal law or regulation specifies what, if any, rights you have when an airline cancels your flight, and those rights vary from airline to airline. In a routine cancellation, you have two basic rights:

1. A seat on the next available flight or
2. A refund of the unused portion of your ticket.

Most airlines offer a meal or hotel room voucher if they cancel your flight for a reason within their control, such as scheduling or mechanical issues. However, they do not assist you when they cancel or postpone the flight because of bad weather or some other *force majeure* factor. Here are some tips to help you if your flight is cancelled:

- When an airline cancels a flight well before scheduled departure time, it often automatically rebooks you and notifies you of any changes. In general, if the airline's solution is at all reasonable, take it; arranging something else is often a hassle. If you do want to make other arrangements, identify possible solutions and present them to the reservation specialist or to the agent at the desk. Many things are negotiable, and most agents would rather respond to a specific suggestion than start looking at alternatives themselves.
- Booking through a travel agent gives you access to their 24/7 services. Having them handle any changes or updates can be key, especially if you are already en route to your destination, out of the country or unable to stay on the phone and on hold for long periods of time.
- Before you travel, download a copy of the airline's customer commitment documents to see what they will cover. For example, some airlines state that, if they can get you to your international destination within four hours of your scheduled landing, they are not required to compensate you.
- If you are bumped from an overbooked flight, check the airline's refund policy and inquire if the free ticket offered comes with restrictions.
- Need more help? Go to a website called **AirHelp**, a great website that outlines passenger rights and can assist with compensation.
- Keep your cool. The agent at the desk didn't cause the cancellation and can't offer seats that aren't there. Getting aggressive is the direct route to less assistance, not more. If you have an idea your flight might be cancelled, start calling the airline and go to the customer service desk immediately. They may be a better bet to help you rebook than the attendant at the gate. You'll be at the head of the long line that will quickly form when the cancellation is announced. As my pilot husband always says, "I'd rather be down here wishing I was up there, than be up there wishing I was down here."

Planes

SEARCHING FOR AIRFARE

Finding the best airfare is a game. There is no magical day, time or formula. The time you put into good planning can really pay off.

Plan your routes. Begin by mapping out your journey on a website called **Rome2Rio** which searches any city, town, landmark, attraction or address across the globe and gives you thousands of ways to get to get to a destination. You may find that taking a train after you land in Europe is more efficient than a connecting flight to your final destination. Another great resource to help you book as few connections as possible is **flightsfrom.com**, which finds airline routes and flight schedules.

Sign up for airfare alerts. Once you have your route, toggle between two websites — **Scyscanner** and **AirFare Watchdog** and an app called **Hopper** — which offer low-fare alerts. Try to stay flexible on dates, times and connection options. Since I'm usually traveling alone, I don't book my flight until six to eight weeks ahead of travel. For a large family or group, however, you should book much earlier or contact a travel agent for the best group rates and seating.

Search flight options. Once you have received your low-fare alerts, an online booking search engine like **Kayak** or **Google Flights** gives you a variety of options. You don't necessarily have to book through these tools, but the exercise provides a good base from which to make the best decisions.
TIP: Make sure you indicate how many checked bags you will have, as well as your carry-on when you filter the flight options, as that will make a big difference in the price.

Be extra careful with basic economy flights. There are often no flexibility or cancellation options, which in this day and age can be crucial, and you probably will be the first to be bumped from an overbooked flight.

Consider searching in incognito mode or opening up a private browsing window. Companies that book travel often keep track of previous searches and use this data to increase your pricing when you return to the site. If you use the incognito mode, it hides your search history and helps prevent price gouging. Browsers differ, but many have menus to the right of the search box, indicated with three vertical dots or dashes. Select New Incognito Window. On some browsers, go to the File menu and click on New Private Window.

Consider breaking up your search into individual legs. This can be cheaper and more flexible than booking every leg of your trip as a package.

Pay attention to connecting flight times. It's important to allow *at least two hours* to connect between flights. Delays, gate transfers, customs and immigration lines can all cause you to miss your connection, especially on your return. Long customs lines, terminal changes, baggage retrieval and re-checking can cause you to miss your connecting domestic flight. In turn, check those super-cheap fares closely. Some have you waiting in the airport for hours, or even overnight.

BOOKING YOUR FLIGHT

Armed with your airline and flight options, booking directly with the airline is often the best choice. Booking through an online booking search engine can get you great deals, but booking directly through the airline gives you the best flexibility and cancellation options. At the airport, it also might assure better customer service and a chance for an upgrade, especially if you are in their rewards program.

Miles or dollars? Of course, this decision is based on cash flow as well as the amount of mileage points you have accumulated. The general rule of thumb, however, is *two cents per mile*. That means, if you are looking at a $1000 airline ticket, 50,000 or fewer mileage points is a great deal; anything over that, paying with dollars is a better deal.

Verify your confirmation and ticket numbers directly with each airline after booking to insure that the flight was actually ticketed and not just "reserved."

Book your seat when you book your flight. It's very frustrating to find out when you board that your seat doesn't have an entertainment unit, is located near the restrooms or doesn't recline. A website called **SeatGuru** pulls up the seating chart on your upcoming flight and shows you the best seats available on the plane. If you have a connection, choose a seat in the front of the plane or near the egress exit. This can make a huge time difference if you need to rush to a connecting gate or a different terminal.

Another good idea is to download your own entertainment on to your mobile device *before* you travel so you always have something you can watch or read without relying on the Internet.

Always try to upgrade or get the exit row at check-in. You can tell the frequent flyers, as they linger at the gate desk with patient smiles. When the true road warriors board, they don't get themselves unpacked and comfortable until everyone has boarded the plane. Then there is a mad dash to grab open seats that also have an empty seat next to them. It doesn't happen all the time, but having another seat to stretch out on is the true score!

Pre-order a special meal when you book your flight. Low-cal, low-carb, vegetarian, Kosher — there are some very good choices available on international flights and the meal will be of better quality than the rubbery chicken/pasta choice. It doesn't cost anything extra, but you must order this when you book your flight. Your boarding pass should indicate that you get a special meal; if you don't see it, inquire with the desk when you check in. Make sure you tell the attendant if you have changed seats, as your special meal order will be attached to your original seat.

Keep your cool at the airport. I would rather be down here, wishing I was up there, rather than up there wishing I was down here.

Pilot wisdom from Captain Odell Isaac

Scan this code to go to the Che Bella Tours Marketplace for direct links to products, books and films listed in this book.

AT THE AIRPORT

For international departures, arrive at the airport at least three hours in advance. International flights require check in at the airline departure desk. You present your passport and check your bag. International flights allow one, 50 pound checked bag for Economy and two, 50 pound bags for First-Class. If you are flying an economy airline such as Spirit or Ryan Air during your travels, you will be allowed one 40 pound checked bag, so plan ahead.

Consider a day pass to the airline lounge. Instead of spending hours in an uncomfortable gate seat or coffee shop, you can enjoy a more comfortable atmosphere. Most airlines offer a day rate to their lounge for about $50. The day pass follows you for a full 24 hours, so you can use it when you arrive at the next airport. There is always a free buffet of light fare, coffee, soft drinks and snacks as well as showers, a full bar, television and magazines. You can work at the business center desks or in a comfortable recliner. The monitors placed throughout the lounge keep you apprised on flight status.

Pack to easily repack. At the end of the book is a packing checklist and a complete list of my favorite carry-on and checked bag supplies. Backpacks are a good carry-on of choice because they release your hands to pull a roller board, shuffle through paperwork or just keep you centered and balanced as you are walking. Struggling with a handheld carry-on bag is cumbersome and leaves you open to pickpockets.

Travel and tour documents can be organized in an accordion file folder and slipped easily into the backpack. Consider putting your laptop or tablet into a **Unik plastic carrier** with the zipper at the top of the backpack opening. Your accordion file folder can lay flat against the carrier, and you'll be able to slip your laptop out and return it without disrupting the contents of your backpack.

Have your one-quart bag of liquids easily accessible. Include travel-size **mouthwash**, **toothpaste** and **toothbrush**. Travel packs of **face wipes, disinfecting wipes and deodorant wipes** really save space. To moisturize and stay hydrated throughout the flight, include **cosmetic counter samples of hyaluronic acid and rich moisturizer. Saline nasal spray, Afrin nasal spray and Aquafor** are my nasal protection team.

Liquid prescription medications don't count as part of these liquids, so you can pack them in a separate liquid quart bag.

Have your identification and boarding pass ready in your hand as you enter the security line.

Watch the lines. A family with strollers and toddlers? Someone fiddling with jackets, belts, keys, watches, change in their pockets and multiple carry-on bags? Move to a different line.

Don't go through the x-ray barefoot. Have a pair of ankle socks or slippers in your carry-on to wear as you go through security.

SANDY'S FLIGHT SURVIVAL GUIDE

My seatmates are always fascinated by my routine. I'm not one for chatting on a plane. En route I'm focused on my tours. On the way home, I'm exhausted from months of solid talking.

Get comfortable. My travel outfit is always the same: black skirted leggings, a wicking cami, soft bra with no underwire, a light breathable sweater and my **pashmina scarf** in case I get cold. Layering is the key. I also pack a **complete change of clothes** in case of lost luggage or an unexpected layover. I wear my boots or heaviest shoes on board to leave more room in my checked bag. I immediately change into my **compression knee socks,** which are key to arriving without swollen ankles and developing Deep Vein Thrombosis (DVT). The ankle **socks or slippers** I used to walk through TSA are again used on the plane. Throughout the flight, I make it a point to get up and walk around every few hours for some calf raises, neck rolls and forward bends.

Inflatable neck and lumbar support pillows make the flight much more comfortable. For some reason, plane seats are designed with a deep C-curve, which doesn't match the natural curve of the spine. Inflatable pillows work best to custom fit to your neck or lumbar, and deflate easily to fit into your backpack.

Disinfect. I wipe down the tray, arm rests, TV monitor and buttons. I stay away from putting anything in the back seat pocket. You never know what you're going to find there.

Dinner service usually begins one hour in to the flight. You never know when the attendants will do beverage service, so I bring a **collapsible water bottle** that I fill after getting through security.

After dinner, I'm ready for my sleeping routine. I wipe the day off of my face with the **facial cleansing wipes** and apply a few drops of **hyaluronic acid** and moisturizer. **Saline spray** provides a good moisture base for my nasal passages, which I follow with a spritz of **Afrin** nasal spray. A few years ago, I was diagnosed with vertigo caused by the amount of flying I do, so the Afrin helps prevent the crystals from forming in my ears. One last layer of **Aquafor** seals in all of this goodness and protects my nose from dry cabin air. When it's time to shut down and check out, the **earbuds** go in, movie is started and **eye mask** is at the ready.

Sleeping. I'm careful not to sleep during takeoff or landing. Your inner ears need time to regulate the air pressure. Pinching your nostrils and blowing your nose, as well as deliberate swallowing during takeoff and landing also helps clear the pressure in your ears. Two caplets of **ZzzQuil** at bedtime usually do the trick and don't leave me groggy the next morning.

Arriving. In the morning, I try to get to the restroom as soon as the lights are on. The lines get very long after coffee has been served. Airline breakfasts don't appeal to me at all, so I carry a bag of almonds and Baby Bell cheese packages, which last me until I can enjoy a proper *cappuccino* and *fette biscottate* at my hotel.

Because I know to choose a seat near the egress exit, I'm one of the first to disembark. I make a beeline to Immigration. By the time the rest of the passengers deplane, get through the bathroom lines and finally work their way to Immigration, I'm usually through baggage claim and out the door.

Before I leave the airport, I do an ATM cash withdrawal so I am sure my debit card is working. This gives me a few days to get it straight with the bank if there is a problem.

MANAGING JET LAG

Our body clock responds to a circadian rhythm of daylight and darkness. It is thrown out of sync when we travel internationally and can take several days to readjust.

Get as much sun as you can in the days leading up to your trip. The **Jet Lag Rooster** website is an online tool that creates a sleep schedule based on your departure and arrival information. Plug in your travel details and the app tells you when to sleep and wake up as well as when to expose yourself to sunlight to make your jet lag as short as possible. When you fly, set your watch to the time zone of the arrival city. Try to sleep on the plane.

International flights usually arrive in the morning and hotel check-in is usually at 2 p.m. Get some sunshine and enjoy an al fresco lunch. Exposure to daylight helps you adapt faster to the new time zone. When you get to your room, try to take no more than a one-hour nap. That first night, stay up until your regular bedtime hour and get a minimum four hours of solid sleep. This is called "anchor sleep" and it helps you adapt to the new time zone. That first night, I take **Sundowns Naturals Melatonin** to help me sleep. If I wake up in the middle of the night, I take a bit more. I sometimes will take another pill the next night. By night three, I am on Italian time.

Get as much afternoon sunshine as you can on the last days of your trip. Most international flights back to the U.S. leave during the day, so it is difficult to fall sleep. Another melatonin tablet for a day or two will help you regulate your sleep pattern.

Trains

You don't always have to have an itinerary. Sometimes it's an adventure to go to the train station, look up at the departures board, pick a destination and go!

Above *The Renaissance Sisters getting ready to board a train from Venice to Florence*

Photo by Cinzia Trivisan

Train travel in Italy is fast, fun and one of the easiest ways to get around. High-speed rail links almost every city and town in Italy. At 175 mph, you can often reach your destination in less time than it takes to drive or fly. Most central train stations are in town and an easy walk or taxi ride to or from your hotel.

Buying tickets online. Tickets are available for purchase about three months ahead of your departure, but can get more expensive the closer you are to your travel date. If all details are confirmed, book in advance for the best prices and times. You also can purchase flexible tickets, which are easy to change if you itinerary shifts. Che Bella Tours will be happy to book train tickets for you, or you can go directly to a variety of online sites including:

Omnio ***ItaliaRail*** ***Trenitalia***

Rail Europe ***Italo Treno***

Make sure you select high-speed rail. Regional trains make a lot of stops and don't offer reserved seating. High-speed rail also provides "quiet car" options. This works for people who are working, so note those coaches when you are choosing your seats. All of these sites allow you the choice of paying in U.S. dollars and will confirm your purchase via an email. Read this email carefully, as it will include a link to the actual ticket with a bar code. Download and print this ticket at home before your trip. On board, the conductor will scan that bar code.

Buying tickets at the train station. You can purchase tickets at the counter in the train station. The clerks speak English and can help if you are unsure which train would be best. Prepare for long lines. You can also use a self-serve kiosk if the lines are long and you need to get on a train. Kiosks have an English language option and are very intuitive to use. Pay attention to your valuables while you are at the kiosk. Just beware of "nice" people who want to help you through the transaction — they will want to be paid afterwards and often will be looking at your credit card number.

The Departure Board (*Partenze*). You will see arrival and departure boards throughout the train station. Below shows how you will find your departing train. See the numbers in red that coordinate with the explanations below.

1. **The train number**

2. **Final destination**

3. **Departure time**

4. **Train delay in minutes**

5. **Train stops on your route.** Check carefully to make sure you see your stop on this list.

6. **Track number (*binari*).** Head to the track as soon as it is posted to give yourself time to board comfortably. Many city central stations now also have security, where you will have to present your passport with your ticket to get access to the platforms.

7. **Flashing lights** as the train is pulling in.

ARRIVAL AND DEPARTURE BOARD AT THE STATION

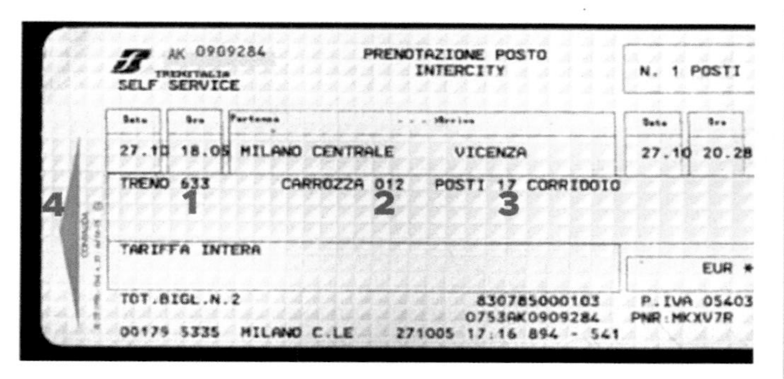

TRAIN TICKET AT THE STATION

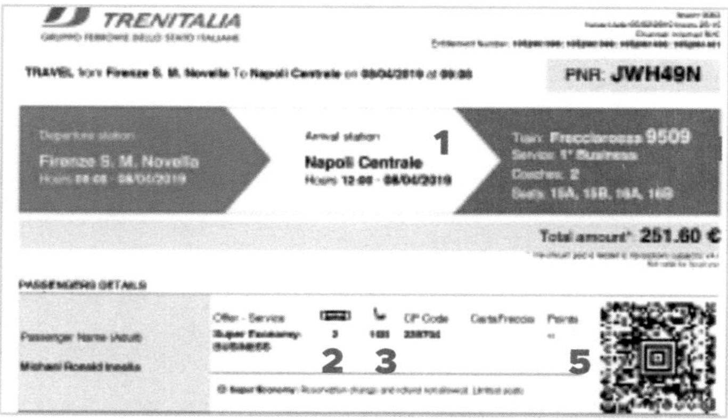

TRAIN TICKET VIA EMAIL

Train tickets can be purchased at the station or via email. On the left, is the ticket you will get at the train station, on the right is the ticket you download from your email. See the numbers keyed on each that coordinate with the explanations below.

1. **Train number**

2. **Carrozza** means coach. Match the number on your ticket with the number on the coach door to make sure you board correctly. Don't mistake the large ***1*** & ***2*** on the coaches, which indicate first and second class.

3. **Posto** is your seat number.

4. **Regionale** means regional trains. These trains offer general boarding without seat assignments. You'll have to stamp this type of ticket by inserting it into the green and grey (or sometimes yellow) machines at the entrance to the platforms to validate the date of travel. If you don't validate these types of tickets, the conductor will require you to buy another one on board.

5. **QR Code** where the conductor will scan to confirm your reservation. If you book online, make sure to download this ticket from your email confirmation.

On the train. First-class tickets include a snack and beverage service. It's also perfectly fine to bring your own food and drinks to enjoy while on board. Don't forget your wine opener! Picnicking as you watch the countryside go by is one of the fun aspects of train travel. Most trains have power outlets for laptops and mobile phones. WiFi login is available for a fee.

Luggage. Most coaches have a luggage rack right inside the doors to accommodate larger suitcases. You'll find ample overhead shelves for carry-ons at your seat. Keep your purse and valuables safe on your person. Only pack what you can physically lift up onto the train. Stops are quick and juggling a lot of heavy suitcases can be a challenge. Some regional train stations don't have elevators, so you will have to carry your luggage down the stairs from the ticketing area, find your track and then lug it back up the stairs to the platform — yet another reason to pack light.

WC* means water closet or restroom.** Look for the ***WC sign at the end of the coach; it will light up green if the restroom is available, red if it's occupied. I always recommend my guests use the WC well before the last stop. Train station facilities are not the most convenient or clean, and they often charge for access.

Prossimo Fermata means "next stop." Stops are listed on the monitors hanging from the coach ceiling and/or on a running LED board above the coach doors. The next stop is announced in both Italian and English well before the train approaches the station. Get your belongings together and move toward the end of the coach when you hear your stop announced. Stops are quick. Juggling heavy luggage, while people are pushing to get off and on, is a challenge. Watch your valuables and make sure you have everything. Once the train pulls out, it's too late.

Strikes. Strikes happen infrequently, are announced long in advance and usually last only a couple of hours. Hotels stay on top of this and can advise you. Most tickets are exchangeable. You will have to go with the flow, but there will be alternatives to get you to your destination within a reasonable amount of time.

Previous page *Stay sharp. Keep your valuables on your person. Nobody will get past this fortress!*

Photo by Vicci Rodgers

Above *"Ferrovia" means train station. It's a place where the next adventure begins.*

Photo by Sandy Gregory

Above *The Milan train station*

Photo by Vicci Rodgers

... and Automobiles

I'm sometimes asked my thoughts about renting a car and driving through Italy. My response always is the same: *"Per che?"* (Why?) Here are my favorite reasons for hiring a private driver:

I'm not a great driver anywhere in the world. It's a fact. Just ask anyone who has white-knuckled through a car ride with me. I'm ok with it. We all have our strengths.

To Italians, rules are merely suggestions — especially on the road. One-way streets, roundabouts, speeding, merging, tailgating, honking, fender-bendering, hands waving and hundreds of scooters weaving through traffic — *mama mia*, why would you want to deal with any of this?

ZTLs are *Zona a Traffico Limitato*, or limited traffic zones. These zones are located in historic city centers, are very poorly marked and very well monitored. Find yourself in one and you'll be puttering along in a sea of pedestrians shooing you over. Soon, a *Policia* will be knocking at your window, cut you a ticket and escort you out of the zone. If you do make it out on your own, know that in a few weeks your rental car company will be charging your credit card the amount of the bill they get from the ZTL camera system. The cameras see all!

Parking in the city? Yellow lines? Blue lines? White lines? Free? Metered? Residents only? FAAAGETABOUTIT!

Parking in the country? They're called hill towns for a reason. It's a real hike to get from the parking lots into the city walls. And at the end of the day, when you walk back down, your luggage might be gone.

Here's my suggestion: City-to-city travel is quicker, easier, cheaper and more comfortable by train and private car. Have Che Bella Tours arrange for a personal driver who will take care of everything. You sit back and enjoy the view, learn a little about the homeland, have wine at lunch, not get lost, be dropped off right at your destination and picked up when and where you desire. You'll be really glad you did.

To Italians, rules are merely suggestions — especially on the road.

I rarely drive myself in Italy, but when I do, it's in a Vintage Cinquecento in Tuscany with my long-time Italian associate, Ales. He leads the way and I pay attention to shifting.

Riding on the back of a scooter is an art. But be forewarned, Italian *motorini* swerve in and out of traffic at very high speeds ... see red lights as more of a suggestion than a rule ... believe sidewalks are not just for pedestrians ... think space between two cars is fair game ... and believe anywhere is a great parking space. So, if you are looking for a little *dolce vida*:

- Hold on tight to your driver and lean the way he leans.
- Don't ride in high heels or tight skirts. Italian women can pull this off, but we cannot.
- Wear a helmet.
- There will be dust and bugs, so fight the urge to smile and don't wear lip gloss!

Above *How many scooters can be squeezed into a small city street?*

Photo by Janette Tepas Images

FREESTYLE PARKING

During a holiday in Rome, my husband and I made plans to meet an old college friend and her new Italian husband at a cafe. As we waited at our sidewalk table, a Smart Car shot out of the roundabout, cut across 3 lanes of traffic, flew up on to the sidewalk, pulled in right next to our table and stopped. They emerged from the tiny car in triumph, smiled at us and said, "Wow, we got a great parking space!"

La Bella Figura

The term *bella* means good. *Figura* refers to a proper behavior, or presenting your best self. Wanting to look fashionable and put together is an integral part of the Italian culture. You'll often see an Italian woman wearing an impossibly tight, short skirt and stiletto heels smoking a cigarette and talking on her cell phone ... while driving a scooter. It's fantastic! Or a man in a crisp Armani suit sweeping the stoop. Even the old nonnas stop traffic as the crowds respectfully part for them as they click along the street shrouded in black designer dresses and well-made shoes. La bella figura is much more than appearance, however, it is about dignity, hospitality and being polite. It is about a sense of self-respect and decorum.

Left *Smartly dressed locals enjoying passeggiata in Santa Margherita Ligure*

Next page *A tour director is always on the job and appropriately dressed for an afternoon of gladiator swordfights.*

Photos by Janette Tepas Images

PURSE OR DAYPACK?

I carry a small **crossbody nylon purse** with lots of organizational pockets and good, sturdy zippers. My hands are free to do commentary or carry shopping bags. A nylon bag is light enough to comfortably and safely lie on my lap when I'm at a restaurant or sitting on a train. I also carry a **purse hook** so I never have to lay my purse on the ground.

If you are a fan of the money belt, **Bandi Belts** are stylishly designed to carry small essentials. I recommend my guests only bring cash and one credit card for the day and keep the rest with their passport in the hotel safe. If you prefer to travel with a backpack, make sure it is a **small daypack**, as many museums and churches require you to check larger backpacks before entering, which is inconvenient and takes up precious tour time. Daypacks leave you vulnerable to pickpockets who come up from behind, so think about what you carry during the day and pack accordingly.

The sun. During my summer tours, I often give the ladies paper Chinese fans. They are a lifesaver in the heat and glaring sun.

The rain. My scientific evidence shows that it doesn't rain if everyone in the group carries an umbrella. When the rain does come, however, digging through your cavernous bag during a downpour is the perfect storm for pickpockets — and the umbrella peddlers. I don't know how many times I spent five Euros on one of these pieces of crap, only to have it last two minutes in the wind before it flew off the stem or buckled inside out. I recommend the sturdy **Kolumbo "Unbreakable" Travel Umbrella**. The rib frame on the Kolumbo is designed to spring back in to shape when the umbrella is flipped inside out during high winds. More and more, however, I have decided **the cheap, disposable rain ponchos from the dollar store** might be better than any umbrella or rain coat, because they weigh nothing and take up zero room. Add to your day pack: a **portable battery charger,** a **travel pack of tissues, Compeed Blister Bandages, sunscreen** and a **water bottle.** You'll be set for the day.

WHAT TO WEAR WHEN YOU TRAVEL

You'll want to be comfortable, but stylish, when you travel to Italy. Here are some guidelines to choosing your travel wardrobe.

- Pre-plan your outfits using pieces that can easily be mixed and matched into different looks. Build around a neutral palette. I am trying to get out of the habit of buying only black travel clothes. It's not just that I need more color in my life, but I wind up with a black cavernous void in my suitcase.
- Choose thin, quick-dry materials that allow for layering.
- Do whatever you can to deflect attention away from yourself. Dress in clothes that do not scream "I am an American!" T-shirts, sweat suits and ball caps emblazoned with American logos and sport teams are not recommended.
- Jeans are absolutely acceptable as long as they are combined with elegant and stylish accessories. A scarf always dresses up an outfit and there are myriad styles to buy in Italy. Men often bring a blazer for the evening, but ties are not necessary.
- Short shorts, spaghetti strap camis and flip flops don't fly in Italy, even during the hot days of summer. Churches require that knees and shoulders be covered. You will be denied entrance or, at some churches, be issued a less-than-stunning paper dress to wear during your visit.

The Anatomy of a Well-packed Suitcase

The most important thing to pack is your sense of humor.

Pack with a purpose when you will be in hotel room after hotel room. Keep everything easily visible and accessible. The less you disrupt your entire suitcase every time you change locations the better. The key is having a system. A place for everything and everything in its place. Packing light makes all the difference when you're rushing for trains, climbing stairs and rolling along cobblestone streets dodging tourists.

There are strict weight rules when flying internationally: One 50 pound bag is the included limit for most coach flights. While first class and business class have more checked-bag options, most tour companies limit you to the one bag and one carry-on rule. You might also be traveling on airlines that have even stricter weight limits.

Weigh your suitcase before you travel. I travel with a **Travel Smart Digital Luggage Scale.** There's nothing worse than a meticulous agent who weighs every item before forcing you to pay extra or repack on the spot.

Love to shop? Pack a rolled-up nylon duffel bag. You can purchase an additional checked-bag allowance on your return flight home. Packing your dirty laundry into the duffel leaves room in your more structured suitcase for souvenirs.

Whether I am traveling for six days or six weeks, I use a **Swiss Gear 20" Expandable Upright Carry-on rollerboard suitcase**. It's super sturdy, and no matter how much I stuff it, this bag never exceeds the 50 pound international (or even the 44 pound discount carrier) weight limit. This size is easy to maneuver through crowds, and the rollerboard slides over cobblestones better than the spinner-type suitcases. The size makes it easy for me to hoist on to a train and store in a small hotel room.

From years on the road, I've learned a few things. As we say in the business, "Lay out everything you think you need to wear and the money you are going to bring, then put back half the clothes and double the cash." At the end of the book is a packing checklist and a complete list of my favorite carry-on and checked bag supplies. .

1. Stuff shoes with their coordinating socks. Stack them on the wheel side of the suitcase so they don't put extra weight on lighter items when the bag is in an upright position.
2. On top of your shoes, stack jeans, pants, shorts and skirts. Fold these items in half lengthwise so that the back pockets face outward. Roll tightly from the bottom to the waistband and align them tightly.
3. Dresses, shirts, sweaters and blouses are placed next. Fold each sleeve backward to create a rectangle, then fold the entire garment in half lengthwise and smooth out wrinkles. Then fold in half again, rolling in any extra material. Place these items vertically, as if you were filing them into a cabinet. This will allow you to view all of your tops at a glance.
4. Pack undergarments and pajamas together in a **packing cube**, as they are the first thing you'll need in the morning and the last thing you'll need at night.
5. Your toiletry bag and styling tools get cushioned in the middle of your bag.
6. In the outside pocket pack two large **Spacesaver compression packing bags**: one for dirty laundry and one as a wet bag. Jackets or items you don't need every day can also go in the outside pocket.
7. Belts, scarves, workout resistance bands etc. go in the outside small pocket.

SOME ADDITIONAL PACKING TIPS:

- Before you travel, take photos and make a list of the contents of your suitcase in case it's lost in transit. This will help you with airline and travel insurance claims. Put a **LugLoc GPS luggage tracker** in your suitcase.
- Have two luggage tags. Put one on the bag and one inside, in case the outer tag gets damaged or ripped off. Do not put your home address on your luggage tag, just your name as it appears on your passport, email and phone (with +1 for U.S. international dialing).
- If you are traveling with a partner, put a set of your clothes in their suitcase. If one of your bags is lost or delayed, at least you will have one set of clothes until your luggage is retrieved.
- Hotel shower caps make great shoe covers.
- To keep toiletries from spilling in your suitcase, stretch a piece of plastic wrap between the bottle and cap then twist to create a seal. Use pieces of the hotel shower cap to replace the plastic wrap as you go.
- Planning to bring home wine or olive oil? You'll be glad you brought padded travel bags that maintain a seal in case the bottles break or leak. I like the **Wine Skin** brand.
- A dryer sheet in your suitcase helps keep it smelling nice throughout your trip.
- Ziplock bags in all sizes are your friend!
- **Tide Pods** or **Sink Suds** are easy to carry and melt quickly in the sink for washing clothing by hand. **Downy Wrinkle Release** really works to remove wrinkles without ironing. Most Italian hotels do not offer an iron and ironing board in your room.
- **A Rubz Ball and Yoga Toes** keep your feet in top shape. spikes on the rubber Rubz Ball hit the pressure points on the bottoms of your feet, and the Yoga Toes hurt so good as they stretch out your toes. At the end of the day, these two little remedies massage your feet and alleviate tension in your legs and back after a long day of walking on cobblestones.
- **The Braun M90 Mobile Electric Shaver** is fully washable under running water and no plug is required. It is powered by easily replaceable batteries, so no need to worry about another converter plug.

Hotels, Villas and Views

"LIFE IS NOT MEASURED BY THE NUMBER OF BREATHS WE TAKE, BUT BY THE MOMENTS THAT TAKE OUR BREATH AWAY."
MAYA ANGELOU

ITALIAN HOTELS

You may be surprised by some major differences between American and European hotel rooms. Many of the quirks of European hotel rooms are due to the fact that they are retrofitted to 200+ year-old buildings.

Space is a precious commodity in European cities. You will not have the spacious two queen bed layout typical in the U.S. Bed configurations are either a "double-twin" (two single beds spaced about five inches apart and made up separately) or a *matrimonia* (two single beds pushed together and made up as one). If you reserve a single, expect one twin bed with little additional room space. Country villas and hotel chains offer more options.

Your room key card or plug-in key often will be required to turn on the electricity in your room. Because of very high electricity costs in Italy, you'll also find that hallway lights are on a timer, or motion sensor that often switch off while you are en route to or from your room.

A small can of Lysol, or package of disinfecting wipes, serve as a quick fix for any germs on doorknobs, faucets, handles and especially the TV remote. I also immediately remove the top cover on the bed because ... eeew!

ELEVATORS

Hotel elevators are often the size of a tiny, coat closet. If you're lucky, the elevator will fit two to three people with luggage. Don't try to overload it — with people or luggage — as you will get stuck.

PRIMO PIANO

In Europe you will find that the ground floor is labeled "0" and the second floor is labeled as the *primo piano* (first floor.) In some of the smaller hotels, there also might be a first floor walk-up before you even get to the lobby — one more reason to pack light.

PERSONAL SAFETY

When checking in, don't allow the clerk to say your name and room number out loud if there are other people around the desk.

Keep the hotel business card separate from your key card. One way is to keep a picture of the hotel information on your phone.

Request a room away from the exit stairway or elevator. Check your room to make sure it is empty upon your return and bring a rubber doorstop to seal yourself in for an added level of security.

If you are staying for only two nights, forgo housekeeping so your room is not accessible to anyone during your stay. The threat typically doesn't come from the staff themselves, but rather when the door is wide open and anyone can walk in. The usual routine of these thieves, called "dippers," is to walk into the room pretending to be the guest saying they forgot something. They grab what they can and walk out.

Hang out the "Do Not Disturb" sign and leave the TV playing at a low volume to give the room an occupied feel.

Above *The beach in Positano*

Photo by Sandy Gregory

PLUGGING IN WITHOUT BLOWING UP

All hotels and villas in Europe have hair dryers, but they vary greatly in quality. Decide what your "do" will do when you travel. But beware, European voltage is 220. If your hairdryer and curling iron from home are dual voltage (like 100V~240V), you'll only need a plug adapter suitable to fit European outlets. However, if your appliance reads 110V or 120V, it is single voltage and will require both an **adapter** and a **converter.** Look for the voltage rating.

Or, based on my personal experience, leave your hairdryer at home. It will short out, but even worse, will blow up the hotel. And if you must bring a curling iron, I love the **ConAir MiniPro Cordless**, which runs on refillable tubes of butane allowed through TSA.

STAYING CONNECTED

Most hotels offer free WiFi throughout the building, but it might be a challenge to find a strong signal.

There are English channels on your hotel TV including BBC World News, Fox News, Bloomberg Television, Al Jazeera English and CNN International. You can also tap into your VPN to get any channel, anywhere.

TOILETS AND SHOWERS

Plumbing in Italy might take a little getting used to. Flushers can be pushed, pulled, stepped on or twisted. Public toilets often do not have seats, or sometimes are simply a hole in the ground, while some require pay for use. Your hotel room will most likely have a bidet (pronounced buh-*day*). The bidet is used for cleaning yourself after using the toilet. They're quite refreshing after you wipe or to freshen up during a hot day. Adjust the temperature and flow of the water, straddle and hover over the bowl facing the controls, splash up with your hands and dry with the small towel provided.

Hotel showers can be compact. Sometimes even turning on the water can require an engineering degree. You might not have unlimited hot water or strong pressure. You often will see a string dangling in the shower. This is not a clothesline, but rather an "I've fallen and I can't get up" alarm that alerts the front desk of an emergency. If you require a tub, request one when you check in.

European hotels often do not provide washcloths, so it's always a good idea to bring your own and carry it in a Ziplock bag.

AIR CONDITIONING

The cost of electricity in Europe is astronomical — about 50 percent more than we pay in the U.S. Heating and air conditioning are also not as powerful as U.S. systems. You rarely will find a heated swimming pool. Italians are not fans of air conditioning, and many think it is bad for your throat. Always afraid of catching a cold, they wrap themselves in fashionable scarves ... even in the summer!

European air conditioning should be considered more of a climate-control system. Most of the time there will be a unit on the wall that turns on with a remote control. Most units have three settings for the fan, plus a "cool" setting, which is nowhere near as frosty as we Americans are used to. In addition, **some hotels automatically turn off the A/C at midnight** — even in the summer — to help contain electrical costs. When you check in, ask the front desk to keep your A/C on all night. Many hotels don't run their A/C from September until well in to April.

SHOWER CAPS

Hotel shower caps make great shoe covers and keep the city dirt off of clean clothes when packed in your suitcase.

Above *A favorite villa in Tuscany*

Left *Che Bella Tours selects hotels and villas that offer a full buffet breakfast that is included in the price of your room. This buffet includes not just the breads and pastries, but also eggs, meats, cheeses, yogurts and fruit to satisfy the American palate. This feast is accompanied by wonderful coffee.*

Photos by Sandy Gregory

Above *Wild beauty sculpted by wind and sea, Capri's jagged coast is encircled by the famous Faraglioni Rocks.*

Photo by Sandy Gregory

Above *A view from Piazelle Michelangelo, San Miniato al Monte stands atop one of the highest points in Florence.*

Photo by Sandy Gregory

Out and About

BE RESPECTFUL TO OTHER CULTURES AND OPEN TO NEW EXPERIENCES. REMAIN PATIENT, UNDERSTANDING AND KIND TO THOSE AROUND YOU. YOU WILL BE PLEASANTLY SURPRISED HOW MUCH MORE YOU'LL GET OUT OF YOUR TRAVEL EXPERIENCE.

ACT APPROPRIATELY

Sprin tourist decorum and increase visitors' awareness of the extreme fragility of the cities and their vast artistic and cultural heritage. There now are penalties for tourists who jump into fountains, walk the streets with alcohol, or eat on the steps of sites or along the fountains in the piazzas. Consider these basic rules:

- Don't block pedestrian traffic when taking a photograph.
- Speak quietly. Europeans love Americans, but think we're very loud.
- Learn a little Italian. Cut out and bring our Italian cheat sheets with you on your trip. The Italians will appreciate your efforts and it will add a new dynamic to your trip.
- Pay attention to traffic signals, cross with the group and watch for scooters zipping in between cars.

BE RESPECTFUL

Refrain from touching, leaning, standing or climbing on the ancient structures or walls.

Throughout the world, different religions and customs have certain behaviors, dress codes and traditions. While some may be out of step with your beliefs, understand that behaviors or jokes in one part of the world may not translate.

GREETINGS

"*Buongiorno*" is used from morning until after lunch as a formal hello.

"*Buona sera*" can be used all afternoon and evening.

"*Buon pomeriggio*" which means good afternoon until dinner time.

"*Arrivederci*" is a formal way to say goodbye.

"*Ciao*" is an informal way of saying "hi" or "bye."

"*Salve*" is a more formal greeting for someone you don't know well.

DRESS CODES

Churches in Italy require that knees and shoulders be covered, so dress accordingly. Many churches will prevent you from entering if you are dressed inappropriately, and some even sell paper dresses to put on over your own clothes. Have a scarf with you to cover your shoulders or to create a quick long skirt. Eating, cell phone use and loud conversation is prohibited. Many churches also don't allow photography or video recording. Your guide will let you know.

ADVICE FOR WOMEN

I have always felt safe while traveling alone in Italy, even in big cities at night, *if* I follow these guidelines:

Stick to the main streets and populated areas after dark.

Avoid empty train compartments.

Know where you are going.

Stride confidently and purposefully.

Ignore any comments or catcalls.

In conversation, *always* be on your way to meet someone who is expecting you at a certain time.

Carry a safety whistle and a tactical flashlight. Sometimes things get dark — power outages, environments with little or no light or natural disasters. It's good to have a powerful flashlight that can guide you, double as a weapon and won't use up your cell phone battery. The brightness of a tactical flashlight can temporarily blind an attacker, helping to create the time necessary to give you the chance to get away. They are legal everywhere, including on the plane. Always be prepared, and even better, be equipped for the unexpected.

SUPPORT LOCALS

Part of the adventure of travel is shopping in the local markets, dining at family run restaurants and supporting the local artisans. Italian artisan products are made by the hands of talented craftsmen, using techniques that often are passed down from generation to generation. Wake up early and enjoy the morning markets. After the day-trippers have left, participate in the local *passeggiata* (evening walk). This is the time when locals meet up with friends and family.

IN-COUNTRY GUIDES AND DRIVERS

One of the great features of a Che Bella Tours is the wealth of knowledge and experience from our in-country associates who serve as guides and drivers. Guidebooks don't begin to provide the sense of place and history you get from a local tour guide. Che Bella Tours maintains close relationships with the best in the business, including published authors, scientists, historians and curators. Our guides are great storytellers and passionately committed to environmental and cultural preservation. They also are great resources for hints and tips about places to eat or shop during your downtime. Sightseeing should be an interactive experience, and our guides are more than just providers of information, they set the tone for your time in their city.

Be prepared. Come ready, on time and dressed appropriately for the experience and the weather. Have the right footwear, a sweater or coat if weather dictates, sunscreen, a hat, and an umbrella or rain poncho. As we say in my home state of Colorado, "There is no bad weather, there are only bad clothes." One person complaining about being too cold, too hot or too tired can spoil the experience for the group.

Be on time. When everyone arrives on time, your guide doesn't have to rush through parts of the tour to make pre-scheduled, skip-the-line reservations.

Follow the guide's lead. Pay attention and don't stray from the group. Your guide might be negotiating crowds or traffic, pacing the walk to reveal a sight at just the right moment, or answering a question. Take advantage of the "comfort" stops so you don't hold up the group when nature calls. We give everyone plenty of time to take pictures. Please be respectful of the group and be ready to move on when directed by the guide.

Lean in, get involved, pay attention and ask questions. A tour is not a lecture, but rather an interaction between the guide, the guests and the sights. Too often people ask questions about information that was just presented. Your guide watches you just as closely as you watch him or her. Engaging commentary feeds off of enthusiastic attention. There is nothing a tour guide loves more than to have guests excited and interested about what is being said.

GRATUITIES

Experienced travelers know that tipping is an expected element of worldwide travel almost everywhere. Please tip guides, drivers, porters, housekeeping and servers. Show them that their work is valued and appreciated. Here is a simple guide to help you plan:

Tour Director:
$9 - 15/day/person

Day Guide:
5 Euro/person/tour

Driver:
2 Euro/person/day

Porter:
1 Euro per bag

Housekeeping:
1 Euro per night left on the desk or nightstand

CURRENT EVENTS

Stay abreast of international news before traveling. *BBC* and *Al Jazeera* cover the world well, and many hotels will have English language newspapers like *USA Today* and *The Wall Street Journal*. It's also helpful to be aware of travel advisories, strikes, holidays or cultural events that may happen upon during your trip.

My Favorite Books

ROME

***SPQR,* by Mary Beard.** To this day, you'll find these letters all over Rome – even on the manhole covers. SPQR means *Senatus Populusque Romanus* (the Senate and the Roman people). In the context of the rise of the Roman Empire, this author focuses on the lives of the average people who lived in the era.

VENICE

***The Politics of Washing: Real Life in Venice,* by Polly Coles.** This is a city perilously under siege from tourism, but its people refuse to give up. They love Venice with a passion. This book is a fascinating window into the world of ordinary Venetians and the strange and unique place they call home.

***Death at La Fenice* and *Blood from a Stone,* by Donna Leon.** Any of her mysteries featuring the fictional hero, Commissario Guido Brunetti, is a winner.

***The City of Falling Angels,* by John Berendt.** This story tells the truth behind the 1996 fire at La Fenice opera house in Venice. This author also wrote *Midnight in the Garden of Good and Evil.*

TUSCANY

***The Agony and the Ecstasy,* by Irving Stone.** I first read this historical novel about the life of Michelangelo when I attended college in Florence. The streets and artwork came alive as I was studying his works while living in this Renaissance city.

***Sixteen Pleasures,* by Robert Hellenga.** This wonderful novel focuses on the "Mud Angels," who helped to clean up and preserve the art and books in Florence after the 1966 flood. Many U.S. volunteers went to help rescue works of art. This is one woman's story of her struggle to help save a waterlogged convent library.

***Decameron*, by Giovanni Boccaccio.** A medieval story of seven young women and three young men who take refuge in a secluded villa outside Florence in order to escape the Black Death. Over ten evenings, to pass the time, each traveler takes a turn as storyteller.

***A Light in the Ruins,* by Chris Bohjalian.** In 1943, the prominent Rosati family was confident their grand villa would protect them and garner favor from the greedy German forces intruding on Italy. Jumping forward to 1955, the story picks up with the brutal slayings and heinous dismemberments of Rosati family members by an unknown assailant. Serafina Bettini, a Florence police investigator, is assigned to the gruesome case. She promptly finds herself immersed in family drama as she pursues the serial killer, who is determined to slay the entire clan. Serafina discovers she has a personal relationship with the maniacal murderer.

THE SOUTH

***My Brilliant Friend,* by Elena Ferrante.** This is a rich story about two friends growing up in a poor, but vibrant, neighborhood on the outskirts of Naples. This story is an HBO series.

***Calabria: The Other Italy,* by Karen Haid.** My grandfather, Dr. Michael Serio, came to the U.S. from Calabria when he was eight years old. My grandfather, and this book, are inspirations to travel there soon.

***The Ancient Shore: Dispatches from Naples, The Bay of Noon* and other books by Shirley Hazzard.** Born in Australia, Shirley Hazzard first moved to Naples as a young woman in the 1950s to work at the United Nations. This was the beginning of a long love affair with the city. My grandmother, Genevieve DelBello Valentine Serio, came to the U.S. from Naples when she was three years old, so this is an inspiration every time I visit this rich and historical city.

Scan this code to go to the Che Bella Tours Marketplace for direct links to products, books and films listed in this book.

***Unto the Sons*, by Gay Talese.** Gay Talese, one of America's greatest living authors, is from Calabria. This is the saga of his family's emigration to America from Italy in the years preceding World War II. It's the story of all immigrant families and the hope and sacrifice that took them from the familiarity of the old world into the mysteries and challenges of the new.

TRAVELING TO ITALY

***The Italians*, by John Hooper.** As a tour director since 2008, I love this study of Italy, where geography, history and tradition weave a portrait of the Italians at their best and their worst.

***Italian Neighbors, An Italian Education and Italian Ways*, by Tim Parks.** Certainly we all have the longing to live "Under the Tuscan Sun" and there have been many books written in the genre. I like this series about an Englishman married to an Italian wife in Verona. Tim Parks is a very good storyteller and observer of people and culture.

***La Bella Figura: A Field Guide to the Italian Mind* by Beppe Severgnini.** This is your book if you want a fun peek into Italian culture through the eyes of a local.

***La Bella Lingua*, by Dianne Hales.** This book is a celebration of the language and culture of Italy. It is the story of how a language shaped a nation. Told against the backdrop of one woman's personal quest to speak fluent Italian, this is for anyone who finds the idea of living the Italian life powerfully seductive.

ART

***Lives of the Artists*, by Giorgio Vasari.** This is an excellent reference book for anyone who is interested in the Renaissance masters. Vasari was born in Arezzo. A painter and architect, he is more famous, however, for his biographies of contemporaries than any of his own works. The talents of the Renaissance artists made them geniuses, but it was Vasari's words that made them celebrities. His book also provides an insider's view of the business of art and the struggles artists faced to thrive in the environment of pleasing their patrons. Vasari also dishes on the artists behind the works: the groundwork laid by Leonardo da Vinci; the showdown between Michelangelo and Pope Julius II over the Sistine Chapel; the competitive subterfuge of Raphael.

***The Stones of Florence*, by Mary McCarthy.** A unique history of Florence, from its inception to the dominant role it came to play in the world of art, architecture and Italian culture.

***Brunelleschi's Dome: How a Renaissance Genius Reinvented Architecture*, by Ross King.** On August 19, 1418, a competition concerning Florence's magnificent new cathedral, Santa Maria del Fiore — already under construction for more than a century — was announced. Of the many plans submitted, one stood out: a daring and unorthodox solution to vaulting what is still the largest dome (143 feet in diameter) in the world. It was offered not by a master mason or carpenter, but by a goldsmith and clockmaker named Filippo Brunelleschi. Starting at the age of 41, he would dedicate his next 28 years to solving the puzzles of the dome's construction. In the process. Brunelleschi reinvented the field of architecture. This book is one of my favorites.

CUISINE

***Italian Food Rules*, by Ann Reavis.** In Italy, they love making rules, but hate to follow them. However, when it comes to cuisine, food rules are carved in stone. And for those of you who have traveled with me to Italy, you know food rules are not merely a suggestion.

***Why Italians Love to Talk About Food*, by Elena Kostioukovitch**. Italy is food and food is Italy: literally, emotionally, historically, culturally and symbolically. This book is organized by region and tells a wonderful story about the history of Italian cuisine.

***Ecco la Cucina*, by Gina Stipo.** Chef, instructor, restaurateur, culinary tour director and my friend, Gina Stipo is another Italian-American who brings groups to Italy. She lived in Siena for many years and ran a cooking school. Her recipes are authentic and easy to follow.

***Honey from a Weed*, by Patience Gray.** This 1986 autobiographical cookbook has been on my shelf for years. It's a story of the author's relocation from London, marriage to a sculptor and travel throughout the Mediterranean. Gray celebrates, through her recipes, the places she loves. In Puglia, she cooked with the local produce, including the weeds. My own grandmother, who came from southern Italy, also used the weeds from her backyard to make wonderful dishes.

My Favorite Films

Big Night. An American movie set in Atlantic City, this film is about two brothers from Italy who open up a restaurant. To save their business, they take a chance and create one epic night of food, friends and family. A Serio family favorite, we make and enjoy the food featured in the movie, especially the timpano. Stanley Tucci wrote and starred in this movie, along with Isabella Rosallini, Tony Shalhoub and Mark Anthony.

The Godfather. It's a classic. The cast. The criminals. The family. The staging. The camera work. The music. If you travel with me, bring your favorite line from the series. My line is, "Leave the gun, take the cannoli!"

Tea with Mussolini. Set in Florence and San Gimignano, this is a true story about a gaggle of Englishwomen caught in the fray of WWII. Maggie Smith, Judi Dench, Joan Plowright, Cher and Lily Tomlin star in this Franco Zeffirelli film. Available on DVD or from the local library. My copy is worn and scratched from the many times I have played this little gem for my guests on my motor coach.

Mid-August Lunch. A charming tale of good food, feisty ladies and unlikely friendships during a very Roman holiday. Broke, and armed with only a glass of wine and a sense of humor, middle-aged Gianni resides with his 93-year-old mother in their ancient apartment. The condo debts are mounting, but if Gianni looks after the building manager's mother during the Pranzo di Ferragosto (the Feast of the Assumption), all will be forgiven. An auntie and a mother-in-law join the party. Can Gianni keep four such lively mamas well fed and happy in these cramped quarters?

The Bicycle Thief. This is a simple, powerful film about a man named Ricci, who joins the queue every morning, looking for work. One day, there is a job for a man with a bicycle. "I have a bicycle," he says! The bicycle allows Ricci to go to work as a poster-hanger for cinema advertisements. Soon, of course, the bike is stolen, no doubt by another man who needs a job. The cycle of theft and poverty is the theme of this movie. In Italian with English subtitles.

Cinema Paradiso. This is a sweet story about a young boy's friendship with a movie house operator and their mutual love of film and fantasy. In Italian with English subtitles.

La Grande Bellezza (The Great Beauty). Rome is the backdrop of this reflective story about 65-year-old Italian socialite who, for decades, seduced his way through lavish parties and romance. Depressed with the high life, a shock from his past causes him to rethink the beauty of life and the meaning of the superficial. Available on Netflix.

Life is Beautiful. A Jewish librarian and his family become victims of the Holocaust. While in the concentration camp, he uses a mixture of will, humor, and imagination to protect his son from the dangers that surround them. Papa tells his son that they are competing with others to win an armoured tank. Everything from food shortages to tattoos becomes part of the contest. This movie was filmed in Arezzo, a place I love to travel with my guests.

THEN THERE ARE THE CHICK FLICKS

The language, the music, the passion toward life — all contribute to the romance of Italy. The first time I stepped foot onto a cobblestone piazza, I was smitten with *la dolce vita*. I'm a sucker for a chick flick about a grown-up woman who's on a beautiful, life-affirming journey. Here are a few of my guilty pleasures:

A Room with a View. Lucy Honeychurch's journey to self-discovery during Victorian England is set in beautiful Florence. As Lucy is exposed to opportunities previously not afforded to women, her mind — and heart — must open. Before long, she's in love with an "unsuitable" man and is faced with an impossible choice to follow her heart or be pressured into propriety. There is a newer version, but I prefer the 1986 movie featuring a young Helena Bonham Carter, Daniel Day Lewis, Maggie Smith and Judi Dench.

Enchanted April. A wonderful movie about new life, rekindled relationships, new beginnings, new friendships and finding love again. Filmed in beautiful Positano. Sometimes a change of scenery can change everything.

Under the Tuscan Sun. When Frances Mayes (Diane Lane) learns her husband is cheating on her, life is turned upside down. In an attempt to bring her out of a deep depression, her best friend, Patti (Sandra Oh), encourages Frances to take a tour of Italy. During the trip, she impulsively decides to purchase a rural Tuscan villa and struggles to start her life anew amid colorful local characters.

The first time I visited Cortona was in 1985 to attend the wedding of some friends from my days living in Florence. At that time, it was a sleepy town that clung quietly to the side of a hill, where I was one of a very few tourists wandering through the steep, narrow streets. Cortona was changed with the publication of Mayes' book in 1996 and the subsequent movie in 2003. Everything under the sun became Tuscan: Tuscan kitchens, Tuscan soaps, Tuscan sandwiches. I returned to Cortona to 2004. The town had grown a bit and was dotted with a few lovely restaurants and boutique shops. By 2009, when I started as a tour director, it was a boomtown. The company I worked for based their marketing on all things *Under the Tuscan Sun*.

At the hotel, we were required to dramatically award someone "The Diane Lane Room" upon check-in. I took many of my guests on a morning hike to the real Bramasole. People were always disappointed when I told them there was no fountain in Signorelli Square.

Today, Cortona is both rustic and elegant, a sophisticated mix of locals and others who have settled there from around the world. The afternoon into the evening *passeggiata* is my favorite time. The day-trippers have left and the shops stay open late. There are plenty of restaurants to enjoy a drink, people watch and maybe dream of one day living under the Tuscan sun.

Letters to Juliet. While visiting Verona, a young woman visits Juliet's house, where the lovelorn drop notes in the red mailbox of Shakespeare's tragic heroine, Juliet Capulet. This story, filled with love and romance, inspired me to go to Verona to write my own letter to Juliet. Like the movie, my note went into the little red mailbox. Curiously, Juliet's 13th century house also had a computer, so I followed up with an email: "Dear Juliet, per my letter in the post, please facilitate promptly as I am 52 and not getting any younger." Three weeks later I met Odell, who became my husband.

Dear Juliet,

IN REFERENCE TO MY LETTER IN [illegible] POST. PLEASE FACILI[illegible]
PROMPTLY AS I AM 52 AND NOT GETTING ANY YOUNGER!

GRAZIE,
SANDY

NOTES

EATING IN ITALY

PARLA COME MANGI = SPEAK THE LANGUAGE OF YOUR FOOD

La Tavola. Italians talk about food. A lot. Talking about food means celebrating tradition. In this culture, a family recipe stems from a sense of region and heritage.

Food saturated every part of my family's life. Most days, you were hit with the waft of garlic sizzling in oil when you came through the door. A maze of freshly rolled strands of pasta draped over brooms and mops stretched down the hallway. The crowded kitchen always had a pot of "gravy" simmering on the stove. We grew up learning how to cook, not from books, but from our mother, grandmothers and aunts who drank coffee, watched *As the World Turns* and cooked up a storm. Italian. Polish. Chinese. Mexican. No matter what they were making, Grandma Gonciarz always said, "Just make it with love."

Our Polish mom was actually the best Italian cook in the family. We all learned the family gravy recipe from her and, after much practice, made it our own. You knew your gravy was up to par when Mom finally gifted you with your own gravy pot.

Sunday Gravy. Sunday lunches were spent at Grandma Serio's house, where three generations squeezed tightly around her long table. As I grew, and my point of view of that table changed, one memory stayed the same: Grandma's enormous ceramic pasta bowl, decorated with swashes of pink and lavender flowers, always filled with something homemade and delicious. All the people I loved sat for hours passing that bowl around the table laughing, arguing and talking over each other, the volume rising as the sun slowly set.

Pastabowlgate. As in many families, years go by and narratives change. Grandma Serio's funeral lunch gathered the family around her table once again. My aunt now positioned herself at the head, draped in Grandma's fur and jewels. I struggled with the catered food in front of me and the silence around the table. I don't know what made me blurt out, "Remember Grandma's pasta bowl? I remember Sunday lunches growing up, and it's the only thing I would love to have as a memory of her." Eighteen sets of eyes bore down on me, and then redirected to my aunt. She looked down the long table with a smile, slowly met my gaze, and quietly and firmly replied, "No."

As guests began to arrive for the funeral reception, my brother and I were putting the lunch dishes away. Something caught Danny's eye. He pointed to an item on the top shelf under a pile of papers. It was *the pasta bowl*. He pulled it down and handed it to me. It was chipped and worn. Like all childhood memories, it was a whole lot smaller than I remembered. This piece of junk had been shoved out of sight, but to me it was a treasure. We peeked out into the living room where the guests milled around the sweets' table and my Aunt was holding court. Danny and I looked down at that bowl, then to each other. "Grandma would want me to have it, right?" With a devilish grin, he shrugged, "Leave the gun, take the cannoli."

Just make it with love.

Marie Gonciarz

Top left *Grandma Marie Gonciarz*

Top right *Daughter, like mother. Gerry Serio*

Bottom left *Daughter, like mother, like grandma. Sandy Gregory*

Bottom right *Sons, like mother, like grandma, like great-grandma. Jackson and Joe Gregory*

The Italian Restaurant Experience

Next page *Preparing truffle risotto in Lake Como.*

Photo by Sandy Gregory

Cuisine is a big part of an Italian travel experience. On a trip with Che Bella Tours, when we gather around the table as a group, it is a celebration of good food and wine, culture and friendship.

Hosting this celebration is one of the joys of my job. On our tours, I take you to my favorite off-the-beaten-path restaurants, guide you through the menu, inspire you to choose something you've never tried before, choose the perfect wine pairings and throw in some local delicacies to broaden your palate and surprise you a bit. When we roll our sleeves up for a cooking lesson, savor a wine tasting, or enjoy a local farm or market tour, you'll go home with new knowledge that will draw you under Italy's spell and increase your hunger for more.

In this chapter, I'll walk you through the Italian restaurant experience, highlight some of the most important Italian products and give you an overview of cooking lessons and wine tasting experiences. Recipes from many of the featured dishes are in my cookbook: *Make it with Love: Recipes from My Italian Travels for the American Kitchen*, at the end of this book.

CONSIDER TAKING A FOOD TOUR

There is no better way to get the taste of a new place than walking through the markets, side street restaurants and food shops with a local guide. The value is not just someone who shows you around their town, but also who gives you their insider's enthusiasm about how food is grown, bought and sold, as well as what — and where — to eat in their city. You will find that your best meals will not come from the Michelin, Yelp or Trip Advisor recommendations, but rather from off-the-beaten path places where the locals eat.

TYPES OF RESTAURANTS

Bar Serves cocktails, coffee and soft drinks, plus a variety of pastries, snacks and sandwiches. Usually has only stand-up counter service.

Gastronomia Like a bar, but with more sandwich and snack options.

Café Like a bar, but with small indoor and outdoor tables. Know that you will pay more for your beverage if you sit at the table rather than stand at the bar.

Tavola Calda Casual a la carte buffet with lots of cold and hot plate choices. Great for the busy traveler.

Osteria A casual eatery serving simple, rustic, traditional food and good, local wines.

Trattoria A casual, family-owned place with a limited menu of fresh seasonal food. Varies in size and price range.

Ristorante A restaurant with a full menu and extensive wine list.

MEALTIMES

Breakfast: *Colazione.* A typical breakfast for an Italian is a frothy *cappuccino* with a *cornetto*, a croissant-style bread pastry, eaten while standing in a neighborhood bar. Italians save their appetite for a proper lunch. Most vacation hotels and villas, however, offer a full breakfast that includes eggs, meats, cheeses, yogurts, pastries and fruit to satisfy the American palate. Be warned, however, that scrambled eggs are often bland and runny, and the "bacon," soggy. Italians do not eat these heavy breakfast foods and are not very good at making them. Be assured, however, that whatever breakfast foods you choose, it will be accompanied by a wonderful cup of coffee.

Lunch: *Pranzo.* Lunch is enjoyed between 12:30 and 2:30 p.m. In small towns, expect many stores to shut down for a proper lunch. Enjoy this tradition while on your own trip and plan your day accordingly.

Dinner: *Cena.* It's important to know, when making plans for dinner, that restaurants generally do not start serving until 7:00 p.m., with 9:00 p.m. prime dining time. Don't be surprised if your 7:00 p.m. reservation takes you to an empty restaurant. Rest assured that come 10:00 p.m., the place will be jumping.

REGIONAL CUISINE

Chefs in Italian restaurants around the world improvise and experiment to create dazzling takes on Italian dishes. In Italy, however, classic recipes rarely change. Just like the differences in language, history and sensibility, each region has its own culinary tradition. Ingredients are simple and the quality of the cuisine is based on the quality of these ingredients. There is no such thing as "Italian Seasoning" in Italy. You will not get a meatball on top of spaghetti. Caesar Salad? Invented in Mexico. Veal or Chicken Parm? Nope. Deep dish pizza? Just a variation of *focaccia*. And no, you will not dig in to a sausage and pepper combo topped with *giardiniera*. But you'll be far from disappointed, because in Italy, discovering regional cuisine means discovering local spirit.

Whether for pranzo or cena, don't feel pressured into ordering all of the courses.

The Italian Menu

Italian menus are presented in courses, with each course ordered separately.

- **APARITIVI**
  Pre-dinner cocktails.
- **ANTIPASTI**
  Appetizers. *Anti* means "before" *pasto* "the meal."
- **PRIMI PIATTI**
  The first course: pasta, risotto, polenta and soup.
- **SECONDI PIATTI**
  The second course: meat, fish and poultry.
- **CONTORNI E INSALATE**
  Vegetables, potatoes and salad.
- **DOLCE, CAFE E DIGESTIVI**
  Desserts, coffee and after-dinner drinks.

Whether for *pranzo* or *cena*, don't feel pressured into ordering all of the courses. While the actual servings are thankfully much smaller and more manageable than those served in the U.S., it can add up. Think about ordering a few plates of *antipasti* to share with the table, your own *primo piatto* and/or *secondo* depending on how hungry you are, and then order the *contorni* or *insalati* for the table. If you decide to have a pasta for your first course and no *antipasti*, then a salad and no *secondo*, expect a little confusion from the kitchen, that are set up to serve in a certain order.

A TIP: Walk past the restaurants that try to pull you in with tourist menus and photos of the dishes. These are usually just overpriced "front of the house" tourist establishments where the food is commissaried in from another location, not made to order.

Your meal will include a basket of bread for the table. In Italy, table bread is more of a utensil than an eat-alone food. It's a base for *antipasti* meats and cheeses, and used to sop up the last of the pasta sauce. No butter is served and no Italian would ever dip their bread into plates of olive oil drizzled with balsamic or grated cheese. That is an American creation.

Water is always offered and it's always bottled. Tap water, *acqua dal rubinetto,* is perfectly safe to drink. You can ask for it, but your waiter will be reluctant to bring it to you. Bottled water is offered. Flat bottled water is *sin gas* or *naturale*; sparkling water is *con gas* or *frizzante*. You can ask for ice. This does not mean you will get it. If you do, it probably will be just a cube or two.

Aperitivi

***Passeggiata* is the evening walk and the main social event of the day.** In every town, village and city in Italy, when the shop doors close, the last of the day-trippers leave and the lights begin to twinkle, this evening ritual begins. *"Andiamo a fare qualche vasca!"* means let's go do some laps. Families take to the streets to mingle. The young meet up with friends. Couples stroll hand in hand. The *nonni* sit along the route, nurse a glass of wine and hold court. Traditional *aperitivi* will be light drinks such as wine, prosecco or a cocktail such as a *Bellini, Negroni, Campari* or an *Aperol Spritz. Birra Moretti, Peroni* and *Nastro Azzurro* are widely available and craft beers have really blossomed over the past 10 years.

Nuts, nibbles and Pringles. Drinks are always accompanied by a variety of savory nibbles such as nuts, cheeses, olives or chips. The Pringles phenomenon puzzles me. For a country whose cuisine is based on the quality and seasonal freshness of ingredients, it's curious how much people love this uber-processed, salted potato product foodstuff that tastes like paper. Served in fancy wine bars. Displayed amidst the shelves of fine chocolates. Stacked ceiling high at the Autogrilles. Maybe the way they're so neatly canned and stacked gives some kind of order to this crazy world of ours. There has been many a waiter, dressed smartly in a grey morning suit, who proudly presents a silver tray draped with white linen cloth. With a proud smile, he points to the array of snacks, "Look, they're Pringles." Hmmm. Go figure.

Salute! Cin Cin!
(*Sa - LU - tay*) (*Chin-Chin*) There are a few traditions that bind wine to good luck in Italy. Do they work? I don't know, but what I do know is:

- It's bad luck to pour your own wine.
- Always look someone in the eye when you are toasting him or her.
- Be like an Italian and do not drink without food.

Above *Venice is famous for its aparitivi tradition of cichètti, tapas-type small plates.*

Menu page photos by Sandy Gregory

SALUTE! CIN CIN!

CICHÈTTI

BIRRA

Antipasti

Appetizers. Italian menus in every region will always offer a charcuterie platter adorned with nuts and olives. Other options will be available depending on where you are in Italy and the season you are traveling. Remember, Italian dinners have many options. Plan to pace yourself and share a few small antipasti plates.

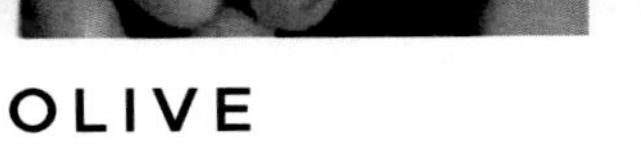

OLIVE

CROSTINI

CAPRESE

NORTHERN ITALY

- Venice and The Cinque Terre pull from the sea with mixed seafood, *frutti de mare,* and salt cod called *baccalà*.
- Venetians dine on meat dishes such as *carpaccio*, thin slices of raw fish or meat served with olive oil, cheese shavings and lemon. Many of my guests travel to Venice for *fegato alla Veneziana* made with fresh calves liver, white wine and onions.
- Piedmont brings anchovies to center stage in a crudité dip called *bagna cauda*. *Acciughe al verde* consists of anchovies in green sauce made of garlic, parsley, olive oil, white wine vinegar and hot pepper flakes spread on bread.
- Lombardy's hearty meals begin with rich cheeses like gorgonzola and crunchy balsamic onions. *Cavolfiore alla Milanese* is made with a combination of cauliflower, butter, onions, grated cheese and parsley.
- The northern most regions of Italy, Trentino-Alto Adige and Fruili Venezia, pull from their Austrian neighbors and serve sausages with sauerkraut and white asparagus. This area is also the home of *speck*, a type of cured, lightly smoked ham.

CENTRAL ITALY

- Tables in the Emilia-Romagna and Tuscany regions start with a simple, but perfect, dish of *Parmigiano-Reggiano* with a drizzle of *Balsamico di Modena,* or their famous meat and cheese boards called *tagliere*.
- *Crostini* are grilled thin, round bread slices with various toppings. Tuscan bread is unsalted, making it the perfect base for salty toppings such as olive *tempanade*, tomatoes or *fegatini,* a creamy chicken liver paté.
- Umbria is all about the truffle. *Crostini* are slathered with truffle butter and called *crostini al tartufo*.
- Le Marche serves up stuffed, deep-fried *olive all'Ascolana***.**
- The Roman table is often laid with artichokes, called *carciofi*. *Carciofi ripieni* are stuffed, baked in olive oil and spices. *Carciofi della Giudecca* is the famous fried Jewish artichoke found in Rome.

SOUTHERN ITALY

- Campania summers bring a burst of color. Fresh tomatoes sit atop *bruschetta* (please note pronunciation: BRU-*sketta*, not Bru-*shetta*). *Bruschetta* is made with thicker slices of bread than *crostini* and toasted over barbecue coals.
- Fresh sliced mozzarella and fresh basil, a dash of salt and olive oil make a *Caprese salad*.
- Popular appetizers throughout the south are *prosciutto e melone*. When in season, *prosciutto* can also be served with fresh figs.
- Zucchini flowers, *fiori di zucca,* are fried, stuffed with herbs and creamy cheeses.
- Coastal restaurants serve mixed fried vegetables called *fritto misto* and fried seafood called *fritto misto frutti de mare*.
- Puglia serves up a variety of soufflés stuffed with vegetables and cheeses called *sformato*.
- Sicilian antipasti are typically *caponata*, a deliciously tangy, sweet and sour mix of fried eggplant, tomatoes, capers and vinegar. Perhaps the most famous starter in Sicily, however, are rice croquettes stuffed with cheese and peas called *arancini*.

FIORI DI ZUCCA

CARCIOFI RIPIENI

PROSCIUTTO E MELONE

Primi Piatti

The first course. Your first course consists of pasta, risotto, polenta or soup. Enjoying pasta is probably one of the main reasons people travel to Italy, but the country offers a variety of first courses for you to try.

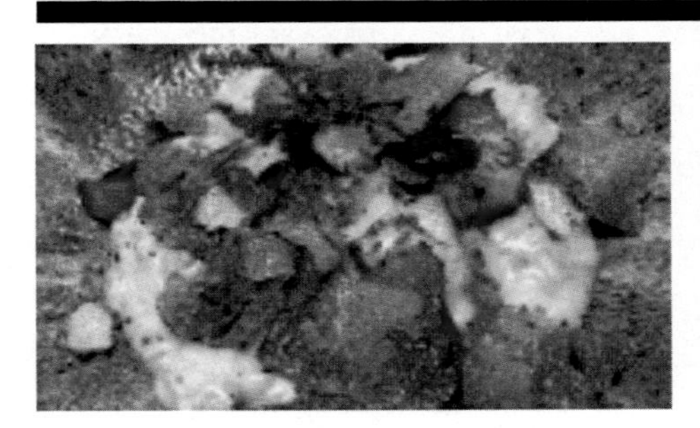

RISOTTO AL TARTUFO NERO

NERO DI SEPPIA E FRUTTI DI MARE

PASTA E FAGIOLI

NORTHERN ITALY

- Venetians love a simple recipe made with rice, pancetta and peas called *risi e bisi.* Menus are filled with dishes pulled from the sea such as pasta in anchovy sauce, called *bigoli in salsa,* and pasta with cuttlefish ink and seafood called *nero di seppia e frutti di mare.* In the colder months, *pasta e fagioli* combines beans and pasta to make a hearty first-course soup.
- Piedmont's exclusive white truffle, *tartufo bianco d'Alba*, is the highlight of *risotto al tartufato alla Peidmontese. Agnolotti* are ravioli-type pasta pillows stuffed with meat, eggs and cheese that are served in a meat broth or butter and sage sauce. *Tajarin*, a thin tagliatelle, are topped with a variety of sauces, including butter and sage, *porcini* mushroom or tomato sauce.
- In Milan, a variety of *gnocchi* and *polenta* dishes make rich, substantial starters.
- Liguria is the home of a short, thin, twisted pasta called *trofie*, slathered with the famous aromatic basil pesto. This also the home of the vegetable soup known as *minestrone.*

CENTRAL ITALY

- The Emilia Romagna offers countless rich choices: *Ravioli* of every kind, *tortellini in brodo, tagliatelle al ragú* and *lasagne al forno.*
- Tuscany, Le Marche and Umbria are known for their pasta with black truffles, or *risotto al tartufo nero.* Plan on rich egg pasta with mushrooms, *tagliatelle con porcini,* or *ribollita,* a soup made from leftover *minestrone.*
- Wild boar are a threat to native wildlife and the environment. These scrappy creatures are notorious for wiping out vineyards and gardens. To do our part, we enjoy heaping bowls of wild boar ragú, *pappardelle al cinghiale,* as well as *cinghiale* sausage, *cinghiale* salami, *cinghiale* bacon *and cinghiale* meatballs. One less boar is a good thing for the land — and our taste buds.
- Abruzzo's most famous dish is *maccheroni all chitarra*, a pasta dish made with a pork, goose or lamb.
- *Bucatini all'Amatriciana, spaghetti alla carbonara* and *cacio e pepe* are the most famous dishes on the Roman tabel. On Thursdays, however, *gnocchi*, potato dumplings with a simple tomato sauce, is often the traditional choice.

SOUTHERN ITALY

- Naples and Calabria are the roots of my family's cooking traditions. Menus in the south offer a simple dish of spaghetti with garlic, anchovies and breadcrumbs, known *aglio e olio.*
- *Penne all'arrabbiata* is a light, spicy tomato sauce. Add anchovies, capers and tomato, and you have savory *pasta alla puttanesca.*
- Naples is the home of Italian wedding soup called *minestra maritata.*
- Positano is a magical place to sit at a beach restaurant and enjoy *linguine a vongole* — pasta, clams and wine — simple and perfect. Carb counters should try eggplant parmesan, *parmigiana di melanzane,* which is not breaded and fried as they do in the U.S., so makes for a much lighter dish.
- Puglia's nonnas roll out fresh pasta called *orecchiette*, which means little ears. The regional specialty is made with broccoli called *orecchiette alle cime di rapa.*
- Sicily's *pasta alla norma* is a baked dish of tomatoes, fried eggplant, grated ricotta salata cheese and basil. *Il timpano* is a complex traditional favorite, a pasta drum filled with pasta, meats and cheeses.

TROFIE CON PESTO

GNOCCHI

PARMIGIANA DI MELANZANE

Secondi Piatti

The second course. Your second course consists of meat, chicken or fish. In Italy, your second course arrives on the plate without any side dishes. You will have to order sides separately.

OSSO BUCCO

BISTECCA

PORCHETTA

NORTHERN ITALY

- Milan is where you go to indulge in the famous veal shank stew served with rice, known as *osso bucco con risotto alla Milanese*. Also enjoy breaded veal cutlets called *cotoletta*.
- Venice, of course, pulls from the sea. A dish of mixed seafood called *frutti di mare* can include a variety of prawns, shrimp, clams, eel and fresh whitefish. One of my favorite dishes is *zuppa di cozze*, steamed clams in a fragrant broth served in puff pastry. You break open the pastry and soak up the juice.
- The Lakes of Como and Maggiore are deep, cold and yield a plethora of freshwater *pesce,* such as char, lake salmon, trout, perch and pike. TIP: A whole fish is usually charged by weight. Be sure to double-check the exact weight (and whether the listed price is total or by weight) before you order.
- Piedmont is all about wild game: rabbit, capon and lamb in elaborate casseroles. *Vitello tonnato* are veal cutlets topped with a sauce made of mayo, flaked tuna, boiled eggs, capers and anchovies.
- Liguria also pulls an abundance of fish from the salty Mediterranean, but also try their local meat specialty, *asado*, a breast of veal slow-cooked in the oven.

CENTRAL ITALY

- Emilia-Romagna serves a veal cutlet topped with a slice of *prosciutto* and cheese called *cotoletta Bolognese.*
- Le Marche's regional *brodetto all'Anconetana* is a broth of garlic and saffron brimming with the bounty of the Adriatic
- Tuscans love their barbecue. Whole pigs called *porchetta* roast on spits in every town market. Mixed grill dishes are called *abbacchio al forno.*
- Florence boasts a Fred Flintstone-size porterhouse, *bistecca alla Fiorentina,* which is served rare with crispy roast potatoes and meant to be shared by at least two people. Every Tuscan menu features veal medallions called *vitello*. These thin, delicate cutlets are served with a variety of sauces such as lemon and capers or mushrooms and wine.
- Umbria's famous lamb roast, *agnello arrosto*, is cooked to tender perfection in a covered roasting pan with rosemary, sage, garlic and oil.
- In Rome, you'll always find a fillet of veal rolled in ham called *saltimbocca*.
- Throughout central Italy, a nice salad lunch with protein is *tagliata di manzo,* a grilled rib eye, thinly sliced on top of a bed of arugula topped with shaved parmesan cheese.

SOUTHERN ITALY

- The Mediterranean, Adriatic and Ionian Seas provide an abundance of mussels (*cozze*), clams (*vongole*), squid (*calamari*), octopus (*polpo*), sardines (*sarde*), tuna (*tonno*), anchovies (*acciughe*), swordfish (*pesce spada*), sea bass (*branzino*) and sea bream (*orata).* All are plucked fresh from the sea in the morning and served whole, grilled or baked with tomatoes, olives and potatoes.
- The most sought after spring lamb in the regions of Lazio and Abruzzo is called *abbacchio*, a four-week-old kid, exclusively nourished by its mother's milk.
- Throughout central and southern Italy, you'll find *cacciatore*, a hearty tomato-based hunter's stew, made with braised chicken. You can order chicken, *pollo alla cacciatora*, or rabbit, *coniglio alla cacciatora*.
- Neapolitans make a beef roll cooked in tomato sauce called *braciole alla napoletana*.

PESCE

AGNELLO

TAGLIATA DI MANZO

Contorni y Insalati

Side dishes, vegetables and salads are ordered separately from the main plates. Think about ordering a variety to share.

- Mixed fried vegetables are called *verdura fritta*, and mixed grilled vegetables, *verdure grigliate*. In the spring, grilled asparagus, *aspragi grigliati*, is a good choice as well.
- Roast potatoes are called *patate al forno*, and french fries called *patatine fritte*.
- Sautéed spinach in oil with lemon and garlic appears on menus throughout Italy, called *spinaci saltati*. For a spicy twist, try sautéed chicory, or *cicoria saltata*.
- White beans, *fagiolini,* are a protein and flavor-packed side dish.
- *Panzanella* is a bold summertime salad of tomatoes and stale bread.
- *Puntarelle* is one of my favorite Roman vegetable dishes. It's a tasty mix of spicy greens, sliced thin and seasoned with olive oil, vinegar, anchovies, salt and garlic.

INSALATA MISTA

Salads in Italy are generally uneventful, with a variety of mixed greens in a bowl. But as you move south, you'll get the wider choice of salad greens such as spicy red radicchio, delicate endive, peppery arugula and a variety of rucola, rocket and frisee. Your dressing will include a squeeze of lemon with extra virgin olive oil, balsamic or red wine vinegar brought to the table. No ranch or honey mustard here.

ASPARAGI GRIGLIATI

PANZANELLA

INSALATA MISTA

Dolce, Cafe y Digestivi

Desserts. A simple plate of *cantucci*, or biscotti as they are known in the U.S., is often the dessert of choice after a multi-course meal. Dipped in *vin santo*, a sweet dessert wine, they are a great finish to most any meal. For those of you with a sweet tooth, an array of *gelati, tiramisu, panna cotta, zabaione, cannoli* and *profiteroles* can be found on the menu as well.

Caffé y digestivi. Dinner is never complete without a *caffé*, usually an *espresso,* never a *cappuccino*. (That is only a morning drink!) Italians obsess over digestion, so your waiter will offer some kind of *digestivi* liqueur to settle your meal and prolong the dining experience — anything from iced cold *limoncello* to sweet *amaretto* or a stiff *grappa*. This might be the time for you to order a *caffé corretto* – a shot of *espresso* spiked with a little *sambuca* and three coffee beans: one for health, one for happiness and one for prosperity — a sentiment that perfectly encapsulates the ritual of *digestivo*.

LIMONCELLO

Italy is the world's largest producer of lemons, and along the Amalfi Coast, the air is perfumed by terraced groves of lemon trees. As is custom throughout Italy, the people here use what is abundant and local to give life to tradition. The ingredients are simple and few: the oil-rich zest of the Sorrento lemon, a little vodka, sugar and 80 days of patience. "*E buono per la digestione.*" "It's good for the digestion."

TIRAMISU

CANNOLI

MAKING LIMONCELLO

Il Conto

The check. Rushing a meal in Italy is not done. It is not the aim of the Italian restaurant to turn tables quickly. What some people think of as slow service is actually your waiter allowing you the time to enjoy your meal. You will never automatically get the check, you have to ask for it. Get eye contact and use the universal writing on your palm signal, or the next time he is near, ask, "*Il conto, per favore.*"

Make sure the bill is itemized. If it's not, ask for "*il conto dettagliato*" or "*il conto lungo*" to make sure you are being charged correctly. On your bill you will see the word *Pane e Coperto*. It is usually about two Euro per person and is essentially a bread and table charge. Non-negotiable.

Tipping. Being a waiter in Italy is a respected profession, done with dignity, professionalism and pride. Unlike U.S. wait staffs who rely mainly on tips, Italian waiters make a living wage and have national healthcare. The service you receive is sincere and not driven by the need to be tipped. Tipping is not the rule in Europe, and most Europeans don't tip. However, it is becoming expected, especially from Americans. If you enjoyed your meal and your waiter did an exceptional job, you can leave a tip. Up to 10 percent is plenty.

Watch out for the "*Servizio.*" Many touristy restaurants include an automatic tip, most neighborhood or locals' restaurants will not. Check the small print at the bottom of the menu. If you see the word *servizio* included in the bill, check the math on your itemized bill. *Servizio* should be 10 percent of the bill. If it's not, speak to the manager and have it removed. You can pay the 10 percent *servizio* if you were pleased with the service, but remember, this counts as the tip so you don't need to leave an additional gratuity.

Paying. In most restaurants these days, waiters bring a handheld machine right to the table and swipe your credit card in front of you. This is comforting. Pay just the amount of the bill with your card. To be assured your waiter receives his or her tip, pay this in cash.

Grazie Mille. *When you're sitting back, relaxing and digesting your meal, you will always get a smile from your waiter if you drill your index finger into the flesh of your cheek, which means, "Tutto era delizioso" or "Everything was delicious."*

Photos by Sandy Gregory

Eating Seasonally

Many of my guests come to Italy with preconceived ideas about what they are going to eat, only to be disappointed if they can't get fresh white truffle shavings on their pasta, or sample the famous fried Jewish artichoke. You must remember, that Italians eat locally grown food that is in season, and menus reflect these seasons. Here is a guide for you foodies who would like to plan your trip around favorite foods.

December, January, February

Winter is all about rich, hearty vegetables and winter lettuces.

- Black cabbage (*cavolo nero*) is the feature of *ribollita Toscana*, a hearty minestrone-based bread soup.
- A wonderful winter lettuce is *radicchio*. It's bitter, spicy and adds color to salads, but is also a great side dish sautéed with lemon and parmesan shavings, or sautéed in pig fat, called *radicchio al lardo*.
- Cauliflower (*cavolfiore*) and leeks (*porri*) are woven into soups. Broccoli (*broccolini*) is served over *orchiette* pasta in Puglia.
- Fennel (*finocchio*), both dried and fresh, appear in bread, *foccaccia*, crackers, *salumi*, soups and salads.
- Blood oranges (*arance rosse*) make their way from Sicily to juicers throughout Italy.

March, April, May

Early harvest brings a plethora of fresh fruits and vegetables to the local markets.

- Asparagus (*asparagi*) both green and white, is at its peak.
- This is the time of year when we go to Rome's Jewish ghetto to enjoy *carciofi alla guidea*. Mammole artichokes (*carciofi*) are deep fried with a tender heart and crispy golden crust. They have been a local favorite since the 16th century.
- Spring peas (*piselli*), zucchini (*zucchine*), spinach (*spinaci*) and beets (*barbabietole*) bring color to the table.
- Spring is a great time to go to the market and pick up some fresh strawberries (*fragole*), kiwi (*kiwi*), and cherries (*ciliegie*).
- Italy is the world's largest producer of lemons (*limone*). The skin of the Sorrento lemon is the essential ingredient in *limoncello*, but lemons are also used on grilled mozzarella with lemon leaves, lemon cakes, lemon *granita* and seafood pastas such as clam sauce (*pasta vongole*) and mixed seafood (*frutti de mare*).

June, July, August

The summer table is abundant with a burst of color and flavor.

- Cucumbers (*cetrioli*), peppers (*peperoni*), zucchini (*zucchine*), tomatoes (*pomodori*), peas (*piselli*) are found in salads, grilled, served on top of pizza and baked inside lasagne and focaccia.
- A favorite Italian summer primo, beautiful and tasty, is *fiore di zucca*. Zucchini blossoms, like you see in the picture above, are stuffed with seasoned ricotta cheese and fried.
- Tomatoes (*pomodori*) and eggplants (*melanzane*) are adorned with handfuls of aromatic basil (*basilico*).
- Summer is when fruit is at its peak including cantaloupe (*melone*), peaches (*pesche*), watermelon (*anguria*), mixed berries (*frutta di bosco*), plums (*susini*), and my favorite, figs (*fichi*) drizzled with local honey.

September, October, November

As the weather cools, the flavors get richer.

- Hearty pasta pillows are stuffed with mushrooms (*funghi*), porcini mushrooms (*porcini*) and pumpkin (*zucca*) dressed with a butter-sage sauce.
- September marks the start of the grape (*uva*) harvest and in November, the olives (*olive*) are picked and pressed.
- November also begins the season for one of the rarest and most expensive foods in the world: white truffles (*tartufi bianchi*). The pungent, earthy truffle is thinly shaved over pasta, *risotto* or an omelette, or stirred into a thick sauce and served with steak.

THE SLOW FOOD MOVEMENT

In the 1980s, the first McDonald's in Italy opened near the Spanish Steps in Rome. The Italian people were outraged. And, being Italian, they protested. A journalist named Carlo Petrini gathered his friends and joined the protest with bowls of pasta. Amidst the screaming, they calmly dished out *penne pomodoro* and chanted their slogan, "We don't want fast food. We want slow food!" They didn't stop McDonald's from coming, but they did lay the groundwork to preserve the way Italians thought about food — The Slow Food Movement.

Here is an excerpt from the Official Slow Food Manifesto, as published in "Slow Food: A Case for Taste" in 2001: *"We are enslaved by speed and have succumbed to the same insidious virus: The fast life which disrupts our habits, pervades the privacy of our homes and forces us to eat fast foods. ... which has changed our way of being and threatens our environment and our landscapes. Our defense should begin at the table with Slow Food. Let us rediscover the flavors and savors of regional cooking ... that is what real culture is all about: developing taste rather than demeaning it. Slow Food guarantees a better future ..."*

The Slow Food Movement is based on food that is good, clean and fair. The focus is on whole foods that are grown locally and eaten in season, dishes made with the health of the body and soul in mind, and meals that are appreciated and shared with family and friends. Today there are over 150,000 members of the Slow Food Movement in 160 countries. The United States has more than 170 local chapters.

slowfood.com

Coffee

ITALIANS LOVE COFFEE SO MUCH THEY CONSUME OVER 14 BILLION ESPRESSOS EVERY YEAR

Legend has it coffee was discovered by an Ethiopian goat herder. One day, he noticed his goats were unusually energetic while eating the berries of a nearby shrub. Curious, he tried one himself and immediately felt more alert and happy. He told his friends and soon word spread throughout the region. The rest is history.

Coffee first found its way to Italy in the 13th century, when Venice was a major trading port between east and west. Venetian merchants charged high prices for this luxury item. The popularity, however, grew in the 1700s with the emergence of coffee bars. Venice's Caffé Florian in Piazza San Marco is one of the oldest. It was a luxury haven for noblemen, politicians and intellectuals to gather, drink and even enjoy an orchestra. The infamous Casanova went there in search of his daily caffeine fix and, true to form, also was looking for female company. Because of Casanova, Caffé Florian was the first in the city to allow women. Today, visitors from all over the world sit, sip and listen to the orchestra that has played every single day since it opened.

The Catholic church originally banned coffee (*caffé* in Italian) because it was a stimulant, calling it the bitter invention of Satan. Pope Clement, however, loved the drink. He said, "This devil's drink is so delicious we should cheat him by baptising it." Who knows if this story is true, but the Pope certainly offered a divine intervention to our morning fix.

To this day, Italians remain passionate about their coffee. They have a light breakfast, typically espresso or cappuccino with a bun or toast; have another espresso after lunch; perhaps a quick shot during the afternoon; and then another after dinner.

"Vorrei un (name your coffee), per favore. Grazie."
Coffee ordering is a two-part system. You pay for your drink at the register first. When you pay, there is usually a tray or plate near the register. You put your money down, and then the cashier takes it and puts your change back on that plate with your receipt. Walk over to the barista with your receipt to make your order. Most Italians drink standing up. This is because your order can cost four times as much if you sit at a table than if you stand at the bar. However, you're on vacation, so sit, let the waiter take your order and savor your cup. It's the perfect time to watch the world go by. And at Caffé Florian, listen to the orchestra. While you're certainly going to pay a steep price, you'll never be rushed.

THE STRONG STUFF

ESPRESSO

If you ask for *un espresso* or *un caffè*, you will get an espresso. Served in a demitasse cup, this dark roast is made to be drunk quickly.

DOPIO ESPRESSO

Make it a double with two shots of espresso.

RISTRETTO

An even more concentrated brew than *espresso*, *ristretto* is prepared with the same amount of coffee, but more finely ground, and with half the amount of water. It's slightly thicker, with less caffeine and more *crema*, the aromatic, reddish-brown froth on top.

CAFFÈ CORETTO

This after-dinner drink is "corrected" with a splash of grappa, cognac or sambuca and served after dessert. In your cup you might also find three coffee beans: One for health, one for happiness and one for prosperity — a sentiment that perfectly encapsulates the ritual of *digestivo*.

Previous page *A morning coffee overlooking the Bay of Naples in Sorrento*

Photo by Sandy Gregory

WITH A LITTLE WATER FOR AMERICAN TASTES

AMERICANO

For those of you who like a lighter, American style drip-strength coffee, *espresso* is diluted with hot water to make an Americano.

CAFFÈ LUNGO

If you are missing your strong mug of Starbucks brew, this is called a *lungo*, or long shot: a double shot of *espresso* or *ristretto* diluted with even more hot water.

ITALIANS DO NOT TAKE THEIR CAFFÈ TO GO

In Italy, you don't see people walking down the street or working at their desks clenching their large paper tumblers of brew. Italians believe in taking the time to stop, relax and enjoy their caffeine break. They walk to the bar, meet a friend, peruse the local newspaper and chat with the barista while their fresh-ground *caffè* is being brewed. There are no mocha, half-caf, skinny, double-pump, caramel lattes. Instead, you have a simple cup of *caffè* made with quality ingredients, served graciously in a real cup and saucer. There is something beautifully traditional about a crowded local bar, watching the barista pound out *espresso* after *espresso* while people take just a moment out of their busy day to stop and enjoy this simple pleasure.

AND SMOOTHED DOWN BY ADDING MILK

CAPPUCCINO

The hefty amount of protein from frothed milk makes *cappuccino* the traditional Italian breakfast drink. The recipe contains equal parts *espresso*, steamed milk and foamed milk. For Italians, this is only served in the morning.

MACCHIATO

A lighter creamed coffee drink that takes the edge off of strong *espresso* is a *macchiato* — *espresso* that is "marked" with just a dollop of steamed milk.

CAFFÈ LATTE

If you want more steamed milk than *cappuccino* and less foam, order a *caffè latte*. This drink is often served in a tall glass. Do not order just a "*latte*" or you will get a tall glass of plain, steamed milk.

CAFFÈ CON PANNA

For a richer treat, have your *espresso* topped with a dollop of rich cream or *panna*.

CAFFÈ GRANITA

A cool summer treat is a frozen dessert made from *espresso* and water, blended and frozen until icy, flaked with a fork and frozen again. And yes ... it's served with *panna*!

THE PERFECT FOOD

Modern pizza was born in the 19th century at the foot of Mt. Vesuvius in the working class neighborhoods of Naples. It was of cheap ingredients found locally: San Marzano tomatoes, mozzarella and fresh basil artfully arranged on a simple crust of flour, water, yeast and salt. Pizza has become a philosophy, a culture and a social activity.

Until Christopher Columbus brought back the tomato from the New World, pizza was a plain flatbread with a little olive oil, garlic and basil. Pizza in Naples is soft and thin, the edges are thick and scorched from the wood-fired oven. Regional styles of pizza have developed. Thin *focaccia* in Liguria. Thick *focaccia* in Sicily. Thick crust fritters called *panzerotti* in Puglia. *Pizza Romana*: thin, large and crunchy, often with no sauce whatsoever, but instead topped with salt, olive oil and chopped rosemary. Even within Naples, it's easy to find different varieties, including rolled pizza, *calzones* and *pizza fritta*, stuffed then fried, and meant to be eaten on the go.

Pizza is a social event. It is not meant to be delivered to the home. Revered pizza chefs, *pizzaioli*, create made-to-order pies and serve them piping hot, straight from the wood-fired oven. Start with a knife and fork, or sometimes with a pair of scissors, and then finish by ripping it apart with your fingers. Pizzas are personalized orders, about the size of a dinner plate and not designed to be shared. You can also get pizza *al taglio* (cut to-go). Just point to the slab that appeals to you and use your hands to indicate how big you want your slice. The *pizzaiolo* weighs it, toasts it up and charges you by weight. This is a great way to try a variety of styles.

You will never find a Hawaiian, meat lovers or buffalo chicken pizza in Italy. Don't be caught trying to add BBQ sauce, guacamole, kale, lemon, Brussel sprouts, cheddar cheese or jalapeños.

Pizza Margherita. Considered by many Italians to be the only true pizza, because less is more when it comes to tasting the fresh ingredients. This simple pizza has a place in history. The first pizza recipe (*marinara*) dates back to 1734, while the Margherita dates back to the early 1800s. Legend has it that the famous pie evoked the colors of the Italian flag – green (basil leaves), white (mozzarella), and red (tomatoes) in honor of Queen Margherita as a symbol of Italian unity.

Marinara. This pizza is nothing more than crust and tomato sauce.

Quattro Formaggi. Four types of cheese — usually Gorgonzola, Fontina, Mozzarella and Parmigiano-Reggiano — make this a "white" pizza. It is served without tomato sauce.

Capricciosa. This is a unique combination of ham, salami, mushrooms, olives, artichoke and tomato.

Diavola. Spicy tomato sauce and spicy salami (*salamino picante*) make this one spicy pizza. Note: Keep in mind that *pepperoni* in Italian means bell peppers. Ordering a "pepperoni pizza" will result in a pie covered with red bell peppers.

Napoli. This is a savory pie with mozzarella, tomato sauce, capers and anchovies.

Pizza ai Funghi. This pizza is all about the mushrooms, which can be served with tomato and mozzarella or as a "white" pizza.

Pizza Quattro Stagioni. Each quadrant of this pizza contains a different ingredient — prosciutto, artichoke, olive and mushroom — representing the four seasons.

Photo by Sandy Gregory

Pasta

I TELL MY GUESTS ON TOUR, "WHEN IN ROME, DO AS THE ROMANS DO." ONE OF THOSE ACTIVITIES IS HONORING THE TRADITION AND PASSION OF PASTA. WE ITALIANS TAKE PASTA VERY SERIOUSLY. PASTA IS THE FOOD THAT TRULY DEFINES US. HERE ARE A FEW TIPS AND TRICKS I HAVE LEARNED ABOUT EATING PASTA.

PASTA RULES

Pasta is to be eaten only with a fork. Spoons are for amateurs. Put the fork into a few strands of spaghetti and let the tines of the fork rest against the curve of the bowl or the curved indentation of the plate. Twirl the fork around to create a small bundle. Too big? Too long? Drop it back into the dish and start again.

Never cut spaghetti ... ever. With the side of the fork, with a knife, never ever ever! The one thing that could bring my boisterous family to silence at the dinner table was a guest who cut their spaghetti. Awkward.

Bread is used to soak up the pasta sauce. *Fa la scarpetta* means "do the little shoe." You form the bread like a little shoe to mop up the last of the sauce. No butter is served on an Italian table and no Italian would ever dip their bread into plates of olive oil covered with balsamic or parmesan cheese. That is an American creation.

Cheese on seafood pasta? No. Fish from the seas and rivers of Italy are mild and delicate. The milky saltiness of cheese overwhelms the flavor of the fish. Cheese is usually made in the land-locked areas of the country where fish is not widely served, so location as well as tradition, makes cheese on fish pasta a no-no.

All that being said, Italians are famous rule breakers. To an Italian, any rule is merely a suggestion. So, take this information and use it as you will — except for the part about cutting your spaghetti. Don't do that. Ever.

Previous page *Spinach linguine with truffle cream sauce and shaved black truffle (linguine agli spinaci con crema di tartufo e scaglie di tartufo nero)*

Above *Linguine with lobster (linguine all'astice) with NO cheese*

Photos by Sandy Gregory

Formaggio

WITH OVER 600 VARIETIES, ITALY MAKES SOME OF THE BEST TASTING ARTISAN CHEESES IN THE WORLD

Every region in Italy produces local cheeses that represent its farming heritage and culture. There are too many varieties of cheese to list. Just ask for your waiter's recommendations. In the meantime, here are some of the most popular:

If you're in the north, you'll find ***Gorgonzola, Grana Padano*** and ***Fontina*** on the menu. ***Taleggio*** is an oozy, pungent melting cheese you'll find in risottos and polenta dishes also from this area.

Italy's most famous cheese, produced in the Emilia-Romagna, is called ***Parmigiano-Reggiano***. The flavor of this hard cheese gets more intense the longer it ages. You'll see this cheese on meat and cheese platters *(tagliere)* or grated over pasta and soups.

Pecorino is a hard cheese made from sheep's milk with flavors that range from nutty to salty, savory to tangy. *Pecorino* is made all over Italy, but the most famous is ***Pecorino Romano***, used in the famous Roman pasta dishes such as *cacio e pepe, bucatini all'amatriciana* and *spaghetti alla carbonara.* It also adds a salty tang shaved over arugula with a light dressing of oil and lemon juice.

***Mozzarella* in Italy is divided into two types:**

1. ***Fior di latte*** is made of cow's milk and produced throughout Italy.
2. ***Mozzarella di Bufala D.O.P.*** is made from rich, buffalo milk and produced exclusively in Campania.

***Mozzarella* is served in a variety of sizes:**

- ***Ovolini*** is the size of a large egg, translating to "bite sized."
- ***Bocconcini*** is small ball of cheese about the size of a campari tomato.
- ***Cigliegini*** are the size of grapes.
- ***Perline*** are the size of pearls.
- ***Affumicata*** is smoked mozzarella.
- ***Stracciatella*** is made from the leftover mozzarella shreds and mixed into a creamy consistency.

Burrata is a close relative to *mozzarella.* Literally translated as "buttered," it's a rich creamy cheese with an almost liquid center. *Burrata* is often served simply with olive oil, salt and pepper on crusty bread.

Marscapone is the cream cheese made from the milk of only Italian cows. It's most famously used to make *tiramisu.* It also finishes and gives the tomato sauce in *penne alla vodka* its creaminess.

Ricotta is the soft cheese Italians use to stuff into pastas such as *ravioli* and *tortellini.*

Photos by Sandy Gregory

Tagliere

TAGLIERE (TA-LEE-ERI) IS A CUTTING BOARD FILLED WITH REGIONAL MEATS AND CHEESES. IT'S ONE OF THE BEST WAYS TO EXPERIENCE LOCAL CUISINE.

If Italy is food and food is Italy, Bologna is the culinary capitol. Striking medieval architecture, the oldest university in the Western world ... and *mama mia* ... the food! Bologna has been nicknamed "La Grassa" or "The Fat." Fat is flavor. Fat is texture. Fat makes everything delicious. Italians are not afraid of fat, which is why their food is fantastically delicious. Fat, salt and time create the delicacies we love. The Emilia-Romagna region is home to the most famous cured pork meats of Italy, their noble cuts are the best parts of pigs raised freely on the slopes of the Apeninnes. Nothing goes to waste.

Walk through the old market *Quadrilatero* district of Bologna and you'll see heaping boards of *tagliere*. Plates of mixed meats and cheeses are a favorite antipasti throughout Italy, but in Bologna, it is brought to an art form. *Buonissimo!*

Prosciutto is a salt-cured ham made from the leg of a pig or a wild boar. There are many varieties:

- ***Prosciutto di Parma*** is produced in the Emilia-Romagna region, where pigs are fed a diet of grains and the whey left over from the production of local *Parmigiano-Reggiano* cheese. Add the salt air of the Mediterranean Sea and you have a delicious, nutty and salty ham.
- ***Culatello*** literally means "little ass," because the cut used to make it is only a small section from the pig's rear leg, with the skin and bone removed. It is salted, massaged and carefully cured and air-dried for a minimum of one year. Also produced in Parma, *culatello* is the king of Italian cured meats — red, fatty and rich. It offers a finer and more intense flavor than *prosciutto*.
- ***Speck*** is another indulgent cured ham if your taste buds prefer the fattier meats.
- ***Prosciutto di San Daniele*** is produced in a small village in Italy's northern region of Friuli Venezia Giulia. It is a darker, leaner meat, with a sweeter taste.
- ***Prosciutto Toscano*** is cured not only with salt, but also with pepper and other local herbs to give it a robust, earthy flavor.

Salumi comes in hundreds of regional variations:

- ***Salumi Toscani*** is a coarsely ground dry salami that has big chunks of fat.
- ***Finocchiona*** is flavored with fennel and coarse pepper.
- ***Cacciatori or cacciatorini*** are bite-size nuggets that hunters once carried in their saddlebags.
- ***Soppressata*** is made from the best cuts of pork coarsely ground and moulded into a fat, round, dried sausage.
- ***Salciccia*** are the dry sausages of all lengths and thicknesses you'll see hanging in Italian butcher shops.
- ***Coppa*** is cooked and pressed boneless pork neck, which is brined, stuffed into a casing and air-dried for six months or more to create a rich, complex purple salami. It has a vein-like system of fat bands radiating throughout the dark meat.

***Cinta Senese* (CHEENTA - senay- zay) pigs.** The *Cinta Senese* is a rustic pig breed that is found free-range grazing in the woodlands above Siena feasting on acorns, olives, chestnuts, tubers and berries. The breed owes its name to its black coat with a white sash (called a *cinta* in Italian). With a very slow metabolism, their fatty meat creates the richest, most flavorful, and expensive, *prosciutto* and *salami* products in Italy.

Mortadella is not to be mistaken for American bologna! This oversized Italian sausage is made of finely ground, heat-cured pork sausage. Cubes of pork fat are then folded into the mixture and flavored with spices, including black pepper, myrtle berries, nutmeg and pistachios.

Lardo is like butta! The essential part to any *tagliere*, lardo is pure cured back fat enhanced with rosemary, garlic, sage, oregano, coriander, anise and cinnamon. Served paper thin, it's a little slice of heaven spread on a piece of bread drizzled with olive oil and a sprinkle of salt.

Photos by Sandy Gregory

PROSCIUTTERIA

Olive Oil

THE OLDEST OLIVE TREE IN ITALY STANDS IN SARDINIA AND IS 3500 YEARS OLD

The olive tree is an ancient, noble plant. Its gnarly roots are a sign of strength and endurance. Even when cut down or burned, new shoots emerge and the tree lives on. Its green/grey leaves are a sign of power and wisdom when displayed on the heads of emperors and poets. Its branch is the sign of peace.

Italy produces some of the best olive oil in the world. Harvest starts at the end of October when temperatures start to drop. Small farms and family co-ops traditionally pick their olives by hand and have their harvest crushed at the local pressing stone. This supplies the family with extra virgin olive oil for the year.

Commercial harvesting is often performed by using a claw-like comb to pull down the olives, or mechanical shakers that cause the olives to drop into nets under the tree canopy. One medium-sized olive tree produces about 22 pounds of olives, resulting in one quart of cold press olive oil. The olives are cleaned immediately, crushed into a paste and then mixed to release the oils and allow the fruit enzymes to develop aromas and flavors. This paste is then placed into a press to extract the oil from the pulp. "Extra Virgin" is the oil that comes out of this first "cold" pressing. It is the oil that contains the healthy stuff: mono unsaturated fatty acids, poly phenols and antioxidants. The leftover mash is then steamed and re-pressed. Italians don't use this second pressing, so it's sent abroad, often to be adulterated with lower grade olive oils or with nut and seed oils.

How are you sure you are getting the good stuff? The first answer, of course, is to join us on a Che Bella Tours trip and buy your olive oil directly from the farm. In the meantime, however, here are some tips on buying olive oil at home:

- Look closely at the label. Look for the words "extra virgin". Don't worry if it doesn't say "cold-pressed." If it is a true extra virgin olive oil, then it was processed at a cool temperature.
- Look for a D.O.P. seal (protected designation of origin), the "Harvest" and the "Best Used By" dates.
- Olive oil should be packaged in a dark glass bottle. Light and heat accelerates deterioration, so it is also best to store your olive oil in a cool, dark place and use within 12 months of harvesting.
- Costco's Kirkland Brand sometimes offers a good choice in January, while supplies last. Look for the tall green bottles with the words: Extra Virgin Tuscan Olive Oil. That's the good stuff.

Next page bottom left
Olive trees can live to be 1,100-yeas-old. Puglia.

Photos by Janette Tepas Images

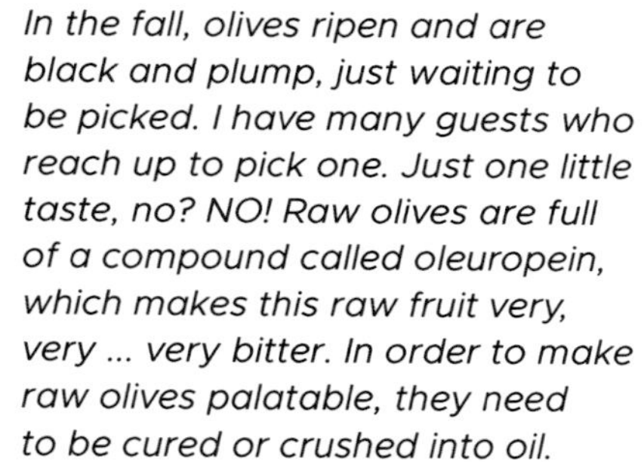

In the fall, olives ripen and are black and plump, just waiting to be picked. I have many guests who reach up to pick one. Just one little taste, no? NO! Raw olives are full of a compound called oleuropein, which makes this raw fruit very, very ... very bitter. In order to make raw olives palatable, they need to be cured or crushed into oil.

Never pick and eat an olive fresh off the tree!

Photos by Sandy Gregory

Balsamico

LIQUID GOLD

In Modena, making balsamic vinegar is a rich family tradition. Almost every household makes their own supply. Ingredients: Grapes, weather, wood and time. True balsamic uses two kinds of sweet grapes: Trebbiano and Lambrusco. The process begins by pressing the grapes and slowly concentrating the juice, seeds and stems over an open flame. The thickened juice is strained and then poured into the largest barrel of what they call a "battery." Nine barrels made of different woods such as oak, chestnut, cherry, juniper and mulberry, make up a battery. As the vinegar ferments, it is moved from barrel to barrel, pulling the taste from the various woods and getting thicker and more concentrated as it ages. Once a year, the finished vinegar is bottled from the smallest cask in the sequence. Each cask is then topped up with vinegar from the next cask up, with the largest cask getting filled with the new yield. None of the casks are ever completely drained.

The tradition of balsamic is not only passed on from barrel to barrel, but also from generation to generation. Parents start a battery for their children when they are born, in hope that one day they will present it to them on their wedding day.

You'll find plenty of bottles that are labelled *aceto balsamico traditionale di Modena* at groceries and upscale markets. The real stuff, however, is only sold in bulb-shaped 100 ml. bottles like you see in the photo on the next page. Join Che Bella Tours in the Emilia-Romagna. You can ship to the U.S., or bring a bottle or two home in your suitcase. Balsamic will keep indefinitely, but store it in a cool dark place to best preserve the complexity of its flavors. It has a rich, complex sweetness that explodes in your mouth with notes of fig, molasses, cherry, chocolate and prune. This is not a cooking ingredient — heating it will kill its distinctive bouquet — and it would be wasted on a salad. Instead, put a few drops on fresh berries, chunks of *Parmigiano-Reggiano* cheese, or creamy desserts like *panna cotta* or vanilla ice cream. It's excellent drizzled over traditional veal scaloppini, a rich risotto, and a meat or game stew.

Next page top left *As vinegar ferments, ages and thickens, it is moved from the largest to the smallest barrel in a battery.*

Next page top right *The sweet taste of balsamic compliments salty cheese.*

Next page right *The bulb-shaped 100 ml. bottles of Modena.*

Photos by Sandy Gregory

Gelato

WE ALL SCREAM FOR *GELATO*!

Gelato is not ice cream. In Italian, *gelato* means frozen. Ice cream is made of milk, cream, sugar and egg yolks. *Gelato* contains a higher proportion of milk, a lower proportion of cream and fresh, seasonal ingredients. It is churned at a much slower rate than ice cream, leaving it denser with a much lower fat content. Served at a slightly warmer temperature than ice cream, *gelato* stays silkier and softer.

Gelato in Italy is a tradition as well as an art form. There are *gelato* shops on almost every block. Pass up the shops whose flavors are displayed in tall mounds of swirls. These are chock full of fillers that keep the shape of these mountainous frozen structures. Instead, look for the "artisan" *gelaterias* that adhere to the "quality over quantity" spirit and use only all natural, seasonal ingredients. It is not about the flash, but rather the flavor. Produced in small batches daily, the good stuff is stored in covered metal containers to keep the flavors fresh.

Other types of frozen treats:

- **_Sorbetto_** is a non-dairy frozen ice, made with sweetened fruit and fruit juice. It is whipped until creamy.
- **_Semifreddo_** is a semi-frozen cream dessert sliced like a cake.
- **_Granita_** is a crunchy, shaved flavored ice. *Caffé granita* is my order when I'm in Italy, except when I'm on the Amalfi Coast, where *granita di limone* is the sweet choice.

How to order _gelato_. On my tours, I always have at least one guest who indulges a few times a day and becomes quite the connoisseur. Just like coffee bars, you make your order and pay at the cash register. You'll choose a size and whether you want a *cona* or a *cuppa*. The size you choose will dictate how many flavors you get. Present your receipt to the gelato server and choose your flavors. Don't be afraid to ask for a sample. And when you're asked if you want a dollop of *panna* on top, you say, *"Si, per favore!"*

Next page *Hail gelato!*

Gelato is heavenly.

Photos by Sandy Gregory, Todd Martin and Janette Tepas Images

Cooking Lessons

Italian cooking is the fruit of centuries-old traditions and varies greatly throughout the regions. What better way to understand "the language" of Italian cuisine than by putting on an apron, rolling up your sleeves and spending a few hours learning how to make local dishes? Rich cooking experiences are found all over Italy. In farmhouse kitchens overlooking the vineyards. In cooking schools with state-of-the-art facilities. In castles and villas. In terraced city apartments. Some are hosted by Italian chefs and cookbook authors, while others are taught by local mamas and nonnas who want to share their passion for their regional cuisine.

From picking herbs and vegetables in the garden to talking with the local farmers at the market, cooking lessons are fun and delicious. Your day can include trips to artisanal food producers, oil mills, pasta factories and bakeries. Passion for pasta? Vegetarian? Seafood lover? There's a course for everyone. You'll learn how to prepare a four-course meal of antipasto, primo, secondo, and dolce before indulging in the results of your hard work.

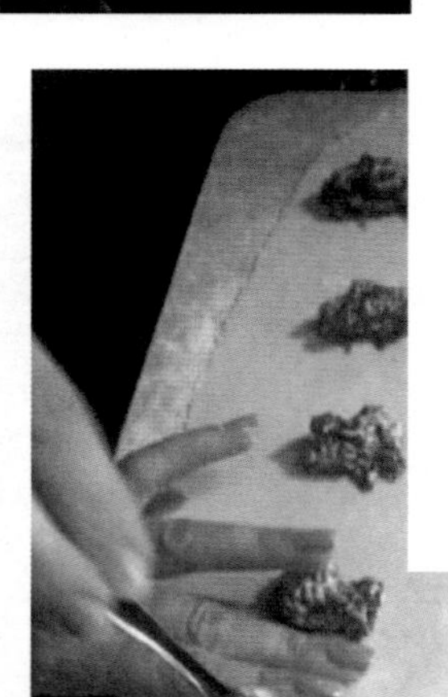

Photos by Sandy Gregory

Wine Tastings

To Italians, wine is much more than a beverage. It serves as an essential part of the Mediterranean diet as well as an essential component of the food culture of Italy. Whether a weeknight dinner, Sunday lunch or a milestone celebration, wine is always present at the Italian table.

Centuries ago, when the Greeks colonized portions of Italy, they called it Oenotria — "the land of wine." With its abundance of warmth and sunshine, sea breezes and varying topography, Italy offers ideal conditions for grape growing. In fact, it produces more wine than any other country in the world. With over 900,000 registered vineyards and 1300 registered grape varieties, the diversity and depth of the country's wine is unparalleled.

What were once the battlegrounds of Italy's war-torn past are now beautiful vineyards as far as the eye can see. Restored castles and villas have been lovingly turned into exclusive wineries where you not only have the experience of an exquisite wine tasting experience, but also a culinary treat.

Great wine tastings in Italy do not merely involve a few minutes of standing and drinking in a large tasting room. Instead, they are more of an immersion into the local culture. As you relax in a beautiful villa dining room or a veranda offering views of the rolling hills, your hosts share the history and story of their family roots, winery lineage, grape varieties and local cuisine.

Photos by Sandy Gregory

APPRECIATING ITALIAN WINE

Evaluating the appearance, nose and palate are important to appreciating a wine.

The appearance. After pouring a glass of wine, look at its color and intensity. Then tilt the glass to a 45-degree angle and see the reflection of the rim on a white tablecloth or placemat. You'll see the differences in color between the core of the glass and its edges. This is referred to as "rim variation." Rim variation is most common in older, complex red wines. Color, intensity and rim variation are not necessarily evidence of a wine's quality, but they do give hints of its characteristics.

- A red wine with deep intensity and a darker color is a fuller body wine with flavors of dark fruits such as black cherries or black plums, and often has a higher alcohol content.
- A red wine with less intensity and a lighter color tends to be medium-bodied, with less or softer tannins and flavors of red fruit such as red cherries and red berries.
- A white wine with deeper intensity and darker color tends to be fuller bodied, with flavors of stone fruit and often with a nuttiness or essence of baking spices.
- A pale-colored white wine tends to have bright and refreshing acidity and lighter fruit characteristics like citrus and apple.

The nose. A wine's flavor is substantially determined by how it smells. Swirl the wine in its glass to release its aromatic compounds. Then, place your nose close to the rim of the glass and take short sniffs while holding the glass at varying distances. Pause to assess and appreciate a wine's various aromas.

- Italian red wines will generally smell of purple fruits such as black cherries or blackberries or red fruits such as raspberries, red plums or red cherries.
- Many Italian reds will give off floral aromas such as roses or violets as well as herbal or spice notes.
- Wines aged in oak barrels exhibit aromas of cedar, vanilla, cloves or toast, adding to the aromatic and flavor complexity.
- Italian white wines will often exhibit floral or citrus aromas with hints of green apples, pears, peaches or apricots.

The palate. Time to drink. Take a sip and swish the wine around gently to coat your entire mouth. Then, draw in a little air. Evaluate how the wine tastes on your tongue.

- Your tongue is sensitive to five basic tastes: salt, sweet, bitter, sour and umami (the savory taste of MSG). By swirling a wine in your mouth, you can activate these various taste buds and appreciate the various flavors a wine offers.
- Notice the wine's body and texture, the flavor intensity and the acidity level.
- Notice how the wine lingers and how it finishes in your mouth.
- Notice the tannin level in a red wine, which will cause your mouth to dry or to "pucker up." Take a second sip to taste how all of the wine's characteristics blend together.

How do you feel about this wine?

- Is the quality of the wine average, good or outstanding?
- What aromas, flavors or other characteristics do you like about this wine?

Wine and food pairings. Italian wine is made to be eaten with food. While the expression "what grows together, goes together" applies throughout the world, perhaps it is never truer than in Italy. Much like its food, Italian wines vary significantly from region to region, so take the opportunity to enjoy the wines of a region with its cuisine. While there are many approaches to pairing wine and food, a few basic principles can guide us in these selections.

- Consider the main ingredient, but also the sauces and sides. For instance, a vegetable salad with a light vinaigrette will go nicely with a *pinot grigio* or a *Vernaccia di San Gimignano*. A meaty ragú or the acidity of a hearty tomato sauce pairs well with a *Chianti Classico*.
- Tannins love fat and fat loves tannins. Fats found in red meats and cheeses can reduce the perception of tannins on the palate. In addition, tannins can cut through the richness and fattiness of these foods. Enjoy a *Vino Nobile di Montepulciano* or an aged *Brunello* with veal dishes or *bistecca alla Fiorentina*.
- Acidity in foods can balance a wine's acidity and enhance its fruit characteristics. Most Italian wines have medium-to-high levels of acidity, and therefore can match the lemons, tomatoes and other acidic elements in many Italian dishes.
- Pair sweet with sweet. If a dish has sweetness, select a wine that has a higher level of sweetness. Desserts go great with *vin santo, moscato* or with a sweet *asti* or *prosecco* sparkling wine.

Above *Enjoying the bouquet.*

Far left *Pour a glass to only about 1/3 full to give the wine some room to breathe.*

Left *Pair the right wine with food and you not only have the experience of an exquisite wine tasting experience, but also a culinary treat.*

Photos by Sandy Gregory and Susan LaBrie

Noteworthy Italian Wines

RED WINE

VINO ROSSO

While delicious and interesting wine is made throughout Italy, certain wines and regions have well-earned reputations throughout the world. Here are some of my favorites.

Northern Italy

- ***Barolo* and *Barbaresco.*** The vineyards surrounding the towns of Asti and Alba in Piedmont make these prestigious wines from 100 percent *nebbiolo* grapes (named for the fog, *nebbia*, that blankets the area's vineyards). These full-bodied wines offer red fruit flavors and high levels of tannins and acidity. *Barolo* must be aged at least three years before release. *Barbaresco* is aged at least two years. Both are aged longer to bring out their true elegance and earthly qualities.
- ***Barbera* and *Dolcetto.*** Piedmont also hails these every day wines. In fact, *Barbera* is referred to as "the people's wine." With big fruit flavors, both wines are easy to drink and easy on the budget.
- ***Valpolicella.*** The Veneto region produces this light, fruity red. The essence of red cherries and spice is perfect with the local cuisine.
- ***Amarone della Valpolicella.*** This wine is intense and full-bodied, with flavors of cherries and dried fruits. It has a high levels of alcohol — with a high price tag to match.

Central Italy

- ***Chianti, Chianti Classico and the Super Tuscans.*** The rolling foothills of the Apennine Mountains provide a stunning landscape for these cellar-worthy, world-class reds. Balanced tannins and acidity with bright red fruit flavors come from the *sangiovese* grape. *Chianti* is actually a wine-growing region and *Chianti Classico* is a region within the *Chianti* region that produces the most superior wines.

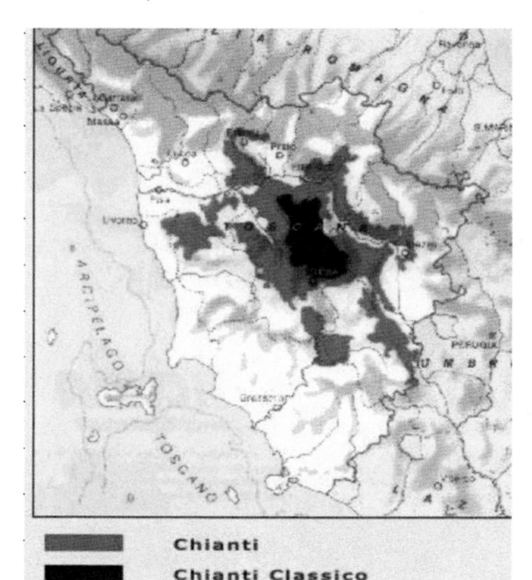

- ***Brunello di Montalcino.*** This powerful red is the most expensive of the *sangiovese*-based wines. The town of Montalcino, perched on a ledge, like many Tuscan hill towns, overlooks the vineyards producing *Brunello*. These wines are powerful enough that they are required to be aged five years before release, but are almost always aged longer. *Brunello* is among the greatest red wines in the world.
- ***Vino Nobile di Montepulciano***, made in southern Tuscany around the town of Montepulciano, provides delicious *sangiovese*-based wines without the expense of *Brunello*.

Southern Italy

- ***Aglianico.*** This full-bodied wine from Campania has high tannins and acidity with flavors of dark fruit. Look for bottles from the Taurasi region.
- ***Nero d'Avolo* or *Nerello Mascalese.*** In Sicily, the quality of red wines has improved dramatically over the last couple of decades. Most are fruit-forward wines meant to drink young, Some are more concentrated, complex and age-worthy wines. Most of these complex wines come from the Etna region of Sicily, where grapes are grown in the hills at or around the still-active volcano.
- ***Primitivo.*** The cuisine from Puglia pulls from the sea and the rich soil, offering light dishes that go well with this light, red wine.

WHITE WINE
VINO BIANCO

Northern Italy

- ***Soave* and *Soave Classico.*** Vineyards east of Verona, in the Veneto region, produce some high quality wines. While most are meant to drink young, *Soave Classico* is often aged longer, developing flavors of almond and honey.
- ***Pinot Grigio.*** The Trentino-Aldo Adige and Friuli-Venezia regions are located in the northeast corner of Italy in the foothills of the Alps. Wines from these regions are rich, with lovely peach and tropical fruit flavors and a refreshing amount of acidity.
- ***Gavi.*** In the southeastern portion of Piedmont, grapes are grown in the hills, where altitude and sea breezes cool the vineyards, resulting in a crisp and light-bodied style of wine.

Central Italy

- ***Vernaccia di San Gimignano.*** The historic village of San Gimignano is the only place you'll find these hearty white grapes. Often called "the white red," *Vernaccia* is a citrus-forward white with a slightly bitter finish. This crisp and bright wine makes a delightful start to a Tuscan meal.
- ***Orvieto.*** Some of the best of the Italian white wines come from Umbria. It has a refreshing profile, with hints of minerality and melon.
- ***Verdicchio.*** Along the coast in Le Marche, you'll find this wonderful and interesting white wine that pairs extremely well with the region's seafood.
- ***Frascati.*** Outside of Rome, in the Lazio region, the *malvasia* and *trebbiano* grapes combine to make this citrus-forward, medium- bodied wine, often scented with floral or orange blossom aromas.

SPARKLING WINE
FRIZZANTE

Italians certainly enjoy their sparkling wines as an aperitivo while sitting and people-watching in a piazza.

- ***Prosecco.*** This refreshing sparkling wine is made in the regions of Veneto and Friuli Venezia Giulia, about one hour west of Venice. To make *prosecco*, a base wine is made from fermenting the white *glera* grapes. The base wine is then transferred to a tank and mixed with a combination of a small amount of sweet white wine and yeast, causing a second fermentation and creating the bubbles. While most *prosecco* is made in a dry style, some varieties have residual sugar, which can make these styles excellent to pair with desserts.
- ***Asti.*** Piedmont produces this sweet wine with fruity flavors of peach and grape, often with some floral notes. Try it with fruit or fruit-based desserts.
- ***Franciacorta.*** The Lombardy region makes the finest sparkling wines in Italy, in a style similar to French Champagne, with balanced acidity, fruit and notes of yeasty bread.

SWEET WINE
DOLCE

- ***Vin Santo.*** *Vin Santo* means holy wine, a truly luscious dessert wine. With flavors of hazelnuts, caramel and honey, creating this wine is a labor of love, patience and faith. It is made from the last grapes picked in the season. These grapes are hung from the rafters to dry until the spring, when they are crushed, strained, sealed and fermented in small chestnut or oak barrels. *Vin Santo* is often served with what we call *biscotti*, but what Italians call *conducini*.

Above *These grapes are hung from the rafters to dry until the spring.*

Photo by Sandy Gregory

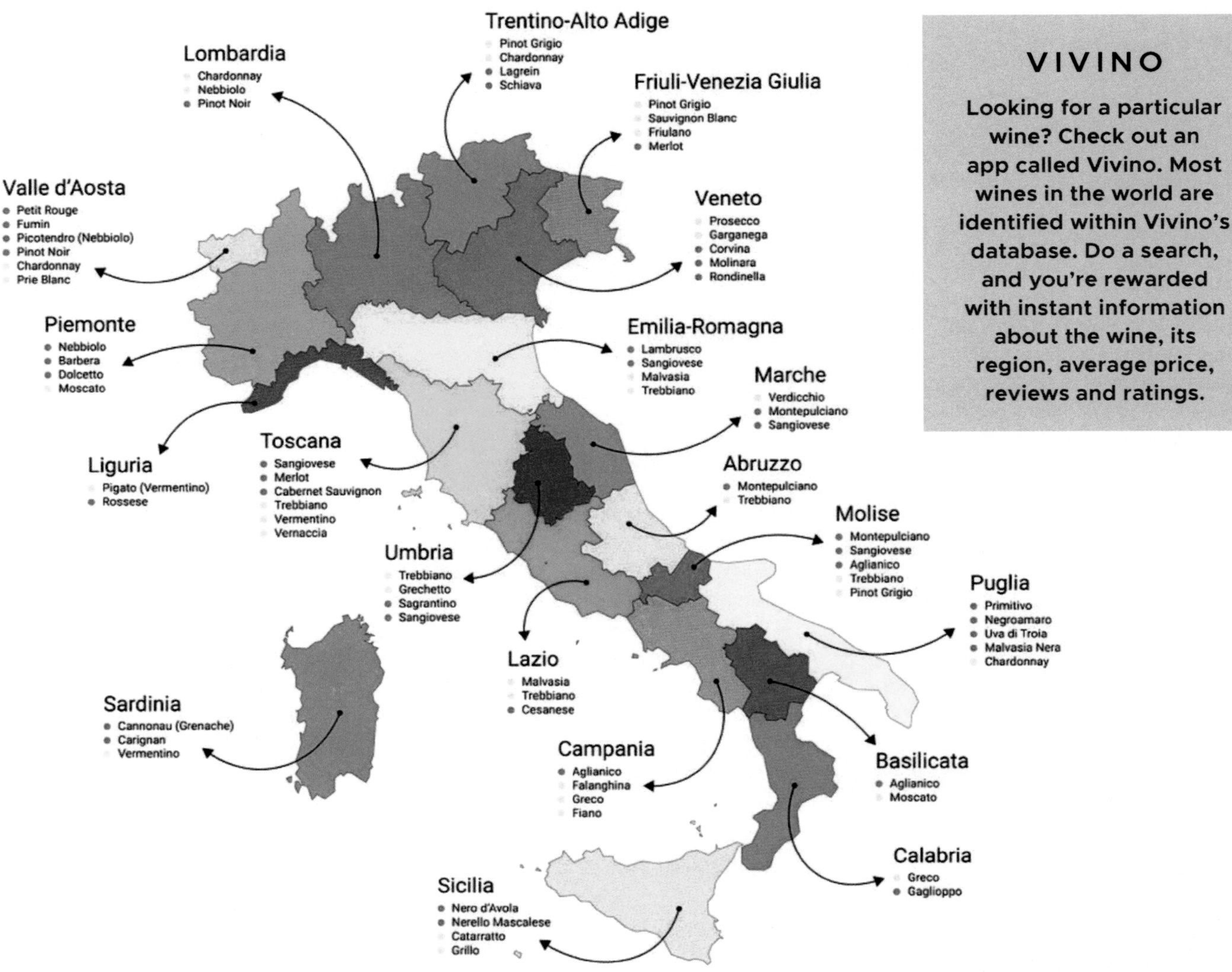

VIVINO

Looking for a particular wine? Check out an app called Vivino. Most wines in the world are identified within Vivino's database. Do a search, and you're rewarded with instant information about the wine, its region, average price, reviews and ratings.

CLASSIFICATIONS OF ITALIAN WINES

DOCG (Denominazione di Origine Controllata e Garantita) These wines have conformed to the strictest standards and therefore have the highest denomination in Italy. To be awarded this classification, DOCG wines must be approved every year by a tasting panel. DOCG wines include such famous names as *Barolo, Barbaresco, Chianti, Brunello di Montalcino* and *Vino Nobile di Montepulciano.*

Riserva These are the wines with both extended aging requirements and higher alcohol levels.

DOC (Denominazione di Origine Controllata) These wines have looser standards. As a result, they are more common and less expensive, often considered high-quality wines.

IGT (Indicazione Geografica Tipica)
These ratings are reserved for wines that may not meet all of the standards of a DOCG or DOC wine, but many are nevertheless considered to be good quality house wines.

Many casual trattorias only serve house wine, locally grown and produced. They vary widely depending on region, year, weather, and even restaurant, but are deliciously affordable.

Don't assume the strictest labels apply to the "best" wines, and vice versa. In fact, some of Italy's best wines aren't DOCG or even DOC. The famous "Super Tuscans," for example, are IGT wines.

THE BLACK ROOSTER

Facing that wall of wine when looking for a good bottle can be simply staggering. The black rooster is a labeling symbol of the prestigious *Chianti Classico DOCG.* So when you are back home and staring at the expansive wine shelf, look for the black rooster, and there is a good chance you have a winner.

A wine pull in Italian is called a cavitappi.

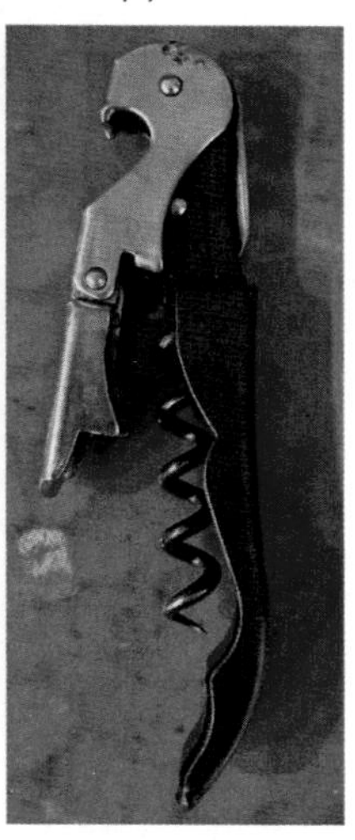

We've all seen the wine bottles covered with woven straw baskets sitting on top of checked tablecloths at our local Italian restaurant. These are called ***fiascos****, which mean bottle or container. During the Renaissance, glass bottles were blown with round bottoms. The basket gave the bottle a flat base, which provided protection during shipping and transportation and also from spilling across the table if it wobbled on the cobblestone floor ... which would be a fiasco!*

DECANTING WINE

Red wines need to be decanted for one of two reasons.

1. Older red wines often have a deposit of sediment which is formed during the aging process. This sediment is gritty and unpleasant and should be removed by decanting. Gently handle the bottle (so as to not agitate the sediment) and slowly pour the wine into a decanter. Watch the neck of the bottle and when you see sediment appear, stop the pour.

2. Younger red wines can benefit from the aeration that occurs from being decanted. By exposing a wine to oxygen, the tannins in the wine can soften, allowing the flavors and aromas of a wine to shine. Younger, full- bodied wines with high levels of tannins, such as *Brunello di Montalcino, Chianti, Barolo* and *Barbarescos* can generally benefit from two-to-three hours in a decanter.

Serving temperature. Red wines generally should be served at 60-65˚F. This can be accomplished by 15 to 20 minutes in a refrigerator just prior to serving. White wines should be served between 45-55˚F. Sparkling and sweet wines should be served slightly cooler than white wines. Bringing these wines out from the refrigeration for 10-15 minutes will allow them to reach the desired serving temperature. Really thirsty? To cool a wine quickly, fill an ice bucket 50/50 with ice and water and place the bottle in the bucket.

NOTES

SHOPPING IN ITALY

ITALIAN SHOES AND OTHER DELICIOUS THINGS

This story is close to my heart and my feet.

For a long time, I thought an obsession with elegant shoes was the indulgence of a select class of women who hobbled around in spike heals in the name of fashion. I'm a Colorado girl, with lots of shoes: Keen sandals, Aosta hiking boots, Sketchers Walkers, Nike trail runners, Sorrel snow boots, Uggs, ski boots and snowshoes. Because shoes should be useful and comfortable, I didn't see the value in fancy footwear. That was, however, until I began to conduct tours in Italy.

Dress shoes were needed for the dinners on my tour, so I popped into a store in Rome. From the corner of my eye I spotted a neutral-colored suede sandal with a platform heel and a flower pattern on the toe. "These will do and will probably match everything I have," I quipped. I put them on. They did more than just "do." A change came over me. It started with a slight tingle in my toes. Then I began to feel taller, longer, leaner. Within minutes, I transformed from a jock with an athletic lumber to a swan gliding above the ground. I wasn't just walking, I was floating. I felt beautiful and sexy, strong and powerful. Wow! These shoes felt great. I was literally swept off my feet. It was a Cinderella moment.

You cannot deny the power of the perfect shoe. Soon I was tapping into my inner Carrie Bradshaw. I began dreaming about shoes. Beautiful shoes. Sexy shoes. Gorgeous Italian shoes made of lush, luxurious fabrics and leathers. Shoes that combined fashion and style with comfort and durability.

Soon people began to notice. My guests asked me where I shopped. I eagerly took them and vicariously lived their thrill. I stalked unknowing Italian women, studying their choices and learning their skill. I began scouring the stores looking for my next find: genuine snake skin sandals, handmade and perfect; red heels, so simple and so very right; boots made of buttery leather and intricate stitching, comfortable yet fashionable.

I hoarded my tips and counted my Euros. Who needs to eat? I can find the deals. *Ti amo! Ho bisogno di te! Lo voglio te!* I love you! I need you! I want you! Who could say if this addiction was manageable, controllable or even understandable?

The intervention. At the end of a particularly long stretch of tours, the packing tips and tricks I give to my guests went out the window as I tried to get the treasured shoes into my own suitcase. (As they say: "The cobbler has no shoes.") In the end, it cost me another suitcase and an additional $150 baggage fee at the airport just to get my shoes home. Right then and there I vowed to manage my addiction.

It's ok. I'm fine now. One day at a time. I know that my shoes will always be there to walk with me, stand by me and lift my soul. But right now, Italian shoes are an extravagance that should be left to the fashionistas. I will focus my efforts on something much more practical — purses.

Planning What You Can Bring Home

BEFORE YOU BUY, THINK ABOUT WHAT YOU CAN BRING HOME AND HOW YOU GET IT THERE.

As of 2021, each passenger is allowed bring home $800 in items duty-free. The combined flat value for a family of four traveling together is $4000. You do not declare what you have shipped home during your travels, just what you are carrying home in your luggage.

Food items that travel well:

- Cheeses that are vacuum-packed. Hard cheeses such as Parmigiano-Reggiano will make the trip home better than the softer cheeses that are perishable.
- Dried herbs, spices, pecorino, mushrooms and sun-dried tomatoes.
- Canned or jarred fruits or vegetables, including honey, jams, mustards, pesto, spreads, truffles and garlic.
- Baked goods, dried pasta, rice, candy, chocolate, nuts, coffee and tea
- Wine, balsamic vinegar and olive oil. I usually ship liquid items directly from Italy to the U.S. But, if you prefer to pack them, you are allowed two bottles total per person in your check-in luggage. I recommend bottle travel protectors such as **Wineskin** in case they break or leak in transit.

Duty free shops have lots of great wines, spirits, olive oil, vinegars, perfumes and other liquids. However, your purchase only works if you do not have a connecting flight. When you land in the U.S., you'll have to re-enter security to get from your international to domestic flight, and all liquids need to meet the 3 oz. restrictions. The TSA screeners will be more than happy to confiscate your *Chianti Classico*.

Food items that stay in Italy:

- Fresh fruits and vegetables.
- Any products made with meat, milk, eggs or poultry, including dried soup mix or bouillon, canned, dried, cured or fully cooked meat such as prosciutto, salami or sausage.

VAT Tax on purchases. VAT (Value Added Tax) is a 22 percent sales tax included in the price of merchandise. A VAT refund is the reimbursement you get if you are a non-EU resident and if you purchase more than $155 worth of goods at one store that participates in the VAT refund program. Refunds generally wind up being about 16 - 18 percent of the final price. If you are a big-ticket shopper, a VAT tax refund is worth it, so plan ahead.

Before you buy, inquire if and how the store handles the VAT refund. You can avoid the VAT tax by having the merchant ship the goods directly to your home address. You'll have to weigh the cost of shipping vs. the cost of the VAT. Note: It often costs more to ship heavy items than the cost of the items themselves. Street and market vendors, sidewalk artists, and many small-town stores don't provide this service.

You need your passport when you make a purchase. The merchant is required to fill out the form and attach it to the receipt. This tax refund is claimed before you leave the EU zone where you have to show all of the VAT paperwork, the merchandise and your passport. You paperwork will be checked and stamped. You can choose whether you want to receive the refund as cash (Euro) or as a credit on your card. Don't expect U.S. currency. Some people go to the local city VAT refund offices during their travels, while some wait until they have made all of their purchases and get their refund at the airport as they leave the EU. No matter which you choose, keep the stamped paperwork and merchandise with you as the customs officer at the airport border control may ask for it.

Airport VAT refund offices are located just before you go through security. IMPORTANT: Make sure you allow plenty of time at the airport to complete this before you go through TSA and get to your gate. If you have an early morning flight home, the VAT office most likely will not be open. There are kiosks at the airport where you can drop your paperwork in an envelope, but I don't recommend this. Refunds don't always happen this way and your address and credit card information is not secure. So, if you know you have an early morning departure, get your refunds at one of the in-town offices during your travels.

Here is a link all of the all of the VAT offices in Italy.

taxfreeservice.com/sedi.asp?Citta=18

Shipping can be an easy option. Vendors, wineries and stores that offer shipping services include the appropriate costs in your purchase price. Packages are shipped via the U.S. Postal Service and other private freight companies who work with U.S. Customs to clear and deliver your goods. Hang on to your payment receipt, as you may have to pay additional customs fees. TIP: Delivery always requires a signature, so plan to have your package delivered to a location where you know someone always will be there to accept and sign for a package.

Here's the rub on shipping. For heavy items, such as ceramics and antiques, the price of shipping from Italy to the U.S. might be much more expensive than the price of the product itself.

When you land in the U.S. You no longer fill out a paper custom form on the airplane before you land in the U.S. Now, U.S. citizens proceed directly to the passport control area and complete the forms at kiosks. Always be truthful with your answers because you could be pulled out by a Customs Officer and checked at any time.

BEWARE OF COUNTERFEITERS

Alongside the true local artisans are hawkers who call out to passers-by with fabulous "copies" of desired luxury items (eg., handbags, watches, shoes, clothing) at unbelievable prices. These counterfeiters set up easily movable displays on sidewalks and perimeters of established markets. If law enforcement arrives, the imp.osters quickly fold up and flee. If you are caught engaging with these criminals, you could pay a stiff penalty of up to 1000 Euros.

Does the allure to buy override the risk? You think to yourself, who would know? Would my friends be able to tell the difference? Who would be harmed? Is it really a problem? Unequivocally, YES.

Selling counterfeit goods violates international laws and costs legitimate manufacturers trillions of dollars. These counterfeit products are made by highly skilled and well-run organized crime syndicates raking in $2.3 trillion dollars through this underground economy. For these crime syndicates, the business of counterfeit products is part of a portfolio that includes drugs, human trafficking and prostitution.

And there is another link you might not be aware of: intellectual property investigations have shown that money gleaned from this trillion-dollar industry also is used to fund terrorism. The money you paid for that fake handbag may fund the training of terrorists, supply weaponry and explosives.

The lure of a fake Fendi is not worth the consequences.

THE HOURS

Especially in small towns, the Italian workday may see quirky to Americans. Visitors are often surprised and disappointed when they arrive at a shop, only to find that it closed at 1 p.m. for lunch and won't be open again until 3 or 4 p.m. In this case, I recommend doing what the locals do — enjoy a wonderful Italian lunch and return to the shops when they open. Most everything in the larger tourist cities are always open, but if you're planning on dipping into a small town for a few hours of shopping, plan your travel itinerary accordingly. The good news is that these shops are often open in the evening, so you can shop and enjoy your *passeggiata* or evening walk.

Photos by Sandy Gregory

TO BARGAIN OR NOT TO BARGAIN

The rule of thumb: If the store is mobile like a market tent, give bargaining a try. If it has fixed walls and a roof, there is usually is no bargaining. A vendor's desire to bargain can depend on the time of day or time of year, how busy the market is, or what you are trying to buy. Their desire also can be influenced if they are bored, if you're cute, or if they need some fast cash.

I recommend you walk through the market and visit several shops to understand the going rate for an item. Then work your way back through to the vendor that gives you the lowest price. It might be appropriate to bargain if you are buying quantities of things, such as ten scarves. If you are making a big purchase, you can try to throw something else into the pot. Most vendors will meet you in the middle. If you still find the price too high, walk away. If the shopkeeper is able to lower it further, they'll find you.

My guests sometimes feel the need to drive a hard bargain. Remember, locals need to make a living. Think about paying a fair price — not the lowest price. Driving a hard bargain can cause real suffering to vendors already living hand-to-mouth. As with everything, you get what you pay for. There are endless rows of shops stocked with ubiquitous souvenirs and inexpensive imports, but try to dig a little deeper. Support local producers, makers and artisans. Think about buying souvenirs as a way to support and learn about local communities.

Have exact change when you shop at the markets. Cash in hand is a quick and attractive way to seal a deal.

Bring currency in a variety of denominations. This way, you won't bargain down something to 20 Euros and then ask the vendor to make change for a hundred.

Be polite and respectful.

Make it fun for everyone.

Know when to cut bait.

Enjoy the game.

My Favorite Things

WHAT TO BUY WHERE AND HOW

During the Middle Ages, artisans were organized into guilds or *arti:* painters, sculptors, glass blowers, leather makers, goldsmiths, mask makers, silk masters and more. Masters helped prepare young workers while benefitting through what we might think of as unpaid labor, while young trainees learned a skill to support themselves in the future, like today's internships. Guilds worked to promote their craft by creating and enforcing regulations for their trade, setting and policing wages, prices and quality.

Today, the streets of Italy are lined with glitzy high-end boutiques and couture chain stores. But tucked away amidst the winding streets are the tiny shops — like mini-museums — where local artisans weave, paint, carve, pound and stitch.

Many of my guests count on me to take them shopping. When we find a treasure, they ask, "Should I buy this here?" My answer is usually, "Yes, if you find something you love and it is created and produced in the region where we are shopping. Don't second-guess yourself. Just buy it. I can't guarantee you'll find it somewhere else."

Remember, generally you have a luggage limit of 50 pounds when you fly internationally. Many of my guests pack a light duffel bag for the flight home. Your dirty laundry and unbreakables go into the duffel so you can wrap your treasures in your sturdy travel bag. Don't forget to bring some **Wineskin** brand sleeves for any wine or olive oil you want to bring home in your suitcase.

Now let's take a closer look at my favorite things to buy in Italy.

Artisan Shops

LEATHER
Florence

CERAMICS
Throughout Italy

OLIVE WOOD UTENSILS
Tuscany and to the South

SILK
Lake Como and Florence

CERAMICS AND HANDWOVEN LINENS
Puglia

BUSATTI LINEN
Tuscany

HAND MADE PAPER
Venice, Florence and Amalfi

JEWELRY
Throughout Italy

FORTUNY
Venice

CARNIVAL MASKS
Venice

MURANO GLASS
Venice

Local Markets

PORCINI MUSHROOMS
Emilia-Romagna, Piedmont, the Alto Adige, Tuscany, Umbria and the Veneto

SPICES
Throughout Italy

SAFFRON
San Gimignano, Abruzzo and L'Aquila

DARIO SALT
Tuscany

TRUFFLES
Piedmont, Tuscany, Umbria, Le Marche

LEMON EVERYTHING
The Amalfi Coast

The Grocery

BACI

POCKET COFFEE

CASTELVETRANO OLIVES

FORMAGGIO

MIELE

The artisan shops of Italy bring you the finest in craftsmanship. Here are a few of my favorite items to bring home.

Artisan Shops

LEATHER

FLORENCE

Italian leather jackets, purses, belts, gloves and shoes come in a wide range of sizes, colors, quality and price.

There really is no such thing as "Italian leather." Italian cows do not make special leather, Italian artisans do. It's all about the quality of workmanship to cut, fit, sew, stitch and hand finish. The first thing I tell my guests is to decide how much they want to spend. A designer bag or jacket is definitely a status symbol, but one that not all of us can afford. No worries though. There are plenty of well crafted, stylish leather products in Florence ... for every budget. Yes, there is a lot of junk, but there also are treasures to be found. As a matter of fact, in 2020, Florence passed a law requiring the markets to get rid of the "junk" in the stalls. They are switching the vendors to showcase local-crafted merchandise. Hopefully, this law will support the talented local craftsman and give us a better foundation from which to buy.

All artisan photos by Sandy Gregory

Follow a few guidelines and you'll find the perfect piece built with good material and quality workmanship – without breaking the bank.

Examine texture closely. You can tell quality leather by touch and smell. It should be soft and supple and smell musky. Don't be fooled by branding: if it doesn't feel luxurious, it's probably not. There are a few grades of leather:

- **Full-grain leather (*pieno fiore*) and Top-grain (*parte grano or cuoio di grano*).** These grades are thick, tough and durable with a hearty grain. And full-grain ages, it gains a beautiful sheen that gets even more beautiful over time. I usually steer toward the natural brown color rather than dyed.
- **Genuine leather (*vera pelle or vero cuoio*).** Genuine leather has no grain even though it may still be supple, rich in color and retain a pleasant aroma. Suede is an example of genuine leather.
- **Bonded leather (*cuoio rigenerato*).** Leather dust, shavings and excess pieces are swept up and pressed together in the factory with the aid of various chemicals, dyes and glues to make this material. Check if it smells like cow or glue.

Look at how the piece is constructed. The stitching should be tight and strong and the hardware sturdy. If the label "Made in Italy" is fully sewn into the leather, it was most likely tanned, cut and assembled in Italy. If one side of the label is sewn into the fabric and not the leather, or glued on, it was made in another country and shipped to Italy.

Use a nourishing leather conditioner right away to protect the finish and so stains can be removed more easily. Regular conditioning helps keep the leather soft, enriching the color after it starts to wear.

CERAMICS

Much of the ceramic work we see throughout Italy is called *maiolica*. This is a technique of painting with ceramic pigments over terra cotta, layering colored pigments on top of a white glaze. When fired in a kiln, this technique imparts bright, shiny colors that pop from a creamy, opaque background. Ceramic afficianados travel to Tuscany and Umbria, where ceramics depict sunflowers, cypress trees and grapevines. To the north, in the Emilia-Romagna town of Faenza, artisans create designs that are geometric, using decorative scrolls in rich blues, ochres and gold. To the south, shops along the Amalfi Coast are brimming with pieces adorned with images of lemons, sunflowers, fish, grapes, the sun and moon.

Shipping ceramics home can be a challenge. Many stores offer shipping and include a certain amount of insurance. This could cost more than the items themselves, but worth the price to assure they arrive in one piece. Make sure you buy from a reputable shop. Most are very experienced in packaging their wares, but here are a few suggestions to make sure your pieces arrive safe and sound.

- Take a picture of the purchased items before they are wrapped and packaged.
- Exchange full contact information including a phone number and email address.
- Pay with a credit card so you can dispute the charge if your items arrive broken or not at all. Get a copy of the receipt and the shipping air bill with a tracking number.
- Ask for your items to be shipped close to the date you return home. International shipping times vary greatly, so you want to make sure you are there to sign for your delivery.

OLIVE WOOD UTENSILS

The dramatic grain patterns of ancient olive trees make stunning kitchenware. This hard wood is durable, resists odors and stains. My guests walk out of my "olive wood superstores" lugging heavy bags of beautiful spatulas, spoons, cheese graters, bowls, honey drizzlers, cutting boards and more.

Proper care and maintenance is required to keep your olive wood products in good condition. In 1998, I purchased a cutting board in San Gimignano. It still looks like new.

- Season periodically with food-grade mineral oil like **Boos Block Mystery Oil.** Avoid using vegetable or olive oil because these products can go rancid. Use a soft cloth to apply the mineral oil and allow it to soak into the wood. After the wood has dried, apply a second coat.
- Clean your utensils after use in warm water using a mild liquid dish detergent and wipe dry. Never put olive wood in the dishwasher.

- Sanitize your utensils every few months. Clean them well in warm, soapy water and then spread them out on a flat surface. Slice a lemon in half and rub into the wood; let sit for 15 to 20 minutes and then wipe dry with a towel. Re-oil as described above.

FORTUNY LINENS

VENICE

At the most elegant shops in the city you'll find Fortuny — one of the most luxurious fabric lines in the world. The price tag is high, but the luminous, unique colors and exquisite craftsmanship make even a small pillow cover, tassel or pendant light a true treasure. The brand was created by Mariano Fortuny, who was born in Spain in 1871 and moved to Venice at the turn of the century. He acquired a Venezian-Gothic Palazzo on the Grand Canal and used it as his home, studio and showroom. Today, the palazzo houses the Fortuny Museum, showcasing his lifetime of art and fashion. In nearby Giudecca, the Fortuny Showroom and Factory still produces his designs and products the same way as was done 100 years ago.

BUSATTI LINENS

TUSCANY

From the medieval Tuscan village of Anghiari, the Busatti-Sassolini family has been weaving linen and cotton from the Apennines mountain sheep since 1842. Their future is in the past. The artisans exercise their craft with pride, skill and a unique passion passed down through eight generations. The weavers at the home factory in Anghairi are a popular destination for my guests, most of whom have left with armfuls of tableware, bedding, bathware and window treatments.

SILK

LAKE COMO AND FLORENCE

Along with breathtaking landscapes, beautiful gardens and a possible George Clooney sighting, silk is another reason to visit Lake Como. Florence is also one of the world's fashion meccas. Italians care for their silk, from breeding silkworms to twisting, hoarding, weaving, and finally dyeing, printing and finishing. And just like everything, you get what you pay for. Here are some things to look for when you're looking to purchase a quality silk item.

- **Take a close look at the weave.** Real silk is shiny and supple. It should feel soft and slippery in your hands. Check the stitching. Edges should be hand folded and hand stitched, with a thread that blends smoothly with the colors.
- **Check the pattern.** High-quality artisan scarves are printed using a traditional silkscreen process, building the design one color at a time.
- **Test the fabric.** If you rub pure silk between your fingers, it makes a distinctive crunching sound. Then, perform "the ring test" by pulling the silk scarf through your ring. If the fabric bunches, making it difficult to pass the fabric through the ring, it's synthetic. Silk will glide through the ring very smoothly.

HANDMADE PAPER

VENICE, FLORENCE, AMALFI

The art of paper making found its way from Asia to Europe via Venice in the Middle Ages. Bookmaking began during the 1450s Renaissance with the advent of moveable type. Traditionally, marbleized paper was used to line the leather bindings in books. The designs were created by swirling oil-based paints into a large pan of water and then laying the paper gently and briefly on the surface to transfer the pattern. At that time, Florentines had extensive libraries and were deeply involved in publishing, printing and bookmaking. Today, you can still find artisans who create rich marbleized paper, elegant stationery and Italian leather bound notebooks that bring back this slower, more artful time. Also made by Italian artisans are gorgeously crafted desk accessories, bookmarks, fountain pens, wax seals
and ribbons.

Amalfi stationery is made by hand from the finest cotton, often incorporating natural elements such as flower petals and herbs. It has a distinctive creamy ivory white color, soft texture, and a delicate edge that exudes elegance and character. The famous watermark proclaims the pride of workmanship that goes into each sheet. The Amalfi Amatruda paper mill is located along Italy's Amalfi Coast, in one of the most renowned paper making centers in Europe, and has produced exquisite stationery since 1380.

JEWELRY

Florence is the place where this amazing craftsmanship was born during the Renaissance. The art of jewelry making is still alive and well throughout Italy. These artisans are the descendants of the ancient *Arti e Corporazioni*, the Guilds of Florence established in the Middle Ages to develop the trade and the economy of the city. In the heart of the Florentine Oltrarno district and dotted around the winding streets of many Italian towns, the artistry continues today. Certainly your style, and your budget, will set the tone. We can set up visits to see the artisans at work. The results are spectacular masterpieces, each unique and designed to tell a different story.

One of my favorite shops is located in Cortona. Enjoy a glass of prosecco dusted with gold and silver flakes while being guided through an ancient olive mill and wine cellar that displays exquisite jewelry, shoes and gifts. This shop created the sunflower necklace (below) that I wear to celebrate my Che Bella Tours logo.

CARNIVAL MASKS

VENICE

Carnival is a traditional festival that takes place during the ten days leading up to Lent. The Venice Carnival is one of the most famous in the world. Three million people descend upon the floating city every February to soak up the scenery, wear extravagant costumes and masks, and be part of the electric atmosphere.

Throughout the long history of Venice, masks protected the identity of people walking the streets. While there is a plethora of cheap, masks made in China, there are still a handful of artisans who make exquisite, made-to-order, hand-sewn Venetian costumes and masks. A traditional mask begins with a base of clay or plaster that is decorated with paint, feathers, jewels, lace, leather and a variety of sparkles and spangles. A few Venetian mask makers still welcome you into their workshops and some even offer mask making classes. Below are my own artistic efforts at mask making.

THE MASTER GLASSBLOWER

Venetian glassblowing techniques have not changed since ancient times. A glassblower is known as a *fioleri*. On the end of a blowpipe, this artisan lifts a molten blob of sand mixed with a variety of materials. He blows, twists, pulls and cuts the blob over a hot flame to form the shapes that will be pieced together to make sculptures, goblets, vases, bowls, chandeliers, jewelry and more.

Shipping these delicate pieces home can be a challenge. I have found that, when insured, you'll get replacement pieces with no questions asked. Most reputable businesses include shipping and insurance in your price.

VENETIAN GLASS

MURANO

Like a broken clock, the master glassblowers of Murano seem to be frozen in time. The small island of Murano, about two miles north of Venice, is home to some of the world's master glassblowers. The glass factories were sequestered on the island of Murano to protect the city of Venice from possible fire hazards caused by their furnaces. The secrets and skills of the master glassblowers were so highly revered, laws were established that actually prevented them from leaving the island. Everyday life in Murano still revolves around the glass making industry.

The quality, style and price of Venetian glass varies widely. Be cautious of counterfeit products sold throughout Italy. To make sure you're getting authentic Murano glass, shop in Murano. If you're elsewhere, look for the foil sticker that says "Made in Murano, Italy," or a holographic sticker etched into the piece that contains a specific number. This number can be used to identify the particular furnace where the piece was made. If there is no sticker, ask the store merchant for a certificate of authenticity that should include information about the artisan who created the piece as well as the production date.

Italian markets are the perfect place to pick up culinary treasures. My favorite is the Mercado Centrale at the famous San Lorenzo market in Florence.

Local Markets

All local market photos by Sandy Gregory

PORCINI MUSHROOMS

Porcini in Italian means "little pigs." The meat-like texture and earthy, nutty flavor make these mushrooms excellent for cooking. You will see *porcini* served from Rome to the Dolomites, adding richness to pasta or rice, sautées, omelettes and veal dishes.

I often stay in Siena with my friend, Chef Gina Stipo, between tours. If I'm lucky to be there any time from August through the fall, Gina and I will join the local *fungaioli* for a mushroom hunt. The early morning will find us hiking through the forest mist, picking our way through the undergrowth in search of fall mushrooms hiding beside the trees. As we take the mushrooms, we also give back. To ensure the mushrooms' survival, we carry our treasures in open baskets that allow their spores to escape. There are many poisonous mushrooms that can be mistaken for the edible ones, so a wild mushroom hunt is only complete after the inspection from the local pharmacist or in some small towns, the mushroom nonna.

Fresh *porcini* doesn't travel, but you can bring home:

- **Jarred *porcini* in olive oil.** Be sure to wrap the glass jar in multiple layers of padding and bag it tightly before you put it into your suitcase. When cooking, reserve the oil and use it to enhance the flavor of your recipe.
- **Jarred *porcini bruschetta* or *porcini* paste.** These pastes are beautiful on grilled bread or mixed into pasta.
- **Dried *porcini*.** A small amount of dried *porcini* can add a lot of punch to a recipe, so it's a great idea to have some in your kitchen. You'll see pre-packaged varieties, but I prefer to choose my own from the market's display baskets of loose, dried mushrooms. Look them over carefully. Choose large, intact slices that are not flaky. Check for pinholes, which could indicate worms. Mushrooms should have a decisively musky scent. If the mushrooms have no smell, then they have no flavor.

To prepare, cover your *porcini* in boiling water and let them steep until they are reconstituted. Keep the liquid and use it to add even more concentrated flavor to your recipe.

Freeze the dried *porcini* mushrooms when you get home. Use a good airtight glass container and your *porcini* will last for months.

SAFFRON

TUSCANY

Spices are displayed beautifully in markets all over Italy. My favorite is saffron. Italians call this spice *oro rosso*, or red gold. There is a staggering amount of labor packed into a farmer's day to make a tiny amount of saffron. It takes roughly 4,000 flowers to make one ounce of saffron powder. The process begins early the morning. As the sun rises, the stigmas — three tiny threads per flower — are separated from the petals. It's a delicate process that takes a skilled and patient hand. As the sun sets, the threads are dried in wire baskets over an open fire, which adds to the richness of the color, the flavor *and* the price.

TRUFFLES

PIEDMONT, TUSCANY, UMBRIA AND LE MARCHE

I always encourage my guests to try *tartuffe*, or truffles. Many people find them too strong, but I think it is because they have not had them prepared correctly. A little truffle goes a very long way which is good, considering it's a pricey purchase. When prepared right, it's a little slice of heaven. Like mushrooms, truffles have a symbiotic relationship with specific tree roots. The woods are full of truffle hunters combing the forest floor with their highly trained dogs. You can join the hunt, but fresh truffles often are confiscated at Customs. Instead, opt for the less pungent, but safe, truffle products such as preserved whole truffles, purées, butters, oils, pastes, sauces and truffled sea salt.

The most popular truffle product online is truffle-infused olive oil. Beware that the majority of truffle oil sold this way is not made with true truffles. The main ingredient is a chemical designed in a laboratory to mimic the aroma of truffles. If you do want to order online, I would recommend ordering from a company called Urbani. They make a product from olive oil and actual truffles. Otherwise, come on my tour and get the good stuff.

The *tartufo nero di Norcia*, the winter black truffle, is in season from November to March. These are the most common truffles that you'll find on Italian menus. The *tartufo bianco d'Alba*, white truffles found only in Piedmont, are too delicate for cooking.This delicacy is thinly shaved raw over risottos and pastas, in salads or on eggs.

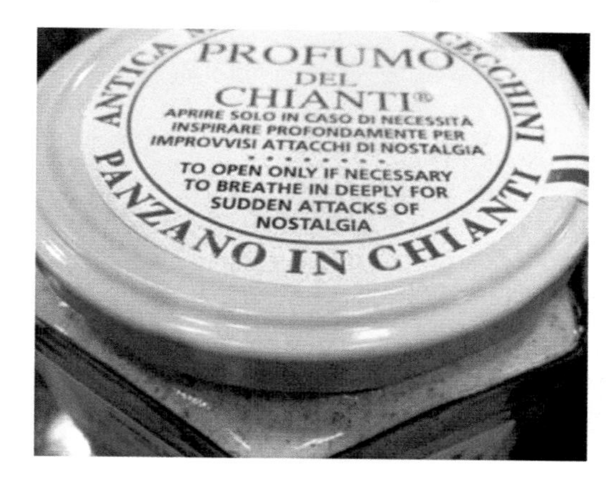

DARIO SALT

TUSCANY

I never come home without a few jars of *Il Profumo del Chianti*. This secret mix of sun-dried Tuscan herbs and sea salt is created by the Mad Butcher of Panzano, Dario Cecchini. Those "in the know" call it "Dario Salt" and it's great on everything. Just a pinch provides the sensation that the forests and meadows of Tuscany are melting in your mouth. Mix it with a little olive oil for a healthy veggie dip.

LEMONS

THE AMALFI COAST

If the Amalfi Coast screams one thing, it's LEMONS! Italy is the world's largest producer of lemons. And, as is custom throughout the country, the people here use what is abundant and local to give life to tradition. Grilled mozzarella with lemon leaves, lemon cakes, lemon granita, pasta vongole, caprese salad with *bufalo* mozzarella, lemon on fish and pasta, lemon soaps, tea towels and lotions. Everything you can and can't imagine is served with lemons!

Forget about the expensive gourmet shops! Stock up at the neighborhood grocery if you want the real deal — and real deals.

The Grocery

PERUGINA *BACI* CANDY

This sweet treat has a silky, dark chocolate shell that envelopes a richly whipped chocolate filling blended with chopped hazelnuts. Each little chocolate is individually wrapped and perfect just the way it is, including the hazelnut crown. But, there's more! Inside the outer foil wrapper is a glassine paper with quotes about love and friendship in French, Italian, German and English. Many a motorcoach ride has been spent with my guests munching on this fine chocolate and sharing quotes with the group. Here are a few notes I keep tucked in my wallet:

The heart cannot be bought or sold, but only given. — Proverb

Grow old along with me; the best is yet to be. — G. Sand

Till I loved, I did not live enough. — E. Dickinson

A true friend knows all there is to know about you yet still likes you. — E. Hubbard

Being deeply loved by someone gives you strength; loving someone deeply gives you courage. — Lao-Tzu

POCKET COFFEE

A shot of espresso in a dark chocolate shell. Eat as is for a delicious pick-me-up, or plop one into a mug of steaming coffee and it becomes a nuclear cup of mocha delight.

CASTELVETRANO OLIVES

Castelvetrano is so much a staple on our family *aperitivi* board that my nephew's first word was "ovive." *Castelvetrano* olives come from southwestern Sicily. These Kermit-green rays of sunshine have a fresh, crisp texture and a rich buttery taste. I often simmer them slowly in extra virgin olive oil and a few cloves of garlic to add a warm, savory addition to our *aperitivi.*

FORMAGGIO

The U.S. Department of Agriculture does not approve any cheeses that are unpasteurized or that have been aged less than 60 days. I bring home the hard cheeses: *Parmigiano-Reggiano* and *Pecorino Romana*. Yes, you can buy these luscious chunks at the Italian village markets. I go to the grocery store right before I fly home, because get the same quality cheese at a much better price, and I am not lugging large chunks during my travels. The vacuum-packed wedges still need to be refrigerated, so I store them in my hotel refrigerator, before packing them in my checked bag. Cargo storage is cold, so I am ok with the cheese making it through a long transcontinental flight. While it may be tempting to pick up some mozzarella at the Naples airport, the soft cheeses rarely make it home without spoiling.

MIELE

Local groceries offer good prices and a wide variety of *miele*, or honey, in different jar sizes for easy transport. *Millefiori* honey — thousand flowers — is made from the nectar of the thousands of flowers that stretch across the Tuscan countryside. It's rich, full-bodied and complex with notes of chestnut, flowers, dry herbs and sweet woody aromas. I also like chestnut honey, a dark, strong honey that works well with pungent cheeses. Honey from the nectar of the acacia tree has a delicate, sweet flavor.

NOTES

HOW TO VIEW ART AND MAKE IT FUN

RESTLESS NOMAD. CREATIVE SPIRIT.

There was no getting away from being a creative spirit in my family. We're writers, sketchers, painters, graphic designers, fiber artists, knitters, chefs, art teachers, architects, woodworkers and horticulturists. Mealtimes were creative expressions of tastes and smells. Gardens overflowed with color and texture.

With sketchbooks in tow, my Aunt Nancy and I sketched Chicago's Northside Art Deco hot dog stands as well as the masterpieces of the Art Institute. My high school art teacher recognized a passion and gave me free access to the art room to create, experiment and grow. As a foreign exchange student in high school, I dug deep into the culture of Oaxaca, Mexico while digging deep into the clay, learning to shape the famous "black mud" pottery. When I was in college, I majored in graphic design, advertising and creative writing, with a minor in art history. So it was no surprise when, as a junior in 1981, I hopped a plane to immerse myself in the art, history, political science, language and culture of Italy.

Florence is one of the most well-preserved Renaissance cities in the world. Boasting over 40 percent of the world's great masterpieces, it is considered the art capital of Italy. I was in the thick of it. Our passionate professors brought the masterpieces to life and we had the luxury of time to learn, engage, reflect and appreciate everything that was around us. It took an entire semester to work my way through the 101 galleries of the Uffizi Museum. Hours sketching in the Accademia's Gipsoteca helped hone the principles of balance, perspective and proportion. Simply walking the streets of Florence was like living in an open-air museum.

I lived with three other girls from my school: Sharon, Mimi and Susan. Our cavernous, one-room apartment on Via Verde was a work of art in itself. Since it was the servants' quarters for a once-grand Contessa, it seemed only right to plaster a poster of Michelangelo's *Creation* on the barrel-vaulted ceiling. We lined our kitchen's half wall with the many empty bottles of wine we enjoyed. The door to our hovel was opened

with a large brass key that measured no less than a foot long and took no less than eight full rotations to activate the tumblers and trigger the lock. The four of us shared one key, with no way to copy, so that key could never be lost. Our class schedule dictated who was to be the "Keeper of the Key" and charged with the quest of egress and ingress to our little queendom.

From our single large window, we looked out on to Piazza Santa Croce and its famed Basilica. The tombs of Michelangelo, Dante and many other of Florence's greatest artists and thinkers were just feet away. Every time we walked out the door, we gave a nod to the inspiration that looked down upon us and wished us a good day. The city tour bus sometimes caught the 8:25 a.m. stop light on our street. As the tour guide delivered her commentary, the tourists on board often enjoyed a sight that was not on their itinerary: a perfect view inside the window of four college girls getting dressed for class.

I was appointed chef for our tight group of friends. We pooled our lira and I shopped for groceries every day after class. My route included the butcher, my cheese guy, the nonna with fruits and vegetables, *Il Fornaio* (the baker) for bread and pasta, and of course, my wine guy. The shopkeepers drilled me on my Italian, shared the local gossip and taught me authentic family recipes. Every night, the gang arrived for the feast. We talked history, politics and art. Florence was our teacher. Europe was our classroom.

The monthly trek upstairs to the penthouse to pay our rent always required tea with the Contessa. On cue, she would make her dramatic entrance through the heavy drapery and sashay her way around the dusty antiques. Her interior design style was inspired by Mrs. Havisham from *Great Expectations*. Her heavily made-up face was like Norma Desmond in the movie *Sunset Boulevard*. I was ready for her at any time to say, "All right, Mr. DeMille, I'm ready for my close-up."

Who could have known in 1981 Florence, that 27 years later I would be a tour director doing commentary at the door of my apartment on Via Verde enroute to Piazza Santa Croce?

Who could have known in 1981 Florence, that 27 years later I would be a tour director doing commentary at the door of my apartment on Via Verde enroute to Piazza Santa Croce?

Top left *Forza Fiorentina 1981 with my roommate, Sharon*

Top right *Florence 1981, the 8:25 tour bus*

Bottom *Doing commentary at the front door of my apartment 27 years later*

Photos by Susan Lentz and Sandy Gregory

Art is Everywhere

Art can be provocative and emotional. It also can be joyous and even silly. Not only are there thousands of museums and galleries throughout Italy, but also statues and fountains light up the piazzas. Ancient structures intertwine with new construction. Foyers and entranceways are adorned with frescoes and sculptures. Storefront windows are beautifully designed. Art students recreate masterpieces with chalk on the streets. Women and men dress smartly and with finesse. Even Italian food is made with the art of *abbinamento* — artistically balancing flavors with colors and textures.

A Che Bella Tours trip to Italy concentrates on two periods of time: Ancient Rome and the periods surrounding the Renaissance. Ancient Rome ruled much of Europe for nearly 1000 years and spread its military, political and social institutions throughout Europe during its rule. As a result, Rome's culture still has an impact in the Western world today. "Renaissance" comes from the French word for "rebirth." It was the cultural, political, scientific and intellectual explosion in Europe between the 14th and 16th centuries. This was the most profoundly important period in Western human development since the fall of Ancient Rome.

Art museums may not be for everyone but, like everything on tour, my job is to make the experience fun and enriching. This chapter is designed to help you prepare for these tours with a short introduction to painting, sculpture, architecture, antiquities, contemporary design and music. This short guide is not meant to be an art history lesson, but rather a tool kit to give you a basic visual vocabulary. Our guides use works of art as a basis for conversation.

- What was going on in Italy at the time?
- What is the value of education?
- What defines a good government?
- What justifies war?
- What determines the worth of individuals?
- What shaped personal and collective identities?
- What did it mean to be a person of faith?

***Above** Art students begin their day on the streets of Florence create masterpieces in chalk. At the end of the day, the midnight street cleaners wash it all away, leaving a clean palette for the artists to begin again.*

Photos by Sandy Gregory

***Next page left** Art and artists are everywhere in Italy.*

Photo by Janette Tepas Images

***Next page right** Che Bella Tours art instructor, Joanna Coke, sketching the view from Piazelle Michelangelo in Florence.*

Photos by Sandy Gregory

The goal of art is to make you feel something. Part of appreciating a piece of art is learning about its history. Do some homework before you travel. We can't help but feel a sense of awe when we learn that:

- Cave dwellers drew stories on walls to summon spirits who would bless the village hunters.
- Etruscan pottery was used during religious ceremonies to make offerings to the gods.
- Religious-themed frescoes and paintings were created to teach bible stories to the illiterate.
- Artists recorded history and rebellion through their works.
- Michelangelo proved that you didn't have to be old to become a master.

Enjoy art without getting overwhelmed. Your trip shouldn't be a giant checklist. Make sure you build in some free time to do what truly interests you. Streetlights are art. Gardens are art. Fountains are art. Fashion is art. Nature is art. Cuisine is art. Sunsets are art.

Ask your tour guide or tour director about off-the-beaten path gems that dig a little deeper into your own your interests.

Give yourself a rest. Sit at a cafe, rent a bike, take a walk in a garden. This way the whole trip doesn't blur into one large, blob of old masters and churches.

A PANDEMIC LED TO THE EMERGENCE OF THE RENAISSANCE

In the 14th century, the bubonic plague (also called the Black Death) was carried by fleas that lived on black rats brought to Italy on merchant ships from the East. This pandemic devastated half of the European population and led to an economic crisis. As trade stagnated, businesses failed and unemployment rose.

The plague changed how Europeans experienced and understood their world. Italian society staged a spectacular recovery. The mental outlook of people who survived changed dramatically. Feudalism, the church, and the old social structure were questioned. No longer was a person's destiny determined by their birth. Laborers became merchants; merchants became noblemen; and the great noble families became patrons of the arts. Trade resumed and many prospered. This all led to keen developments in art, science, astronomy, philosophy, language and writing.

The invention of the printing press brought information more quickly to the masses. Important achievements in art and architecture established a new realism. Perspective was developed. Light and shadow were studied. Human anatomy was examined.

All of this was the result of a pandemic.

Painting

Part of appreciating art is learning what was happening in the world at the time the work was created.

All photos in How to View Art and Make it Fun by Sandy Gregory and Janette Tepas Images

Your Che Bella Tours local guide provides an overview of the artist, the time period and geographical location of the artwork. As you dig deeper, he or she will elaborate on any historical context necessary to help tell the story of the painting.

What do you think the artist is trying to say? Take a moment to stop and focus squarely on the painting. Some grab your attention immediately while others need some time to unfold.

- Is this work is a portrait, a historical event, a scene from religion or mythology, a landscape or a still life?
- Does the size of the piece command the room or is it small and delicate?
- Does it look like it was created for a specific space such as a government office, church or family home?
- What is the subject of the painting?
- How are the people dressed?
- What are they doing? What relation do they have to each other and to the viewer?
- Is the artist responding to something going on in the economy? Politics? Personal life? Apply your own knowledge about what was going on in the world at the time and create a story in your mind.
- What would you like to ask the artist about his or her life experiences that might have influenced or inspired the work?

How do you apply meaning to the picture? As you dig deeper into the work, your guide will point out interesting details. What does the way the artist portrays a person tell you about that person? Skulls, for example, were often included in portraits of the wealthy to remind them that wealth was fleeting and meaningless. Serpents and snakes indicate the reason for the fall of mankind, or something evil. A swan symbolized purity, and of course, the apple represented evil as in the forbidden fruit.

What is the medium? Oil? Watercolor? Fresco? Notice the type of paint the artist chose and how it was applied to the surface. Step as close as possible to the painting and look at the brush strokes, the thickness of the paint and the use of color. Then step back to allow your eyes to blend everything together and appreciate the work as a whole.

How does your eye travel through the picture?

- Is the composition symmetrical or asymmetrical?
- Where is the focal point? Can you see where light is supposed to be coming from?
- Is there three-dimensionality with horizon lines and vanishing points? Are there optical illusions that seem to move when you gaze at the picture?
- Are the lines straight, with sharp angles, or curved and organic? Are they mostly horizontal, vertical, diagonal, or circular?

How does the subject make you feel?

- What makes this work pass the test of time?
- In your opinion, is it a masterpiece?
- Does the work have meaning to you?
- Do you like it?

Some of My Favorite Italian Paintings

THE BIRTH OF VENUS

1486. Sandro Botticelli. Galleria degli Uffizi, Firenze

This painting depicts the Roman goddess of love emerging from the sea on a large shell. At the time Botticelli painted The Birth of Venus, artists were moving away from religious images and enjoying the freedom to produce narrative scenes from literature, history and ancient mythology. This is considered one of the first paintings depicting a confident and beautiful woman. Ironically, her image has been used to sell Reeboks, suitcases and Adobe Illustrator software. Beyoncé, Lady Gaga and two of the Bond girls channeled Venus. Versions of Venus have graced the cover of *The New Yorker*, influenced Andy Warhol paintings and have been mocked by Monty Python. We call the painting Venus on the Halfshell. To me, this makes art fun.

I placed Venus on top of our wedding cake – along of course, with The David.

THE DOGE AND THE PATRIARCH WELCOMING HENRY III, KING OF FRANCE

1593. Andrea Vicentino. The Doges Palace, Venice

A Triumphal Entry refers to a conquering ruler being greeted and being paid homage by his new subjects. In 1574, Henry III of Valois spent a few days in Venice on his journey to sit on the French throne. Venice staged an elaborate multimedia spectacle at which, ostensibly, the guest of honor was celebrated. In reality it proved to be a strategy of political propaganda for the glorification of the Venetian state. When the king arrived, he found an extraordinary atmosphere full of luxury, glitz and beauty. An imposing triumphal arch and covered loggia presented his ship with a grand welcome. What he didn't know was that the arch and loggia were actually made of paper mache, and the detailed sculptures, of sugar. The structure sat on a barge that moved through the city's canal system as needed during the King's visit.

I don't fully agreed with George Orwell who said, "all art is propaganda," but I do think this was an earnest, effective — and very humorous — presentation of defiance.

THE LAST SUPPER

1495. Leonardo da Vinci. Santa Maria delle Grazie, Milan

The Last Supper captures the moment when Jesus announces that one of his 12 apostles would betray him. Outstretched arms, tilted heads, pointing fingers and the ceiling beams all converge to the vanishing point on the head of Jesus.

It's one of the world's most famous works of art. Maybe the divine gift of *The Last Supper* is the fact it's still here at all. It was painted on the wall of the dining hall of Santa Maria delle Grazie, an ancient Dominican cloister in Milan. Traditionally, murals were done in fresco, applying color pigment directly to fresh plaster. Leonardo, however, wanted to work slowly, so he spread a white primer directly on the wall and used it as his canvas. Years of cold winters, humid summers, soot and cooking grease took its toll. Obviously, the monks didn't know what they had as they also cut right into Jesus' feet at the bottom of the mural to make a larger door to the kitchen.

The Last Supper began deteriorating a mere 20 years after Leonardo completed it. To make matters worse, the space was used as a stable, storeroom and barracks. Occupying French soldiers threw stones at the Apostles and gouged out their eyes. Napoleon's soldiers used *The Last Supper* for target practice. During World War II, a bomb landed just 80 feet away from the mural. The building was virtually demolished. The roof caved in, the cloister collapsed and three walls were blown out. You can see from the picture how much of the church was destroyed. Miraculously, when the dust cleared, the wall the mural was on was still standing.

There have been multiple attempts to repair and preserve the mural. I was able to walk right into the cloister by myself in 1981. A lone restorer was up on a tall ladder. With her tiny spotting brush and a cotton ball, she painstakingly cleaned the masterpiece inch by inch. Today, however, the room is strictly controlled, allowing only small groups of visitors access in 10-minute shifts.

The Last Supper was given yet another chance when the famous food store, Eataly, paid to have a temperature controlled air filtration system installed. Maybe this Italian food company can be the one to save the most famous meal in history.

STREET SIGNS

Clet Abraham. Florence

Clet Abraham is a French artist who has lived in Italy for over 20 years. His clever "guerrilla" art is just one manifestation of his often surreal and colorful approach to the world. I love to show my guests his artwork as we walk around Florence and even take them to his small shop as we wander up to Piazelle Michelangelo. While not entirely legal, his whimsical "alterations" of road signs are a harmless, humorous and rebellious way to dress up the ugly road signs in this beautiful city. His simple creativity appeals to me as a graphic designer.

SUPERWOMEN STREET ART

Lediesis. Florence

In 2019, I began to notice some vibrant, entertaining street art popping up in Florence. The subjects were iconic women in pop culture — dressed as Superman — winking at passers-by. Frida Khalo, Mother Teresa, Princess Leia, Barbi with a shopping bag and Lara Croft with a rolling pin. They were friendly and witty, their expressions looked right at me as if to say, "You too are super!"

The art is from an entity called Lediesis who are anonymous, but said to be two friends from Florence. Rome became the second stop for this "guerrilla" art, with more empowered women tucked into the streets near Trastavere. At the moment we have no idea how many works have remained because many have been removed or vandalized. The artists have slowly been accepted into galleries and museums throughout Italy, but still remain invisible. Maybe that's *their* superpower.

Sculpture

Take a close look at the craftsmanship and imagine the artist in the studio working with the raw materials. Then step back to appreciate the finished work as a whole.

Your Che Bella Tours local guide provides an overview of the artist, the time period and geographical location of the artwork. As you dig deeper, he or she will elaborate on any historical context necessary to help tell the story of the sculpture.

Here are a few tips on adding a three-dimensional element to your viewing.

What do you think the artist is trying to say? Take a moment to stop and focus squarely on the sculpture. Some grab your attention immediately and others need some time to unfold. Walk around the entire sculpture. Sculpture in the round offers multiple points of view, designed to lead a viewer around the work. Sometimes the story changes with the point of view.

- How does your gaze move around the work as you explore it?
- Does the size of the piece command the room or is it small and delicate?
- Does it look like it was created for a specific space such as a foyer, a garden or the entrance to a building?
- What is the subject of the sculpture?
- What is the body like? Young and supple or mature and defined? Are the bones and muscles angled and geometric or fluid and soft?
- How does the pose and gesture tell the story? Are the arms outstretched? Are they pleading? Do they reach out to dominate the world? Is the form standing or crouching (active), seated (passive)? Is the face upturned and welcoming, turned aside in grief, or slouching downward in weariness?
- Is the artist responding to something going on in the economy? Politics? Personal life? Apply your own knowledge about what was going on in the world at the time and create a story in your mind.
- What would you like to ask the artist about his or her life experiences that might have influenced or inspired the work?

What is the medium? Marble, clay, bronze, wood, gold, or found objects? Working with marble and wood, the artist sculpts down to create the form. See if you can find rough chisel marks, and compare to where the marble is more finished and polished.

With clay that is cast into bronze or gold or using found objects, the sculptor builds up the form. See how the artist molded the clay, and imagine him or her creating the fine details. Take a close look at the craftsmanship and imagine the artist in the studio working with the raw materials. Then step back to appreciate the finished work as a whole.

How does the subject make you feel?

- What makes this work pass the test of time?
- In your opinion, is it a masterpiece?
- Does the work have meaning to you?
- Do you like it?

Some of My Favorite Italian Sculptures

APOLLO CHASING DAPHNE

1625. Gian Lorenzo Bernini. Borghese Gallery, Rome

Gian Lorenzo Bernini was the chief papal artist of architectural and artistic projects under two powerful Roman families, the Borghese and the Barberini. He was a prolific artist who filled almost every corner of Rome with his masterpieces the high alter of St. Peter's and the Fountain of the Four Rivers in the Piazza Navonna.

Bernini sculpted the Apollo Chasing Daphne at the age of 24. It tells the story of Daphne, a mythological nymph, who was famous for being incredibly beautiful. The story goes that she caught the eye of the god, Apollo, who fell deeply in love with her. Daphne, however, was determined to remain unmarried and untouched by a man and rejected Apollo's relentless advances. This masterpiece depicts the moment when Apollo finally catches her. As soon as he lays his hand on her, however, Daphne calls to her father, the river god Peneus. To save his daughter from Apollo, he turns her into a laurel tree.

What I like about this sculpture is how Bernini transformed hard, cold marble into warm movement and life. When you move around it, you can actually see her changing. A close looks shows you the skill it took to form the delicate illusion of soft human flesh, translucent laurel leaves and thin branches that stretch from Daphne's fingertips.

PAOLINA BORGHESE AS VENUS VICTORIOUS

1808. Antonio Canova. Borghese Gallery, Rome

Napoleon Bonaparte commissioned the great Italian sculptor, Antonio Canova, to do a sculpture of his beloved sister Pauline. Napoleon's favorite sister was widely recognized as the most beautiful woman in Europe. A bit of a loose cannon, Paolina had a reputation for promiscuity. The Emperor's sister enjoyed nothing more than courting controversy and raising a few eyebrows in polite society. The artist wanted to depict her as Diana, the chaste goddess of the moon and the hunt, a role that would have her clothed. As you can see below, Paolina had other ideas. Guess who won? Paolina is Venus, the goddess of love, sex, beauty and fertility, reclining on a pillowed couch, obviously comfortable in her own skin.

THE COLUMN OF MARCUS AURELIUS

193 AD. Piazza Colonna on Via del Corso, Rome

Maybe it's because I'm short and I spend most of my life looking up, but the sheer scale of the architecture, triumphal arches and columns that fill the streets of Rome are awe-inspiring. Most columns were erected to honor the glory of the emperors, military life and wartime victories. There are four triumphal columns in Rome and each is a feat of engineering, imagination and artistic skill.

Marcus Aurelius was emperor between 161 and 180 AD. Often called the "philosopher on the throne," he was one of the greatest warriors of the Roman Empire. The column is built of 28 blocks of marble, hollowed out with a spiral staircase inside to reach the platform at the top. It stands 128 feet tall and commemorates his campaign up the Danube River through Germania and Hungary. Like a movie, the scrolls tell the story as they unfurl upward, showing scenes of actual events. The visual propaganda depicts not just the battles, but the military campaigns and public works of Roman forces as they advanced throughout Europe. This column was once a beautifully painted soaring monument of resplendent color. Today, the it towers over the Palazzo Chigi, the official residence of the prime minister and the seat of Italian government.

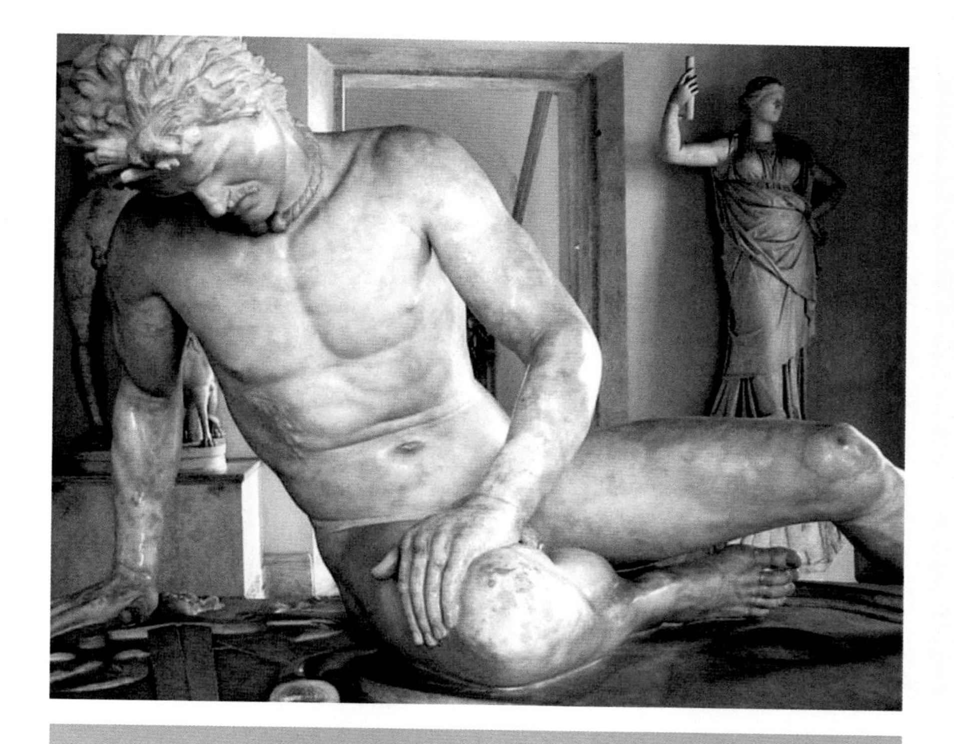

THE DYING GAUL

200 AD. Capitoline Museum, Rome.

If you love sculpture, take some time to go to the The Capitoline Museum. The grand statue of Marcus Aurelius on horseback welcomes you to the entrance in the Piazza dei Campidoglio on Capitoline Hill. The museum's enormous array of ancient Roman, medieval and Renaissance art tell the story of Rome's ancient imperial history. Gorgeous marbled rooms, filled with tapestries and frescoes, set the stage for the statues.

This sculpture is probably the most famous sculpture in the museum. It's a 1st century copy of a Greek original and it celebrates the Greek's defeat of the Galatians.

Dying Gaul was found in the gardens of the Villa Ludovisi in the 17th century. The sculpture is a Roman copy of a Greek bronze original from the 3rd century BC. It was initially identified as a gladiator. But telltale symbols on the base of the sculpture prompted historians to correct that designation. Dying Gaul portrays a Gallic warrior in his final moments, his face contorted in pain as he falls from a visible fatal chest wound. It's a very emotive piece. The sculpture shows both courage in defeat and composure in the face of death.

STENDHAL SYNDROME

It's all in your head ... and your eyes ... and your heart.

As defined: The typical victim of Stendhal Syndrome experiences aesthetic overload after viewing too many masterpieces in too short a time or in too confined a space.

It's true. This scientific study proved some people can become so overwhelmed with the beauty of Italy that they develop symptoms of claustrophobia, dizziness, chest pains and hallucinations. Thankfully, I've had only a few guests reach this level of emotion.

Most guests finish a morning tour describing their experience as "incredible," "breathtaking," "fascinating," and "the thrill of a lifetime!"

Some need a bit of time to soak it in. "I'll never be here again, so I need to look at this until it burns right into my brain, so I'll never forget."

Some are happy they checked a box.

One little boy did cry, "Please Mommy, don't make me look at any more penises!"

And of course, some of my guests glaze over in total boredom.

Michelangelo

1475 - 1564. Michelangelo Buonarotti was a famous sculptor, painter and architect. Along with Leonardo da Vinci and Raphael, Michelangelo is regarded as one of the three giants of the Renaissance.

Michelangelo was celebrated for his complexity, physical realism, psychological tension, and thoughtful consideration of space, light and shadow. He did not just depict the human form, he glorified it. He was a master at depicting the body with such technical accuracy that marble was seemingly transformed into flesh and bone. Here are three of his masterpieces.

THE PIETÀ

1490. St. Peter's, Rome. In Christian art, a *pietà* is any portrayal of the Virgin Mary holding the dead body of her son, Jesus. It means "the pity." During his lifetime, Michelangelo sculpted four *pietàs.* This one, which he sculpted when he was only 25 years old, is my favorite.

As a mother myself, I am overwhelmed by the fragility of Mary holding her dead son on her lap. Her face is youthful, yet wise — so soft and delicate in contrast to the sinewy muscles and veins of the lifeless Jesus. The sculpture represents the moment where her lifetime of fear knowing her son would die became a reality. Her left hand gestures up to heaven, giving you a sense that she is letting go, her eyes resigned to this fate.

Booking an early morning VIP tour for my guests allows us to view this exquisite sculpture in peace, before the crowds ascend into St. Peter's.

THE DAVID

1504. Galleria dell'Accadamia, Firenze. While most artists depicted David holding the head of Goliath after their epic battle, Michelangelo's David is set at a different time of the story. He is prepped with his slingshot in one hand and a stone in the other. He is a strong and assured man, but he stares into the distance in concentration. His brow is furrowed and abdominal muscles engaged as he anticipates the battle. This is a figure focused on the future rather than one celebrating the victory. At the time, Florentines viewed David as a perfect symbol of their city, as he captured the unwavering courage, unexpected strength, and historic perseverance they saw in themselves as they battled their enemies.

The original marble sculpture was moved into its commemorative gallery in the Accadamia in 1910, replaced by a life-sized replica in its original location in front of the Palazzo Vecchia in the Piazza della Signoria.

THE SLAVES

1505. Galleria della Accadamia, Florence. Since college, Michelangelo's "unfinished" slaves (sometimes called prisoners) have been my favorite sculptures in the world. In 1505, the sculptor was commissioned by Pope Julius II to design his tomb. Michelangelo's labor of love was to include a series of 40 figures that eventually would be placed around the tomb. Unfortunately, work on the tomb was abruptly put on hold when Julius changed his mind and insisted Michelangelo paint the ceiling of The Sistine Chapel instead. The tomb was never completed, but years later Michelangelo revisited the figures.

Today, four of the figures welcome you to the great Hall of Prisoners that culminates in the center of the Tribune where Michelangelo's David stands under a halo-like dome.

Are the works unfinished? Michelangelo believed he was a tool of God, not creating but simply revealing the powerful figure already contained within the marble. The visible grindings of the chisels allow the viewer to comprehend the artistic effort invested in the sculptures. The slaves seem to be trying to pull themselves out from the rough stone, their torsos straining and muscles bulging while they struggle to be free. At this time in his life, Michelangelo was questioning his faith and the church. Perhaps he meant the slaves to represent mankind's eternal struggle to break free from our material trappings, never quite succeeding.

Architecture

Buildings can make you feel many things: inspired, threatened, awed and uplifted. Their design can send a message of wealth and power, of pride, of control, or of being a provider and protector.

Italy is filled with architectural wonders. In ancient times, the Romans borrowed ideas from Greeks. They soon broke the mold. Rounded arches and carved portals became the dominant fashion for churches and important buildings for centuries. Medieval Gothic architects discovered the amazing strength and stability of pointed arches, while Renaissance architects placed emphasis on symmetry, proportion and geometry. By the 1700s, Baroque architects ushered in glorious grandeur and drama.

Your Che Bella Tours guide provides an overview of the building, the time period and the importance of the location. As you dig deeper, your guide will elaborate on any historical context necessary to help tell the story.

Here are a few tips to help you better understand architecture.

- Before you travel, learn a bit of the area's history. Look at the buildings in context to their surroundings. Many people find that it's not the buildings themselves that impact them the most, but the spaces between the buildings — the roundabouts, the passageways, the viewing platforms, the gardens or parks.
- What buildings draw your attention? Towers? Government buildings? Traditionally, cathedrals were the most important structures in the city. Their domes and spires were purposefully built to commanded attention and reach toward the heavens.
- Much of Europe is an eclectic mixture of old and new. How does modern design contrast with medieval architecture?

Check out the different vantage points. Go up to the roof. Go down to the cellar or catacombs. Look down the nave of a church from the vantage point of the priest. Check out the courtyard or gardens. Often, viewing architecture from a different viewpoint gives you an idea of why and how it was designed.

What do you think the architect was trying to say?

- Is the architect responding to something going on in the economy? Politics? Personal life? Apply your own knowledge about what was going on in the world at the time and create a story in your mind.
- Is the building rich in details or austere in design?
- Does the building evoke a message of wealth and power, pride, control, or being a provider and protector?
- Does the building make you feel inspired, threatened, awed or uplifted?
- What would you like to ask the architect about his or her life experiences that might have influenced or inspired the work?

How does the building make you feel?

- What makes this work pass the test of time?
- In your opinion, is this a masterpiece?
- Does the work have meaning to you?
- Do you like it?

THE DIFFERENCE BETWEEN A CHURCH, *DUOMO*, CATHEDRAL AND *BASILICA*

A **church** is a house of worship.

A common misconception is that the term ***duomo*** is Italian for dome. *Duomo*, however, is actually Italian for cathedral. A ***cupola*** is a dome.

A **cathedral** is a church that is also the seat of the bishop and the center of the administration of the diocese. Each city has only one cathedral, and it is not necessarily the largest or grandest.

The word ***basilica*** originally referred to a large building that housed large groups. As Christians began to gather together, the *basilica* became an important church designated by the pope to honor some kind of special spiritual, historical, and/or architectural significance.

Some of My Favorite Italian Architecture

BRUNELLESCHI'S DOME

1420. Santa Maria del Fiore, Florence

Filippo Brunelleschi is credited with originating the Renaissance style of architecture. His great *cupola* (dome) is one of the wonders of Renaissance Florence. In 1420, he was given the commission to cover a 140 foot diameter space spanning the already existing cathedral. Inspired by the Pantheon in Rome, and using a deep understanding of the laws of physics and mathematics, his design was as innovative as it was impressive. To displace some of the weight, he utilized ribbed vaulting and inner and outer shells to support a red brick herringbone pattern to create a self-standing dome. There were no buttresses or exterior supports. He invented much of the equipment needed to construct this massive structure, including intricate pulley systems to haul up stones and bricks and floating kitchens to keep the workers on the job. It remains the largest masonry dome in the world, rising above the city and reminding all of Tuscany of the power of the Florentines. Think about avoiding the long lines to climb to the top of the Duomo. Instead, climb nearby Giotto's Campanile to get a bird's eye view of the exterior of the Duomo.

THE FACADE OF THE CA D'ORO

1300. Grand Canal, Venice

My tour season usually begins with a morning arrival into Venice via water taxi. As we move through the maze of twisting canals, my heart flutters with familiar anticipation. Water laps at the walls to the rhythm of the gondoliers' accordions. The morning fog lifts as the sunshine dances on the water, reflecting the palaces that line the Grand Canal. Venice makes you feel as though you have stepped onto a movie set. It looks almost exactly as it has for a thousand years. There is a rich and diverse architectural style, the most famous of which is the Venetian Gothic. Pointed arches dramatically intertwine with the intricate Byzantine stonework filigree, lined with geometric patterns influenced by Moorish Spain. The buildings hang on to each other for dear life, their skin peeling and foundations swaying with the tide. Once the stately residences of noble patricians, rich merchants and artists in search of inspiration, these ornate structures have many stories to tell. One of my favorites is the Ca' d'Oro, the House of Gold, named for the gold gilding that once graced its bejewelled facade. Today, the facade is pure white, but the graceful and delicate cornice and cresting make it one of the most elegant and elaborate on the Grand Canal. Ca 'd'Oro is now a museum that houses the art collection of Baron Giorgio Franchetti, who spent his life studying music, collecting art and restoring the palace to its former glory.

THE TOWERS OF SAN GIMIGNANO

San Gimignano is a favorite stop. The medieval town offers a glimpse into what Tuscany looked like during the Middle Ages. The town developed from a small Etruscan village into a prospering community. In the 11th century, it was an important stop on the Via Francigena, the ancient Christian pilgrim route from Canterbury to Rome. The production of saffron and wine helped the town continue to prosper, but it was in the 12th century that it gained claim to fame.

The towers tell the story of security, prestige and neighborhood dominance. A dispute started between two economically powerful families: the Guelfs, who were sympathetic to the Pope, and the Ghibellines, who were sympathetic to the German (Holy Roman) emperors. As a result of this rivalry, each family built a tower to show its economical stability and power.

As the hilltown region became a major commercial and banking center, more noble leaders and ruling class merchants moved from their grand rural castles into the towns. Each grand family tried to outdo each other with the heights and widths of their towers. Many towers housed personal armies in case of a battle or a feud, some were simply empty chimneys. By the end of the Medieval Era, 72 towers jutted up from the town. Fifteen of them still stand today. Torre Grossa is the tallest of the remaining towers, offering a beautiful view of the Tuscan countryside.

THE ROOF OF THE MILAN DUOMO

The duomo towers over Milan. You can't help but admire the sheer amount of sweat, time, talent and money that went into making the building. This great Gothic cathedral took five centuries to complete. Architects, artists and sculptors worked tirelessly on its construction, creating a massive structure of beautiful white and pink marble that merged the Gothic and Romanesque styles.

Covered in dripping white spires, the exterior boasts 3,400 statues, 135 gargoyles and 700 figures all topped off with the famous Milano Madonnina, a 13-foot high golden statue of the Virgin Mary — the symbol of the city and protector of the Milanese people. No new constructions can be built higher than the revered statue.

Che Bella Tours always adds a rooftop visit to our tour of Milan to see the sculptural details up close as well as enjoy a stunning view of the city.

THE PANTHEON, PIAZZA DELLA ROTUNDA, ROME

The site of the Pantheon is significant in Roman history as it marks the spot where the founder of Rome, Romulus, was carried off by eagles upon his death. The original structure was built around 25 BC. by Marcus Agrippa as a memorial to celebrate the victory of the emperor Ceasar Augustus over Antony and Cleopatra. It was destroyed by a fire in 80 AD and rebuilt by Emperor Domitian, only to be burned down again in 110 AD. In 126 AD, The Pantheon we see today was built during the reign of Emperor Hadrian as a temple to honor the Roman gods. It's uncertain why, but Hadrian put Agrippa's original inscription on the portico. which reads "Marcus Agrippa the son of Lucius, three times consul, made this."

The highlight is the Pantheon's 5000-ton, 142-ft diameter concrete dome — the largest of its kind when it was built. The circular opening at the top is called an "oculus" which acts as a sundial and illuminates the interior. The dome has awed and inspired engineers and architects throughout the centuries, including Michelangelo (St. Peter's in Rome), Brunelleschi (Santa Maria del Fiore in Florence) and Thomas Jefferson (Monticello in Virginia).

Throughout history, many of the treasures of the Pantheon have been pillaged and repurposed. Destruction of the entire temple was avoided by its consecration as a church in 609 AD. Church status for any building in Italy makes it tax-exempt and privy to the vast wealth and protection of the Vatican. However, Pope Urban VIII, who was a member of the Barberini family, famously took the bronze from the Pantheon's portico in 1631 to construct cannons for the Vatican, giving rise to the saying '*quod non fecerunt barbari, fecerunt Barberini*' (what the barbarians didn't do was done by the Barberini). Masses and weddings are performed at the church. It is quite dramatic when the rain pours in from the oculus and drains from the gently sloping floor into 22 well-hidden holes. The Pantheon is the final resting place of the first two kings of unified Italy: Vittorio Emanuele II, and his son Umberto I who lies in rest in front of his wife Queen Margherita of Savoy. The artist, Raphael, rests in an adorned tomb, next to his fiancée, who died in the plague before they could be married.

My favorite hotel room overlooks the Pantheon. During the day, the Piazza Rotunda is filled with tourists. I sip my morning coffee while enjoying this view in quiet solitude, then hop inside for a quick peek of the oculus sundial as the day begins.

THE FOUR HORSES OF THE BASILICA OF SAN MARCO

To the victor go the spoils. Venice's Byzantine style basilica is ornately adorned with the columns, capitals, bas-reliefs and statues the Venetians looted from the territories conquered in the Middle East during the 4th Crusade. This battle culminated in a horrible massacre during the conquest of Constantinople. The looting was so widespread that almost all the churches of Europe came to have treasures from Constantinople. The Four Horses that tower over the entrance of St. Mark's were Venice's greatest prize. Although often described as bronzes, they are actually made mostly of copper, and are thought to be created some time in the 2nd or 3rd century AD. They towered over St. Mark's square for nearly 600 years, until Napoleon arrived in 1797.

The Four Horses were a primary target. Taking them represented the end of the Venetian Republic. Once again, plunder and looting weren't merely to grab trophies. The conquered had to cover the cost of being conquered. As they swept across Europe, Napoleon's armies were followed by antiquarians, scholars and curators, with instructions to grab key works of art. This is why the Louvre is such a rich museum.

Compared to their centuries of repose in Venice, however, the horses' stay in Paris was over in the blink of an eye. They adorned the top of the Arc du Carrousel for a mere 17 years. Following Napoleon's final exile to St. Helena after his defeat at Waterloo in 1815, the horses were lowered from the arch under guard by Austrian soldiers, ferried across the lagoon and placed back on the basilica. There they stood until pollution forced their removal to the basilica's museum in the early 1980s and replaced by replicas. The museum is on the second floor balcony area of the church, overlooking St. Mark's Square. There, you can see up close the gold mosaics, a nice collection of paintings and artefacts and most importantly, the original gold horses of St. Mark's.

A ROOM WITH A VIEW

In 1981, my Florence apartment's single large window provided a great view Santa Croce Square. The basilica of Santa Croce houses the tombs and memorials that honor centuries of artists, theologians, scientists, writers, humanists and politicians. The statue of Dante Alighieri towers over the square. Every morning began with a nod to this inspiration that looked down upon me and wished me a good day. The piazza has hosted markets, jousting tournaments, the annual Calcio Storico match (a violent game similar to rugby), and even beach volleyball. It was my home and inspiration. I love that I am part of its rich history. Today, I take my guests there, teach them about *fresco* painting, enjoy whatever might be happening. We lunch at the same restaurant I frequented in 1981 and, of course, visit my old apartment.

THE STAR OF DAVID ON THE BASILICA OF SANTA CROCE

Construction of Santa Croce began in 1294 and took a century to complete. It was the largest Franciscan church built in the Middle Ages. Overseen by a series of prominent architects, the interior was designed as a massive chest of art, history, frescoes and sculptures.

The exterior was left as rough stone. At that time, churches were not designed to inspire awe to the outside observer, but rather to provide a respite for the medieval faithful. With the wealth that came during the Renaissance, the addition of magnificent façades became a symbol of the city's superiority.

Architect Niccolò Matas was charged with the task of designing the façade. What makes Matas' design is not the characteristic white, red and green marbles adorned Florence's churches at the time, but rather his Star of David window. Variations of the Star of David had been linked before to the Catholic religion, but Matas incorporated it because he was Jewish. It was his way of being part of the legacy of Santa Croce. He requested to be buried amidst his fellow architects, many of whom had honorary tombs in the church's crypt, but was denied due to his religion. He installed the controversial window just before his death. Fourteen years later, The Italian Parliament honored his contribution by relocating his grave and placing him under the basilica's steps, below his Star of David.

Antiquities

Some see rocks, others see history.

Why would someone stand in scorching heat amidst a pile of rocks when they could be sipping an Aperol Spritz in the Piazza Navona? Because antiquities and archaeological sites are some of the most culturally significant reminders we have of past civilizations. Archaeologists often say: "It's not what you find, it's what you find out." Ancient art was not art for art's sake. The rocks tell the story of the civilization and culture that existed at the time:

- How people lived
- What technologies they had
- What their homes and public spaces looked like
- How they interacted with other groups
- How leaders gained and maintained power

Some sites remain well preserved, while others have decayed with time, weather or the onslaught of human destruction. Antiquities are the story not just of building, but also of destroying. Antiquities represent conquering enemies, looting and pillaging, natural disasters, recycling and re-purposing. At times whole quarters were levelled by fires, floods and earthquakes. Centuries of debris and garbage covered ancient landmarks. Builders constructed structures on top of the remains of ancient structures. Sometimes ancients sites were purposefully stripped and covered to make way for a new era of leadership.

When you're standing on a foundation, surrounded by a few walls, a column, and parts of statues, you have to use your imagination. Yes, you must visualize what it might have looked like, but you must also think about what might have happened there. Your Che Bella Tours guides will turn a pile of rocks into an unforgettable story. It's their job to create a visual picture of what the site must have been like in all its glory.

To make your experience richer, educate yourself on the history of the site *before* you travel. After your tour, think about visiting one of the local museums. On display will be the artifacts that will further help you to understand how magnificent the site was during its greatest moments.

Some of My Favorite Italian Antiquities

The Roman Forum defined supremacy, war and peace. It is at this site where you'll learn about the stories of the Roman Empire. You will hear about the power and decadence of its emperors, the games and gladiators, the senators, vestal virgins, politicos and plebeians. You'll learn about defeat and ruin. Because of its very significance, the center of the Empire was sacked, lost and re-conquered, leaving many of the most stunning Roman architectural achievements in ruins.

Rome started out as a small, hilly settlement by the Tiber River. As the population boomed and spread, the valley below developed from pasture land to a desirable downtown. The Roman Forum grew into a commercial center, with shops and markets, temples, law courts and the Senate House. It was the setting not just for selling and trading, but for elections, public speeches, criminal trials, social gatherings and religious ceremonies. As Rome reached its imperial heights, a sprawling city of a million people encircled The Forum, and its marble, high-class real estate was the center of the world.

CROSSING THE RUBICON

Julius Caesar was a general in the army of the Republic of Rome. When he led his troops to conquer Gaul (modern day France) in 49 BC, he paused on the end of a bridge that stretched over the Rubicon, a river that separated Gaul from what is now Italy. As he stood, he debated whether or not to cross the Rubicon, contemplating the heinous crime he was about to commit against the Republic.

When Julius Ceasar decided to proceed, he knew the die was cast. In Roman times, gambling with dice was popular. Just as it is today, once you cast (or throw) the dice, your fate is decided. The future of Rome was cast with that river crossing. Today the phrase "crossing the Rubicon" is an idiom that means to pass a point of no return.

The crossing of the Rubicon started a five-year Roman civil war, which ended in Julius Caesar being declared dictator for life and the Roman Republic becoming the Roman Empire. Upon Julius Caesar's assassination, his adopted son, Octavian, overtook Egypt, resulting in the death of Mark Antony and Cleopatra. As the unchallenged ruler and first declared Emperor of Rome, Octavian assumed the title of Caesar Augustus.

Rome successfully expanded its empire into modern France, Spain, Britain, northern Africa and Asia Minor by extending some form of citizenship to many of the people it conquered. The Romans did not try to turn everyone they conquered into a Roman, but rather allowed them to maintain their existing cultural and political institutions. In return, the conquered had to pledge complete allegiance. A major requirement was that cities provide soldiers for military campaigns. Military expansion drove economic development, in the form of enslaved people and loot brought back to Rome. This, in turn, transformed the cities and cultures throughout the Empire. Roads extended military and economic power. Citizens engaged in trade across the Mediterranean Sea. They minted coins, managed huge farms, and built sewer systems, baths and aqueducts. Victorious generals built temples to their gods, arenas and circuses to occupy the locals during times of difficulty, and grand political buildings from which they managed their empires.

THE COLOSSEUM

The Flavian Amphitheater was commissioned by the Emperor Vespasian and completed in 80 AD by his son, the Emperor Titus. Located just east of the Roman Forum, it was created to be a gift to the citizens of Rome. Today, we know it as "The Colosseum." Measuring 620 by 513 feet, the massive stone structure was the largest amphistheater in the Roman Empire. Much, though not all, of public entertainment was free. Roman emperors and provincial governors sponsored lavish entertainment events to demonstrate their generosity and justify their retention of power. The distinctive exterior had three stories of arched entrances, supported by semi-circular columns. Inside, it had seating for more than 50,000 spectators. They were placed according to their rank in the social hierarchy. Slaves, women ... and tour directors ... stood in the rafters. Senators and vestal virgins (priestesses of Vesta, goddesses of the hearth) were seated near the arena floor. A place of honor was reserved for the emperor himself, who sat in the imperial box at the center of the long curve of the stadium. From here, his every reaction was scrutinized by the audience. Awnings were unfurled from the top story in order to protect the audience from the hot Roman sun as they enjoyed public executions, re-enactments of battles and theater productions, wild beast hunts and, of course, gladiator duals. The animals, gladiators and scenery that made up this grand spectacle were brought into the Colosseum through an underground tunnel and housed beneath the arena in a warren of cells, chambers and passageways. When it was showtime, they were hoisted up in elevators leading to different corners of the arena. They emerged from below to the roar of the crowd.

In the early 5th century, the Empire began to slowly fall. It was a combination of Imperial incompetence and decadence, empty coffers, military problems and the emergence of Christianity. As Rome weakened, enemies from the north arrived and plundered the city. Thousands of Roman citizens were killed, and both the Forum and Colosseum were ransacked. In a sprawling metropolis designed to hold a million people, Rome was now a ghost town. Those who left migrated to the once empty district across the river, where Christian settlements were forming around the edge of the city. The Forum, Colosseum and surrounding area became little more than quarries. Temples and columns toppled. Buildings were looted and burned. Piles of stone and brick were stolen and recycled. Centuries of the Tiber's strong current and floods eventually buried what was left. What used to be the center of the Roman Empire became a cattle field.

EXPOSING ROME'S ANCIENT HEART

Napoleon begins to peel away the layers. When Napoleon Bonaparte was conquering much of Europe, his army occupied the city of Rome. After the war, he worked to restore stability by instituting reforms in such areas as banking, education, as well as supporting science and the arts. In 1809, his occupational government, or "*consulta*," established a commission to inspect and preserve Roman monuments. There is little doubt that the monuments of Rome benefited from French funding, and little doubt that Napoleon's motivation was his own identification with the ancient Roman Emperors. He hired Italian archaeologists to begin to excavate the large cow pasture behind the Capitoline Hill. This could arguably be the most important piece of real estate that has ever existed in the history of the world. During the next 50 years, archaeologists, scientists and eager treasure hunters from all over the world came to Rome to uncover, study and open the remains of ancient Rome to the public.

Il Duce alters the landscape. By 1922, Fascist Italy was ruled by Benito Mussolini. He didn't invent the idea of violent authoritarianism, but he did put a name on a new and terrible breed of it. This was a low moment in human history as well as the landscape of Ancient Rome. The Emperor Augustus was of particular interest to Mussolini, who sought to connect the ancient Imperial Capital with his own achievements. The Emperors built their great Forum, so Mussolini built a road right through it. The road was planned as a traffic artery and parade route. Processions and military ceremonies began at Mussolini's office on the Piazza Venezia, with a nod en route to the Memorial of King Victor Emmanuel III and finished at the Colosseum, with the forums of the Roman emperors as a backdrop. The self-proclaimed Marshal of the Empire changed the city's urban landscape, paving over Roman relics while carving new monuments into the heart of the city. Mussolini's new Rome had to grow to surpass the city of Augustus. Controversial politics aside, he is responsible for the Rome we experience today.

Photo by Janette Tepas Images

THE ETRUSCANS

Virtually everything we consider "Roman" was actually inherited from the Etruscans. The Etruscan civilization flourished in central Italy between the 8th and 3rd century BC and tell a rich story. They did not leave behind manuscripts or architecture. They used perishable building materials such as wood and clay. Etruscans did, however, care very much for their afterlife, and equipped their tombs and graves with artifacts, frescos and imagery.

From these tombs, we know much.

The Etruscans were engineers. They drained marshes and built roads and temples to develop the earliest cities in Europe.

The Etruscans were skilled artists. Rich gold jewelry and stunning painted tombs showed how they dressed and styled their hair.

The Etruscans were visionaries. Frescoes showed what sports they engaged in and musical instruments they played, as well as how they were responsible for spreading writing, religion, and government throughout the Italian peninsula.

The Etruscans were feminists. Etruscan women may have enjoyed more equal status with men than in other ancient cultures. In the tombs, husbands and wives occupied the same chamber, with the sarcophagi more or less equivalent in size and placement. Frescoes and urns depicted scenes of banquets where women played an active part in social dining events. Images also celebrated the woman's role in the house, in childbirth and in religious activities. There were female priestesses and oracles. They took pride in adorning themselves, confident in visible and public roles. Women were literate, could own property and even retain their own surname.

There are many museums throughout Italy that have Etruscan artifacts and documents. Here are a few of my favorites:

Rome. *Museum Villa Giulia.* Located in Villa Borghese area, this magnificent Renaissance villa was built as a country retreat for Pope Julius III. Since then, it has become the most important Etruscan museum in the world, housing some of the most famous masterpieces of this civilization — over 6000 objects distributed in 50 rooms, on an exhibition area of over 3000 square meters. The story of the Etruscan people is presented through fashion and funerary art, including the masterpieces Sarcophagus of Spouses and Apollo of Veia.

Volterra is one of Tuscany's oldest towns, a former Etruscan settlement with a majestic amphitheatre just below the city. The *Museo Etrusco Guarnacci* houses hundreds of funerary caskets and other artifacts and documents.

Arezzo and Cortona. Arezzo is one of the oldest cities in Tuscany. It has been inhabited since the 8th or 7th century BC, first home to the Etruscans and later the Romans. Nearby Cortona has become an important centre for archaeological research with the opening of the Etruscan Museum, where you can find the famous bronze chandelier known as the *Lampadario Bronzeo*, the *Tabula Cortonensis* (one of the longest and most important texts in the Etruscan language) and a chest from the tomb of the prince known as *Melone II del Sodo*, that contains beautiful golden jewelry. In addition to the museum, you also can visit nearby Etruscan burial mounds of *Melone II del Sodo* from the Archaic period and the tomb of Camucia.

Chiusi was one of the most powerful cities during the Etruscan age. The *Museo Nazionale Etrusco* has numerous ceramics, sculptures, urns and vases. After you visit the museum, go out into the countryside to see the tombs: *Tomba della Pellagrina, Tomba della Scimmia* and *Tomba del Granduca.*

Orvieto has some of the best Etruscan artifacts as well as a tour of the system of tunnels and caverns carved by the Etruscans.

THE VERONA ARENA

The Arena was originally used to host gladiator, circus acts, dancing, music and equestrian events. The original meaning of the word *arena* was "sand or sandy place." It evolved to the Latin "place of combat," representing the enclosed space in the middle of Roman amphitheaters. The central stages of Roman amphitheaters were strewn with sand to soak up the blood from the gladiatorial contests and battle reenactments. The Verona Arena was built in 30 AD and is thought to have been the third largest of its time. During its prime, the arena could hold up to 20,000 people. Today, Verona is one of my favorite Italian cities. You can see the footprints of a rich, ancient history, as Roman ruins are incorporated into the everyday fabric of the city's infrastructure. Today the arena is still in excellent condition and hosts events, operas and open-air performances. Like in the arena's ancient times, grandiose stage sets are erected and the elliptical shape gives the space excellent acoustics. I've gone their to enjoy open-air movie nights, and even a performance of Aida with my guests.

HERCULANEUM

The cities of Pompeii and Herculaneum were famously destroyed by the eruption of Mount Vesuvius in 79 AD. The eruption began by showering the cities in a deep layer of volcanic ash. The ash fell much deeper, however, in Herculaneum than in Pompeii. After the ash eruption, fast-flowing rivers of lava cascaded down the side of the volcano with intense speed and ferocity, burning Pompeii and most of its buildings. Herculaneum, however, experienced a different fate. The burning lava, mixed with the top layer of ash, created a type of meteoric stone which essentially vacuum-sealed the city. This made Herculaneum one of the best preserved sites in the world. Many of the buildings look virtually the same as they would have before 79 AD, with beautiful mosaics and murals.

To get the real details, check out the artifacts on display in the Naples Archeological Museum. The museum's Secret Cabinet, or *Gabinetto Segreto*, displays a wide variety of erotic images unearthed from both cities, as well as vignettes of life during that time. For many years the cabinet was only open to gentlemen of "high moral standing." Over time, it became rather infamous, and in the year 2000, the collection was finally opened to the general public.

When we think of Italian design, we think of timelessness, elegance and a sense of purpose.

Iconic Italian Design

AmericanAirlines

DUCATI

CINZANO

bloomingdale's

UNITED COLORS OF BENETTON.

S I S L E Y

When we think of Italian design, we think of timelessness, elegance and a sense of purpose. Highly skilled artisans, designers and engineers incorporate line, shape, space, value, color and texture to create beautifully sophisticated products. Two of my inspirations were Italian-born, Massimo and Lella Vignelli.

Working in both Chicago and Italy, they spanned nearly every field of design including advertising, identity, packaging, product, industrial, interior and architectural design. They believed that beautiful design meant understanding human nature, and designed in a very clear and concise manner with no clutter or unnecessary material. The iconography is still familiar today both in Italy and the U.S.

I became a graphic designer in the early 1980s because I wanted to be like them — part of the highly expressive, influential, fast world of advertising and graphic design. It was an exciting time to be a graphic designer in Chicago. Advertising was a creative force and the development of graphics software took us from the time-consuming production world of cut and paste to computer software that offered endless possibilities. It was our job to help make businesses look elegant, intelligent and contemporary. My time living in Italy greatly influenced my work.

On the next page are a few of my favorite iconic products. When you see them you can't help but think of Italy.

The *Vespa*. The word *vespa* is Italian for wasp. Immortalized by movie masterpieces such as Fredereco Fellini's "La Dolce Vita," this true Italian icon has become synonymous with style, freedom and all things Italian.

The *Cinquecento*. Liberate your passion for life and take to the open road in a Fiat 500 (*Cinquecento*). This car truly represents Italian culture, and played starring roles next to Marcello Mastroianni, Vittorio Gassam and Federico Fellini.

The *Ferrari*. Enzo Ferrari devoted his life to designing and building the most beautiful sports cars in the world. The Prancing Horse is an icon of style, luxury and speed. Sixty years of motorsports history has made Ferrari synonymous with Italian pride. You can't help but stop and stare.

Ferragamo shoes. Salvadore Ferragamo went from small-town cobbler to shoemaker for the stars. He engineered shoes no one had imagined before, making custom-made designs fitted to the client. The flagship store and museum is housed in Florence in a Medieval Palace originally built in 1289.

Missoni knitwear. Missoni's zigzag is one of the most iconic patterns in fashion. Bold shades weave together through a range of geometrical shapes and lines. Embodying old world Italian sensibilities with a modern aesthetic, the Missoni family has stayed true to their carefree Italian roots keeping this a true family business and one of Italy's most recognizable styles.

Borsalino hats. Borsalino is the definition of "lifestyle." Popularly called "the fedora," this was the iconic headwear of Indiana Jones, Hemingway, Bogart, Sinatra, Garland, Hepburn, Bergman, Madonna and Beyoncé. Craftsmanship, utility, simplicity and beauty are the ideals that Borsalino embodies in his Piemont workshop.

The *moka*. The engineering of this sleek, octagonal stovetop espresso maker is simple: steam pushes hot water up through the coffee grounds to perk a perfect cup of coffee.

The pasta machine. The hand crank pasta machine is found in every kitchen throughout Italy. This classic machine helps create all kinds of *pasta fresca*.

The Speedo. Italian stallions have ball-breaking confidence when it comes to their beachwear — no matter what body shape, age or size. Sometimes you just gotta take a snap of one of the good ones. You're welcome.

Music

The Italian language is like a romantic melody.

Above *A free outdoor concert in Plazza della Signoria in Florence*

Next page *Harpist in San Gimignano*

Photo by Sandy Gregory

Italy has played a significant role in the history of European music. The beauty and diversity of the country's nature, historic sights and rich cultural heritage makes music yet another art form to enjoy while traveling. Music bursts from every corner of the country. Ancient arenas and mountains become the natural backdrop for mega-events. Prestigious castles and acoustically-perfect churches become the stages for concerts and performances. Wide piazzas and intimate street corners welcome musicians who beckon people to stop and listen.

Focus and concentrate. Close your eyes and really listen to the music. Find the main melody and listen to how it evolves.

Ask yourself:
- What is this piece about?
- Is it full of laughter, yearning, nostalgia, bitterness, rage?

Picture the music as a painting.
- Do you feel rolling waves?
- A slow sunrise?
- A chaotic street?
- Or do you see energy in an abstract form?

Watch the individual musicians. Watch the cellist or percussion artist carefully throughout the piece. See how they move and the passion they have for playing their instrument.

Know the story. Operas are often sung in Italian, so you want to know the story before you go. Consider printing out the summaries of each act to help you appreciate the performances, setting and spectacle.

Start short. There are churches and venues all over Italy that offer nightly concerts that only last an hour or so.

How does the music make you feel?

- What makes this work pass the test of time?
- In your opinion, is it a masterpiece?
- Does the work have meaning to you?
- Do you like it?

Some of My Favorite Italian Music Venues

Rome. The opera season in Rome runs from January through November, but the performances move outdoors from June through August. Once the ancient Roman baths, the *Terme di Caracalla* seats up to 20,000 guests. It has been hosting summer opera performances since 1937.

Verona Opera Festival. Italy's most famous opera festival has taken place each summer from mid-June to early September for nearly 100 years. The setting couldn't be more beautiful — an ancient Roman amphitheater located directly in the center of the city. Performances traditionally begin at dusk and spectators on the stone seats of the arena bring small candles to light as darkness falls and the performances begin.

Lucca and Florence. The Puccini Festival at Torre del Lago has run from July through August since 1930. This seaside venue honors Giacomo Puccini, the composer known for the beloved operas *La Boheme, Tosca, Turandot* and *Madama Butterfly*.

Parma. In September and October, Parma hosts the Festival Verdi, a popular event celebrating music in Italy. Performances take place in the Teatro Regio di Parma.

Umbria. The Umbria Jazz Festival is one of the most important jazz festivals in the world. It has been held in July since 1973, offering performances in venues in Perugia and the surrounding Umbrian cities. The Umbria Winter Jazz Festival is the most popular music event in the winter. Starting in December, this is a lovely way to ring in the new year.

Milan. The Teatro alla Scala in Milan is among the world's most famous opera houses. Most of the greatest singers of the past 200 years have appeared here. Performances are held all year long.

Venice. La Fenice opera house opened in 1792 and has survived two fires. If you love, or are at least interested, in opera, this is the place to enjoy it. Concerts and ballets are held throughout the year.

If you don't think you can sit through a whole night of classical music, join me for an hour to see the Interpreti Veneziani, an entertaining classical orchestra that plays nightly at the Chiesa di San Vidal. This early 18th-century church, with its Palladian façade, is filled with superb paintings and has beautiful acoustics.

Just off St. Mark's square, you can enjoy performances of Vivaldi's *Four Seasons* and other works played by the St. Mark's Chamber Orchestra at the *Ateneo San Basso*.

Ravello. The Ravello Festival is popularly known as the Wagner Festival. It is an annual classical music festival, held from spring through fall in various venues along the beautiful Amalfi Coast.

Pesaro. The Rossini Opera Festival is an international music festival held in August on the banks of the Adriatic Sea.

Macerata. Sferisterio Opera Festival is held in one of Italy's premier opera venues. Set in the scenic countryside of Macerata in central Italy's Marche region, it runs from late July through August and is just south of Pesaro.

Florence. If you don't happen to be in Italy during these specific festivals, there is music all year round in most major cities. In Florence, the Santa Felicita church performs baroque music with original historic instruments all year long. Italian opera in Santa Monaca Church is performed along with a dining experience. If you are not a fan of classical music, Firenze Rocks is no doubt one of the biggest music events of the summer.

Lake Maggiore. The Stresa Festival is one of the prime events in the Lake Maggiore area. Held mid-July to early September, famous artists and ensembles perform in churches and historic buildings all over the province.

Taking Great Travel Photos

A photograph is worth a thousand words and learning how to take great pictures when you travel is worth a thousand memories. Great light, strong composition and a sense of moment are the elements of a good photo. Here are a few tips and tricks I have learned on the road.

Be curious. The art of travel photography is not simply snapping postcards, but rather creating visual stories of your trip. When you're curious and become involved with your surroundings, the resulting pictures become more intimate.

Enjoy the moment. Don't be a snap-and-go traveler or experience your entire trip from behind the lens of a camera. Take the time to look at your surroundings. Think about the shot you are trying to create, the moment you are trying to capture and the story you are trying to tell.

Tell a story. Capture all of the angles when telling your story — the overall view, the medium view, the portrait, the close-up, and the point-of-view shot. All angles are building blocks of visual storytelling.

Above *St. Peter's in Rome. Even the clergy enjoy capturing the moment.*

Use the rule of thirds. Turn on the camera's gridlines to break down the image into thirds, both horizontally and vertically, so you have nine parts in total. According to this theory, if you place points of interest in the intersections or along the lines, your photo will be more balanced and level.

Find different perspectives. Even iconic subjects look fresh and exciting when you come at them from a different angle. Look for shapes in the clouds, details in nature, symmetry in buildings or colors that compliment each other.

Focus on one subject. A great photo is often defined by what is left out as much as by what is left in. Your subject should fill the frame. Go tight into the subject and let the details create a pattern. Small details often tell a more intimate story.

Use leading lines. There's a line that draws the viewer's eye toward a certain part of the frame called leading lines. They can be straight or circulinear — think staircases, building facades, train tracks, roads, or even a path through the woods.

Use natural framing. Use what's around you to "frame" the subject you are trying to capture. Tree branches, archways, tunnels, door frames or windows — all can be used to separate your subject from its surroundings, draw the eye into the photo and tell the story you want to tell.

Incorporate people. Putting a person into a landscape or scene makes the picture personal, more memorable and gives the scene a sense of scale and place. Experimenting with angles, cropping and depth of field can help to create a story, not just a street shot.

Flatter your subject. If you want your subjects to shine, have them turned so the sun shines on their warm faces.

Use natural light. The half hour or so before sunrise and after sunset provide lots of low ambient light to add mood and atmosphere. These times of day pull out the detail in buildings and people.

Take candids. Posed photos can be great for the sake of memories, but candid shots can be far more interesting as they capture the emotion and essence of a moment.

PICTURE PERFECT

Pictures serve as memories that can last a lifetime. I understand that for many of my guests, it will be the one chance they experience a place. I don't take this for granted, and when on tour, give them as much time as they need to see, absorb and capture the moment. Some of my guests come fully equipped with cameras, tripods and a bag full of lenses. Others snap with their smart phones that are compact, lightweight and great for taking photos quickly and discreetly. Others simply stand in the moment.

Caroline broke the piggybank to get to Italy. It would probably be her only time there, but she would vividly remember every single detail — not with a camera, not with a smart-phone, but with her eyes. Everywhere we went, she stopped to take a long pause and focus her attention. After each of these moments, she would say, "I'm never going to be here again, so I need to burn this into my brain." On a tour of Pompeii, our guide brought us into the ancient amphitheater. You can imagine what a performance must have been like almost 2000 years ago, when the people of Pompeii gathered here on a warm summer's night. That day, however, we were entertained in a different way. When the guide asked if anyone was a singer, Caroline jumped right in. Who knew? We were anticipating a classic aria as she took her place at center stage. Bracing, she took a deep breath, and began ...

"On top of spaghetti ... all covered with cheese."

The perfect acoustics bounced her voice throughout the theater, and the murmur of the crowd quieted.

"I lost my poor meatball ... when somebody sneezed."

With lots of giggles, our group joined in.

*"It rolled off the table ... and on to the floor.
And then my poor meatball ... rolled out of the door."*

With that, many of the crowd chimed in.

*"It rolled in the garden .... and under a bush ...
And then my poor meatball ... was nothing but mush!"*

I'm not sure what a lot of the tourists were thinking, but every American in that theater whooped and applauded when Caroline took her bow.

Right *Assisi doorway*

Next page *Environmental art in Venice*

Photos by Sandy Gregory

Right *Small boy in San Gimignano*

Next page *Vatican Museum staircase*

Photos by Sandy Gregory

Every time you leave home,
Another road takes you
Into a world you were never in.

When you travel, you find yourself
Alone in a different way,
More attentive now
To the self you bring along,
Your more subtle eye watching
You abroad; and how what meets you
Touches that part of the heart
That lies low at home.

A journey can become a sacred thing:
Make sure, before you go,
To take the time
To bless your going forth,
To free your heart of ballast
So that the compass of your soul
Might direct you toward
The territories of spirit
Where you will discover
More of your hidden life,
And the urgencies
That deserve to claim you.

May you travel in an awakened way,
Gathered wisely into your inner ground;
That you may not waste the invitations
Which wait along the way
to transform you.

May you travel safely, arrive refreshed,
And live your time away to its fullest;
Return home more enriched, and free
To balance the gift of days which call you.

– John O'Donohue

Above *When you travel, you find yourself alone in a different way.*

Opposite page *Church candles in Sicily..*

Photo by Sandy Gregory

PB

NOTES

MAKE IT WITH LOVE

RECIPES FROM MY ITALIAN TRAVELS FOR THE AMERICAN KITCHEN

Exploring a country through its recipes is an adventure in itself. I have taken cooking lessons throughout Italy, relentlessly pestered the chefs at my favorite restaurants, and spent many lazy afternoons with my Italian friends in the kitchens of their countryside homes.

After years of eating in restaurants all over the world, the COVID-19 pandemic forced me to rediscover my own kitchen. I gathered a few of the favorite recipes from my tours. With my brother, Chef Danny Serio, I spent the winter months of 2020 in "The Che Bella Tours Test Kitchen" adapting the measurements for the American kitchen. The olive oils, spices, vinegars and salts I brought home from my travels found their way from the darkness of my cabinets to the counter, bringing my collection of Italian recipes to life. Every sizzle of garlic, splash of balsamic and whiff of truffle flooded my senses with memories of my trips.

I hope this cookbook inspires you to open your palate to an authentic cuisine that will draw you under its spell and increase your hunger for more. Make a few of the recipes before your trip to anticipate your culinary adventure, or recreate the memories from your vacation when you return.

Buon appetito!

Sandy Gregory

Founder, Che Bella Tours

chebellatours.com

sandy@chebellatours.com

Above *Sandy Gregory and Chef Danny Serio in "The Che Bella Tours Test Kitchen."*

RECIPES

Let's cook!

TIPS AND TRICKS TO COOK LIKE AN ITALIAN CHEF 200

MAKING PASTA 202

RECIPES BY REGION

VENETO .... 206 - 211

- *Aperitivi Cocktails: Aperol Spritz, Bellini and the Negroni 208*
- *Nero di Seppia Frutti di Mare............ 208*
- *Seafood Secrets................................... 209*
- *Pasta a Fasioli....................................... 210*
- *Pandoro.. 210*

PIEDMONT .... 212 - 217

- *Bagna Cauda.. 214*
- *Tajarin con Tartuffe 214*
- *Agnolotti del Plin.................................. 215*
- *Brasato al Barolo con Polenta 216*
- *Torta Gianduia 217*

LOMBARDY .... 218 - 221

- *Osso Bucco 220*
- *Risotto alla Milanese 220*
- *Cotolletta alla Milanese........................ 221*

LIGURIA .... 222 - 225

- *Focaccia 224*
- *Trofie con Pesto 225*

EMILIA-ROMAGNA .... 226 - 233

- *Ragú alla Bolognese con Tagliatelli . 228*
- *Lasagne Verde al Ragú........................ 229*
- *Tortellini en Brodo 230*
- *Ravioli di Pere con Balsamico............. 231*
- *Panna Cotta... 231*

TOSCANO .... 232 - 237

- *Fagioli alla Toscana.............................. 234*
- *Budino al Formaggio 234*
- *Crostini Fegatini 235*
- *Vitello con Porcini................................ 235*
- *Gnudi al Forno Filling 236*
- *Ravioli di Gnudi 236*
- *Ribollita 237*

UMBRIA/MARCHE .... 238 - 241

- *Olive all'Ascolana 240*
- *Brodetto All'Anconetana...................... 241*
- *Baci Mousse Al Cioccolato.................. 241*

LAZIO .... 242 - 247

- *Cacio e Pepe.. 244*
- *Spaghetti alla Carbonara..................... 245*
- *Bucatini all' Amatriciana...................... 246*
- *Saltimbocca alla Romana 246*
- *Giovedì di Gnocchi............................... 247*
- *Tiramisu... 247*

CAMPAGNA 248-253

- *Salsa di Pomodoro Classico 250*
- *Italian Sauce Deconstructed.............. 250*
- *The Battle of the Sauces...................... 251*
- *Carciofi Ripieni.................................... ..252*
- *Melanzane alla Parmigiana................ 253*
- *Linguine Vongole 253*

PUGLIA .... 254 - 257

- *Orecchiette con Cima di Rapa............ 256*
- *Braciole al Sugo Pugliesi...................... 257*

SICILY .... 258 - 263

- *Caponata.. 260*
- *Arancini.. 260*
- *Cannoli.. 261*
- *Il Timpano.. 262*

Tips & Tricks to Cook Like an Italian Chef

BY CHEF DANNY SERIO

Start with your *mise en place*. *Mise en place* is a French phrase that means "a place for everything" and is one of the first things you learn in cooking school. A proper *mise en place* includes everything from the cooking oil to the pre-chopped ingredients to the finishing spices. It may seem like it's just more dishes to wash, but once you see how much easier your recipe unfolds, those prep bowls will feel like a good investment. A good *mise en place* forces you to read the whole recipe before cooking, make a plan and follow it. I have burned the garlic looking for the pepper mill and have had to substitute spices when I realized I was out. This is especially important if you are entertaining and taken off task because someone wanted your famous Negroni.

Use quality ingredients. When we list olive oil in our recipes, we mean first-press extra virgin olive oil for both cooking and seasoning. Make dishes with produce that is in season. Choose good quality cheeses and vinegars. They don't necessarily need to be imported. Not all imported items are good. They are just imported and the travel can affect their quality.

Save your Parmeseano-Reggiano cheese rinds. Keep them in a Ziplock bag in the freezer and add one to your soup, stew or sauce to infuse an extra umami and richness to the dish. This will draw the milk solids out, flavor your sauce and give it a sheen.

Invest in demi-glacé. Demi-glacé is a reduced, thickened veal, beef or chicken stock. Chefs often substitute stocks and demi-glacé for water in their dishes. Just a tablespoon or two will add richness and depth to soups, stews, sauces and gravies. You can buy demi-glacé at specialty stores, online or make your own. Save your meat bones and slowly cook them down to thicken. Use ice cube trays to freeze them into single servings, then store them in Ziplock Freezer Bags and you'll always have demi-glacé at the ready. If you are going to buy stock, look at the ingredient statement and make sure it says chicken first if it is chicken stock, beef first for beef, etc. Custom Culinary, Minors or Better Than Bullion are good brands. Any other cubed or powdered bullion is simply salt with coloring.

Roast tomatoes. Cut your fresh tomatoes in half, brush them with olive oil, and roast them before you add them to your recipe to add an extra depth to your dish. This gives them a slight char and releases the sugars and acids. If you do use canned, I like the Cento San Marzano brand. All canned tomatoes have a varying level of sodium added, which can affect your cooking. The range can go from 80mg to 700mg per serving per can, which is a huge difference in the saltiness.

Caramelize your tomato paste. Add a few tablespoons of caramelized tomato paste to any recipe to intensify the flavor. Sauté the paste in olive oil on a low flame stirring constantly for a few minutes. It should go from a bright red to a deep, brown brick red. You can also finish this with a pinch of baking soda to mellow out the acidity.

Always have *soffritto* on hand. The combination of diced onion, celery, and carrots cooked in olive oil and seasoned with salt and pepper is called a *soffritto*. It is the base of many Italian dishes, similar to *mirepoix* in classic French cuisine.

Don't burn the garlic. Heat your pan before you add oil, and then add the garlic, increasing the heat slowly. Let it cook to a golden brown for a nice toasted flavor, but watch carefully so you don't burn it. If I am adding it to my *soffritto*, I hold off until the soffritto is almost done.

Blanching vegetables brightens up their color. A quick 5-second dip in boiling water before you sauté keeps your veggies colorful. If you are making veggies for your crudités or dips like bagna cauda, blanch them for 15-30 seconds and then chill immediately. Salt the water for green veggies and add a splash of vinegar or lemon juice for all other colors.

Sauté your dried herbs. Herbs in a dry pan releases the oils before you add them to your dish. Watch the shelf life. Seeds like peppercorns, coriander and mustard last about 18 months, leaf and ground herbs for one year and paprika holds for only six months.

Remove fresh basil in sauces. Adding fresh basil is an easy way to level up any sauce, but if it's cooked too long the flavor burns off and it can become bitter. For a fresh basil taste, tie a bunch of basil together and put into the saucepan for a minute or two at the end of the cooking time, then remove it and discard.

Never rinse mushrooms. Brush the dirt off with a towel or soft brush.

Use shallots. I substitute shallots for onions or include a shallot with the onions when I want a mild, sweet flavor that isn't overpowering.

Use the right onions. Yellow onions work well in almost any Italian recipe. They mellow out as they cook and caramelize easily. The longer you cook them, the sweeter they get. They work best in dishes that require long cooking times or as the base in stews, stocks and soups.

Sweet onions like vidalias don't have the sharp, pungent flavor that other onions do, which makes them great raw in salads, on sandwiches or roasted with other vegetables.

Red onions are much milder, so are great raw in salads and sandwiches. They are used in soups and stews if you don't want a strong onion flavor.

Store onions in a spot that's cool, dark and dry.

Don't crowd your pan when sautéing. Heat the pan, then the fat. Be sure you can see the bottom of the pan between the pieces of food. Too much food will lower the temperature of the pan, creating a lot of steam, meaning you won't get good browning. It's also important to dab everything dry before sautéing it and to make sure the pan is good and hot before you start.

Don't cook meat or seafood straight from the refrigerator. It's always best to let it sit at room temperature for at least 15-20 minutes to make sure it's tempered. This will promote more even cooking.

Calibrate your meat thermometer. Place your thermometer in a glass of ice water for a couple of minutes and adjust it to 32 degrees. This is done by turning the nut behind the dial where the stem is attached. Most thermometers have a built in wrench for this in the protective cover, or make it easy and buy a digital.

Always let meat rest a few minutes after cooking. This allows the juices to redistribute and relax into the fibers of the meat. Carving too soon will cause the juices to spill out onto the cutting board and leave the meat dry and lifeless.

Know your salts. All salts consist mainly of sodium and chloride, as well as additional trace minerals like calcium, potassium and magnesium. Sea salt is made from drying salt water into crystals. Table salt is mined in underground salt deposits, heavily refined and usually contains additives including iodine, fluoride, monosodium glutamate (MSG) and bleaching compounds. Kosher salt can be produced by either method. It's coarseness makes it best for brines, pasta water and seasoning big cuts of meat. Salt flakes are considered a finishing salt, which adds a final bit of flavor and crunch to dishes once they're done.

Your ingredients — as well as your palate — will dictate how much salt you should use. Taste the dish throughout the cooking and add salt as needed. When you're sweating onions, add a small pinch of salt. Season your meat before you cook it. Add another tiny pinch after you de-glaze. If you taste as you go, you'll create a nuanced dish that is enhanced, not overwhelmed, by salt.

Pull your *al dente* pasta into the sauce pan with a bit of the pasta water. The starchy water helps the sauce cling to the noodle and ensure there's sauce in each bite, making it savory and rich.

Finish your tomato sauce with butter. The fat mellows the acid from the onion and the tomatoes and acts as an emulsifier, giving you a thick, velvety sauce.

Add one or two anchovies. Finishing with anchovies adds a rich umami depth to your sauce. Don't worry, no one will taste the furry fish.

SANDY'S TRANSLATION OF ITALIAN MEASUREMENTS

Getting a recipe out of an Italian is always a challenge. We just cook by hand. But an exact recipe? Not so much. A handful of basil, a few sprigs of parsley, a good 'pour' of olive oil, a 'glug' of wine ... that is about all you'll get out of us. My grandmother used the word "q.b.," or *quanta basta*, which means 'as much as you need.' Here are a few more Italian measurements that may or may not be helpful:

***un pizzico* - a pinch**

***circa* - around**

***nu pug* - a handful**

***all'occio* - by eye**

***un po* - a bit**

My good friend, Lisa Courtney, always asked: "How much do you put in?" "Some." "How long do you cook it?" "Awhile." So she simply invited herself over to watch. So until you give me a call, these recipes are my best shot to get you started. But do make them your own ... and with love, of course.

When in Rome, do as the Romans do. One of those things is honoring the tradition and passion of pasta. Italians take pasta very seriously, it's the product that truly defines them.

Making Pasta

Pasta making is both an art and a science. In Italy, of course, pasta is the hero of the dish; the sauce is a tasty garnish. Hundreds of pasta shapes are made to match with certain sauces. Fresh pasta is not "better" than dried, but rather two completely different types of pasta. The delicate texture of fresh pasta makes it perfect for light tomato, cream- and dairy-based sauces, while the firmness and rough texture of dried pasta allows it to hold up and cling to the heartiest of sauces.

Dried pasta is made with semolina flour and water and set out to air-dry. The heavier dough stands up to the extruder which forms the tube pasta such as rigatoni and penne, whose ridges hold up best to the chunky meat sauces. Dried strands of bucatini, spaghetti, and angel hair also cook up *al dente* and are good for the heavier meat, thick cream and tomato sauces. Dried pastas are best bought at the grocery for our recipes that call for them. Always look for 100 percent semolina flour. All pasta flour is Durham, but semolina is the finest of the grinds of Durham wheat.

Fresh pasta is made with "00" wheat flour and eggs, rolled out to be used immediately. The light dough is rolled out into thin sheets and cut into various size strips for tajarin, tagliatelli, tagliolini and pappardelle. This pasta is also rolled into sheets to make stuffed pillow-pastas such as ravioli, tortellini or agnolotti, or hand-formed into *trofie* and *orecchiette*. All of these pastas are used in recipes in this cookbook. We'll start with our basic dough.

All recipe photos by Sandy Gregory

1. Ingredients and equipment

I have taken cooking lessons all over Italy and every chef has his or her own recipe. After all of the complicated measurements and additions, I have decided it comes down to two ingredients: flour and eggs. Yes, Nonna made the dough by hand, but a Kitchen Aid, a nice rolling pin and a good old hand-crank pasta machine get the job done.

INGREDIENTS FOR 1 LB. OF DOUGH

- 2 cups Caputo "00" or all-purpose white flour
- 3 full eggs + 1 yolk. If you live in a dry climate or your dough is dry and crumbly, add another egg to moisten.

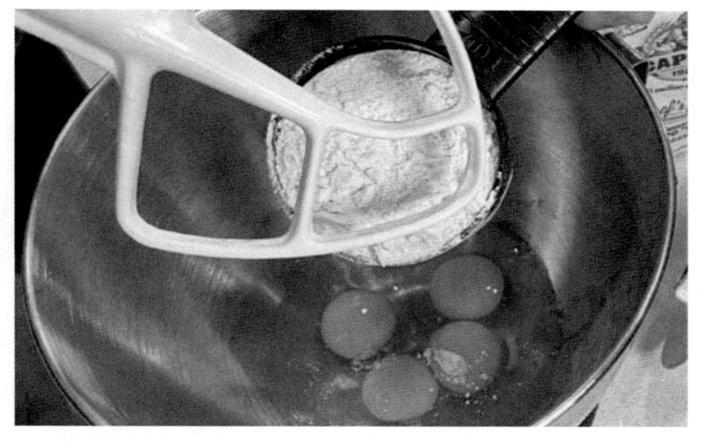

2. Make the dough

Start with the flat beater. Add half of the flour mixture to the eggs and mix 20 seconds on speed two. Add the rest of the flour mixture and mix an additional 20 seconds. Do not overbeat. Remove the flat beater and scrape off the dough. Exchange the flat beater for the dough hook. Knead the dough for two to three minutes until a dough ball is formed. You might have to use a spatula to bring the flour down into the wet mixture. If the dough is still crumbly, add a bit of water, a few drops at a time, until the dough ball forms. If it's too wet and sticky, add more flour. When it forms into a smooth ball, stop the mixer. Don't over mix.

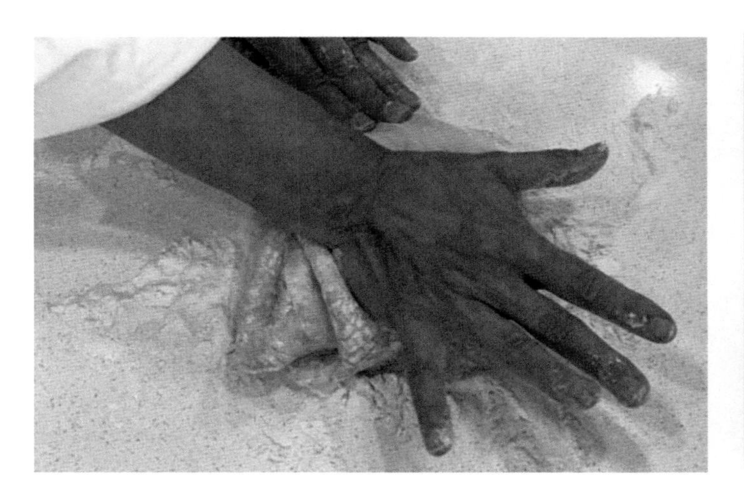

3. Knead the dough

Dust your workspace with flour. Remove the dough from the bowl and hand-knead for two to three minutes. Press into the dough with the heel of your palm, then fold the dough in half, knead again, turn and repeat. NOTE: Good pasta dough should be elastic and pliable, but firm. If it is sticking to your fingers, add more flour by dusting the workspace and kneading the flour into the dough. If it's too dry, wet your hands and knead some more, continuing to wet your hands a little at a time and knead until the right consistency.

4. Rest the dough

When ready, the dough should bounce back when you push it with your finger. Put the dough ball in a lightly oiled bowl, cover with a clean, cotton towel and let it rest for one hour at room temperature. If you live in a dry climate, wrap the oiled dough ball in plastic wrap and then cover it with the towel to rest. When the dough bounces back to the touch of your finger, it is ready.

5. Roll out the dough

Dust a few baking sheets with flour and set aside. Cut the pasta dough ball into three equally sized pieces. Place one piece of dough on a lightly-floured work surface and, with the rolling pin, flatten it enough so that it will fit into the widest setting of your pasta machine.

6. Form the pasta sheets

Start with the widest setting on your pasta machine. Guide the flattened mound of dough smoothly, but quickly through the slot. You'll want to gently support the exiting end with the flat of your hand. Send it through this first setting one more time until it passes through without resistance. It should have doubled in length. Be steady and consistent. Never reverse the crank.

7. Laminate the dough

Laminating means thinning the sheets to break down the gluten to create a smooth texture. Fold the thick pasta sheets into thirds, dust it in flour and feed the folded package into the machine, fold side first, at the largest setting. Repeat this one more time.

8. Thin the sheets

Reduce the thickness of the rollers and run the sheets through. As the sheets become thinner and longer, cut them in half crosswise for easier handling, always supporting the exiting end with the flat of your hand. Dust with flour as needed. Thin the dough until it's almost translucent and you can see the outline of your hand as a silhouette. For most hand-cranked pasta machines, finish on the second-to-last setting, number two, for ribbon pastas such as spaghetti or tagliatelli and the last setting, number one, for stuffed pillow pastas such as tortellini or ravioli. Cover the pasta sheets in plastic wrap until you are ready to cut the ribbons or fill the pasta pillows.

9. Cut the pasta

Keep the dough in plastic wrap until ready to cut. The dough should be room temperature. Crank the sheets through the cutter smoothly as you support the ribbons with your other hand. Do not reverse the crank or the machine will clog. Lay the cut pasta on a rimmed baking sheet dusted with flour. Pasta can be cooked immediately or allowed to air dry, uncovered, for up to two hours. You can also freeze the pasta ribbons for future use.

Spaghetti or Tajarin: 1/16" wide

Linguine: 1/8" wide

Tagliatelle: 3/16" wide

Fettucine: 1/4" wide

Pappardelle: 1" wide

Helpful pasta tools:

- Large, heavy wooden cutting board — to create a good workspace. You can also attach the pasta maker if you don't have a lip on your counter.
- Dough scraper — to clean your work surface.
- Pastry cutters — to cut and create pasta pillow shapes.
- Bicicletta — to cut even strips for pasta pillow strips and lasagne noodles.
- Brush — to glue the dough when making pasta pillows.

10. Cook the pasta

Pasta should be cooked at a rolling boil in water and salt. You often hear the water should be "as salty as the Mediterranean Sea." Since I don't salt my homemade pasta dough, I use this measurement:

1 pound of pasta + 2 tablespoons Kosher salt into 4 quarts (16 cups) water

Fresh pasta is done when it rises to the surface of the water, which can take minutes. Dried pasta will cook a bit longer, and is done when it is *al dente*, which means "to the tooth" or firm to the bite. You can tell if it is *al dente* if there is a tiny bit in the cross-section of the noodle that is not cooked. Never rinse cooked pasta with water or coat it with oil, as this prevents the pasta from absorbing the sauce.

Instead of draining the pasta in a colander, use a pasta scoop or tongs to pull it. Let it drain slightly before you add it to your sauce. The bit of starchy water helps the sauce thicken and cling to the pasta.

11. Clean the pasta machine

Do not wash or put any parts of the pasta machine in the dishwasher. Instead, remove the detachable parts and knock off any excess dough with a dry brush. Use a wooden skewer for hard to reach places. Wipe the parts thoroughly with a damp cloth and dry completely. Keep the pasta machine in its original box to keep it dry and prevent it from warping or rusting.

APEROL SPRITZ, BELLINI AND NEGRONI

PASTA NERO DI SEPPIA FRUTTI DI MARE

Veneto

AS A MAJOR TRADE CENTER, THE VENETIANS GAINED ACCESS TO UNUSUAL AND RARE INGREDIENTS, SO THE REGION'S CUISINE IS A FUSION OF CULTURES AND CUSTOMS. FISH AND SEAFOOD FROM THE VENETIAN LAGOON COMES STRAIGHT FROM THE FISHERMAN STALLS OF THE RIALTO SEAFOOD MARKET INTO THE LOCAL DISHES. RICE AND BEANS ALSO PLAY AN IMPORTANT ROLE IN THE REGION'S CUISINE.

PAIR THESE WINES WITH THE RECIPES FROM THE REGION: VALPOLICELLA, AMARONE, SOAVE AND PROSECCO.

PASTA A FASIOLI

PANDORO

APERITIVI COCKTAILS

APEROL SPRITZ These iridescent orange cocktails brighten up every café in Italy. They look sweet, but are surprisingly dry and refreshing.

- 2 oz. Aperol, chilled
- 3 oz. prosecco, chilled
- Splash of sparkling water, chilled
- Orange slice and blackberries for garnish

Pour the Aperol and prosecco over ice and add a splash of sparkling water to taste. Garnish with the orange and berries.

BELLINI Created in Venice at Harry's Bar, this refreshing cocktail is one of the most popular in Italy.

- 3 ripe peaches, chilled
- 2 tbs. fresh lemon juice
- Bottle of prosecco
- Mint leaves for garnish

1. Bring a pot of water to a boil. Prepare an ice-water bath. Score a shallow X in the bottom of each peach with a knife, then place in boiling water for one minute. With a slotted spoon, transfer peaches to ice water bath and let cool. Peel the peaches, remove the pits, add the lemon juice and blend until smooth. Freeze until slushy.
2. When you are ready to serve, divide the peach ice among six champagne flutes (about 2 tbs. each). Top with the prosecco, stir, garnish with mint and serve immediately.

NEGRONI Bitter yet sweet and very refreshing.

- 1 oz. each: London dry gin, Campari, Vermouth Rosso, shaken over ice. Garnish with a lemon wedge.

NERO DI SEPPIA FRUTTI DI MARE

If you have never tried squid ink pasta, then you are missing out on a classic Venetian treat. The squid ink makes the pasta taste "like the sea" and finishing it in a quick shrimp stock enhances the flavor even more.

INGREDIENTS
4 - 6 SERVINGS

- 1 lb. Linguine al Nero di Seppia
- 5 lbs. mixed seafood of your choice, such as shrimp with the heads, scallops, mussels and clams washed and rinsed in cold water thoroughly.
- 1 small onion, 1 carrot and 1 celery stalk, diced
- 1 medium shallot and 5 garlic cloves, minced
- 9 tbs. unsalted butter and 2 tbs. olive oil
- 1.5 cups dry white wine
- 1/2 cup cherry tomatoes, sliced in half
- 1 tsp. red pepper flakes, salt and pepper to taste
- Garnish: chopped fresh parsley and lemon wedges

DIRECTIONS

1. Make a stock out of the shrimp shells. Peel and devein the shrimp. Put the shells and heads into a small pot with 2 cups of water, the onion, carrot and celery and simmer down for about an hour to make a stock. Strain and set aside.
2. Heat a large pan over high heat and add 4 tbs. of the butter and the olive oil. When it begins to smoke, sear the peeled shrimp and scallops 2 to 3 minutes. Remove from the pan and set aside.
3. Add the remaining butter, garlic and shallots to the pan. Sauté these ingredients for 2 to 3 minutes.
4. Stir the white wine into the pan mixture and bring to a simmer. Add the shellfish, cover the pan and simmer until the shells begin to open. Discard any shells that do not open fully.
5. Cook the pasta in boiling salted water for just 5 minutes. Pull the partially cooked pasta into the seafood mixture with a little pasta water. Add the shrimp stock and cook the pasta for another few minutes. It should still be *al dente*. When the pasta is about ready, stir in the cherry tomatoes, lemon zest, parsley and crushed red pepper flakes. Simmer for 2 minutes.
6. Add the shrimp and scallops back to the pan. Toss gently to meld the ingredients and salt and pepper to taste. Garnish with parsley and lemon wedges.

SEAFOOD SECRETS

If you don't live near the water, consider buying frozen fish. Buying fresh seafood is simple ... when you live near the water. For the rest of us, however, "fresh" does not always mean "fresh-caught." Commercial fishing boats can go out to sea for up to 14 days. If the first catch was on day three and it took the full 14 days to fill up the boat ice storage, some of the product is already 11 days old when the fishermen pull back into shore. Adding another day at the processor for cleaning and packaging, and then transporting the product to the grocery, makes "fresh fish" not that fresh. More and more, however, commercial fishing boats are equipped with blast freezers. Blast freezing lowers the temperature of the fresh caught seafood so fast that it reduces cell wall breakage and increases the moisture retention of the product. This gives in-landers the option to have "fresh-caught" seafood regardless of where they live.

Quality frozen seafood has one ingredient: seafood. Check the ingredient statement. If it says sodium tri-poly-phosphates, sea salt, water or other additives, skip it. These additives are called "pump." Pumps are used by substandard suppliers to stretch the product or cover up older seafood they need to sell. are notorious for including pump. When buying frozen scallops and shrimp, look at the ingredients list. They look decent in the bag, but not on the plate when the pump cooks out.

Buy all of your fish at a quality market and get to know the butcher or fish monger. They will advise you what to buy, what not to and what they recommend that day. There is excellent farm-raised and horrible wild-caught seafood. There really is no set way to tell which one is better. It depends on the species, part of the world, and most importantly, the feeding practices of the supplier. Read the ingredients.

Store your fresh seafood carefully. Ask your butcher to wrap the fish and then put it in a bag of crushed ice for your trip home. Keeping it very cold is key. For the best flavor and quality, fish should be prepared for eating within 24 hours of catching. If stored properly however, it is safe to keep them for 2 to 3 days. Vacuum seal the fish and keep it in a cooler filled with ice and water. The ice water is much colder than your fridge. If you don't have a vacuum sealer, place the fish in a colander or perforated dish, cover with kitchen wrap and then lay crushed ice over it. Place this on a pan to catch the drips and refrigerate immediately.

Some seafoods, like tuna, contain histamines, so perforate the package as you thaw them to let the histamine escape.

Don't be afraid of cooking seafood. Invest in a good digital thermometer. Use it often in your cooking and soon you will learn the timing of cooking to produce better meals. Fish should be cooked to no more than 135°F internal temperature, measured at the thickest part of the fillet. Take into consideration that all food continues to cook after it is removed from the heat.

Shellfish will close when they are raw and alive and will open when you cook them. If they are open before cooking, discard them. If they don't open when cooking, discard them. Scallops can be cooked to about 125°F. Keep them very cold until you are ready to cook them. Pat them dry. A light sprinkling of sugar and then flash cooking them in butter on high heat will get that nice caramelized char. Shrimp should cook on a high heat very quickly so they are not rubbery and served immediately. As soon as the pink emerges, remove them from the heat.

PREPPING SALTWATER FISH

by Ben Martin. Founder of the Hunt Regs hunting app; experienced tarpon first-mate; longtime fisherman and hunter in South Florida; passionate wild game chef.

huntregsapp.com

Salmon. Tuna. Snapper. Swordfish. Grouper. Cod. Hake. MahiMahi. Likely one of the most critical fish meat care practices is also the least known. Many people will rinse their saltwater fillets with fresh water before they season and cook them. While this is perfectly fine for freshwater fish, it will compromise the quality of your saltwater fish. Saltwater fish obviously live in saltwater, so by rinsing them with freshwater, you are causing diffusion to take place between filet and the surrounding water, and actually ruining the quality of your fish. To guard against this, I create a saltwater ice brine for my fish when I am filleting, using a bucket of sea water and some ice. This brine not only keeps any diffusion from happening, but also drops the temperature of the water to below 32°F, helping your fillets cool quickly and stay firm. If you do not have the luxury of processing your fish at the dock, or if you are prepping store bought saltwater fish to cook, you can make a brine using regular table salt and cold water. The goal is to make your brine as salty as the ocean, so just use your best judgement.

Defrost frozen fish in an ice-water brine. It seems counterintuitive, but your fish will defrost in a few hours this way. It will lose much less water during the process, helping keep your fish from getting dry during the cooking process.

PASTA E FASIOLI

This is a regional bean soup served with both potatoes and pasta. It's a hearty carbfest — perfect for a cold winter's night during Venice's February Carnivale.

INGREDIENTS

4 - 6 SERVINGS

- 1.5 1bs. dried cannellini or white beans or 3, 14.5 oz. cans of beans, rinsed well
- 7 oz. pancetta
- 2 medium yellow onions, 1 large shallot, 1 carrot and 2 stalks of celery
- 1/2 cup dry white wine
- 4 plum tomatoes, fresh or canned, hand-crushed
- 1 tbs. tomato paste, caramelized
- 1 sprig rosemary, 1 sprig fresh thyme, 4 bay leaves
- Parmigiano-Reggiano rind
- 2 medium Yukon Gold potatoes, peeled and chopped
- 1/2 lb. dried elbow pasta
- Garnish: fresh parsley, grated Parmigiano-Reggiano and a drizzle of olive oil

DIRECTIONS

1. Prepare the beans. Rinse well and soak overnight in a glass bowl. The next day, rinse the beans again. Quarter one of the onions and add water until just an inch over the beans; simmer with 2 bay leaves for 90 minutes until tender but not mushy. Discard the foam as it emerges. Pull the beans out from the water, discard the onion quarters and the bay leaves and save the bean broth.
2. Make the soffritto. Peel and mince the other onion, shallot, carrot, celery and pancetta. Heat a thick-bottomed heavy soup pot or InstaPot until smoky. Heat 1 tbs. olive oil and sauté the pancetta until crispy. Add the onion, carrot and celery and sauté until soft. De-glaze the pan with the white wine and add the rosemary and 2 bay leaves. Cook until vegetables are soft and translucent. Caramelize the tomato paste in a separate pan until brick red, then add to the pot along with the beans.
3. Add the bean broth and Parmesean rind. Bring to a very slow simmer and cook, uncovered, for about 1 1/2 hours.
4. Discard the rind. Pull out half of the beans with a slotted spoon. Discard the rosemary sprig and bay leaves. Blend the remaining soup with an immersion blender until smooth and consistent.
5. Add the potatoes and whole beans back into the puree. Cook until the potatoes are done. Cool and let the soup set overnight.
6. To finish, cook the pasta and add to the reheated soup. Salt and pepper to taste. Garnish and serve.

PANDORO

Pandoro means 'golden bread'. It's a sweet, buttery cake from Verona that is served at Christmastime. My nephew, Nick, and I make this every year, but it took a few tries to get it right. Allow a whole day to get this done. This isn't just a recipe, it's a relationship.

INGREDIENTS

- 1/4 cup warm water (105°F to 115°F), this temperature is important to get the yeast to activate correctly
- 1 (1/4 oz.) package dry yeast
- 2 cups all-purpose flour
- 5 egg yolks (separated) + 1 whole egg
- 1/2 cup plus 1 tbs. granulated sugar
- 2 sticks unsalted butter, 3 tbs. room temperature and the rest frozen
- The zest of 1 lemon and 1 orange
- 2 tsp. vanilla extract
- 1/2 cup heavy cream
- Garnish: powdered sugar

DIRECTIONS

1. In a small bowl mix the yeast with the water, let it sit for about 5 minutes, then add 1/3 cup of the flour, 1 of the egg yolks, and 1 tablespoon of the sugar, plus enough water to make a soft dough. Cover the bowl with a kitchen towel and let rise in a warm place for 2 hours or when doubled in bulk.
2. In a large bowl, sift 1 1/3 cups of the flour and combine it with 1/4 cup of the sugar. Add the rising dough, 3 egg yolks and 3 tbs. of the butter. Beat on low to combine the ingredients. On a floured work surface, shape the dough into a ball. Cover it with a cloth in a floured bowl. Set aside to rise again for another 2 hours.

3. In your Kitchen Aid use the pastry hook to fold in the remaining 1/3 cup flour, 1/4 cup sugar, the whole egg and remaining egg yolk. Knead the dough well until it is homogeneous; again shape into a ball and put it back into your clean, floured bowl. Cover it with the cloth, and let it rise for another 2 hours.
4. Spread the dough out on your floured work surface and knead in the lemon and orange zest, the vanilla extract, and then the cream, a little at a time, until it is completely absorbed.
5. Shape the dough into a rectangle using a rolling pin. Cut the remaining cold butter into small bits and distribute them over the center of the sheet of dough. Fold the sheet into thirds, and then roll it out again. Let it rest for 30 minutes, and repeat this folding, rolling and resting two more times.
6. Preheat the oven to 400°F. Put the dough into a greased and floured pandoro pan. If you don't have a pan, you can line a deep thin pot with parchment paper to create a cone in which the dough can bake. Bake for 30 minutes. Then reduce the heat to 350°F and bake for another 30 minutes. Unmould the cake immediately and cool it on a rack. Dust with powdered sugar.

The temperature of the water is important to activate and not kill the yeast. 110°F to 115°F average is safe.

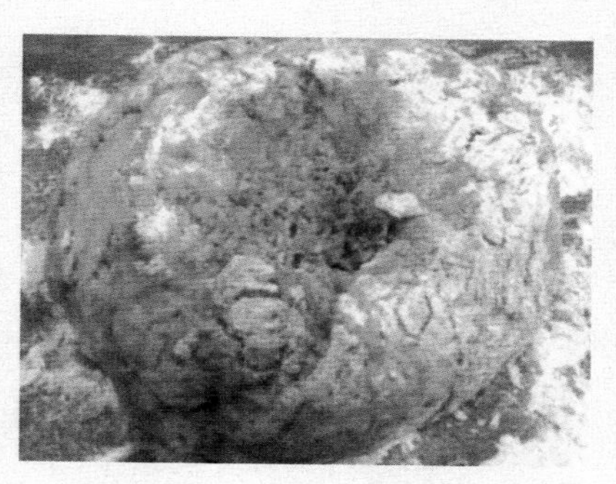

Heavy cream can be 30 percent, 36 percent or 40 percent fat content. As fat is flavor, 40 percent is the best.

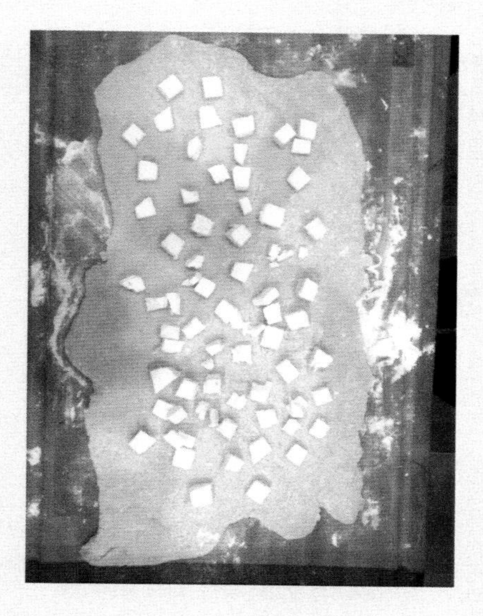

Frozen unsalted butter folded into the dough makes a flakier pastry. If the butter is too warm, it will melt into the dough, making it hard to work with and the cake tough and rubbery.

BAGNA CAUDA

TAJARIN CON TARTUFFE

Piedmont

PIEDMONT IS A REGION CELEBRATED FOR ITS BEEF, RICH DISHES AND CREAM SAUCES ENHANCED BY STRONG FLAVORS SUCH AS GARLIC AND ANCHOVY. ALBA IS THE WORLD'S WHITE-TRUFFLE MECCA. THESE STRONG FLAVORS BLEND WELL WITH THE REGION'S ROBUST RED WINES.

PAIR THESE WINES WITH THE RECIPES FROM THE REGION: BAROLO, BARBARESCO, DOLCETTO, BARBERA D'ASTI, MOSCATO D'ASTI AND GAVI.

AGNOLOTTI DEL PLIN

BRASATO AL BAROLO CON POLENTA

TORTA GIANDUIA

BAGNA CAUDA

Bagna Cauda (pronounced *banya cowda*), means "hot dip" in Italian. It's a simple warm oil dip made savory with anchovy, served with in-season vegetables and toasted crusty bread.

INGREDIENTS
6 - 8 SERVINGS

- 3/4 cup olive oil
- 8 to 10 garlic cloves, very finely chopped
- 12 anchovy fillets
- 4 tbs. (1/2 stick) unsalted butter
- About 8 cups trimmed, cut-up vegetables such as sweet peppers, broccoli, carrots, cauliflower, fresh fennel, celery and boiled and cooled new potatoes.
- Slices of crusty bread

DIRECTIONS

1. In a small saucepan over low heat, combine the olive oil, garlic and anchovies. Cook, mashing the anchovies with the back of a wooden spoon, until smooth, about 5 minutes. Remove from the heat and stir in the butter.
2. Quickly blanch the broccoli, carrots and cauliflower to soften slightly.
3. Pour the mixture into a warmed chafing dish or fondue pot over a warming candle or spirit lamp. Serve immediately with vegetables and crusty bread for dipping.

TAJARIN CON TARTUFFE

November is truffle hunting season in Piedmont, and tajarin (pronounced *tie-yah-REEN*) reigns as the region's most popular pasta. Together, they make a wonderful rich egg and truffle dish. Use your spaghetti width when cutting the pasta dough.

INGREDIENTS
6 - 8 SERVINGS

- 1 lb. of pasta dough
- 1 tbs. olive oil
- 1 small shallot, chopped
- 1/4 cup dry white wine
- 8 tbs. (1 stick) unsalted butter
- White truffle butter to taste. You can order wonderful truffle products from a company called Urbani. *shop.urbani.com/collections/all-products*
- Salt and pepper, to taste
- Garnish: 3 tbs. Pecorino Romano or Grana Padano cheese, grated, chopped parsley and 6 egg yolks for extra richness

DIRECTIONS

1. 1 lb. of pasta dough and cut the tajerin strands. Boil salted water in a large pot.
2. Heat a heavy frying pan until smoky. Add 1 tbs. olive oil and sauté the shallot until soft.
3. Add the white wine to de-glaze. Once the wine is reduced by half, reduce the heat to low and add the stick of butter. Melt.
4. Begin to add the truffle butter, a pinch at a time, to taste. Some people like a robust truffle flavor and others just a hint. Salt and pepper to taste. Remove from the heat and add 3 tbs. cold water to reduce the heat.
5. Cook the tajerin in the boiling salted water until it rises to the top. It should take just minutes.
6. Add 3 tbs. of the grated cheese to the butter mixture, stirring to combine. Return to the heat and pull the pasta from the water, bringing with it a bit of the pasta water as you add it to the sauce. Combine gently.
7. Garnished with fresh cheese and fresh parsley.
8. For a bit of flare, a raw egg yolk on top of the pasta adds a lovely richness. The heat of the pasta and sauce will cook the egg yolk.

AGNOLOTTI DEL PLIN

This popular Piedmontese dish gets its name from the regional dialect for "pinch." *Fare il plin* or pinching the dough creates these savory, stuffed pasta pillows.

INGREDIENTS
6 - 8 SERVINGS

- 1 lb. of pasta dough

For the Agnolotti filling:

- 1 tbs. unsalted butter and a splash of olive oil
- Small yellow onion, finely chopped and 1 garlic clove, thinly sliced
- 1 sprig fresh rosemary, leaves only
- 1/2 lb. each ground veal and ground pork
- 1/2 cup red wine
- 10 cups fresh spinach, roughly chopped
- 3/4 cup freshly grated Parmigiano-Reggiano
- 3 large eggs
- 1/2 tsp. sherry vinegar
- Freshly-grated nutmeg, salt and pepper to taste

For the sauce:

- 1 cup chicken stock, 1 stick unsalted butter, 4 whole sage leaves
- Garnish: Fresh parsley and grated Parmigiano-Reggiano

DIRECTIONS

1. Make the dough. While it's resting, make the filling.
2. The filling: In a large, heavy saucepan, add 1 tbs. of the butter and a splash of olive oil over a high heat. Sauté the onion. Add the garlic and rosemary and cook until the garlic is light golden brown, about 2 minutes. Add the meat and cook until brown and caramelized. Add the red wine and reduce, 1 to 2 minutes. Mix in the sherry vinegar, egg, Parmigiano-Reggiano and nutmeg. Salt and pepper to taste. Let cool.
3. Put the cooled filling into a food processor and pulse to form a rough paste. Form and fill the agnolotti. See the instructions to the right.
4. Bring a large pot of salted water to a boil and cook the filled pasta pillows until very *al dente*, about 3 minutes, or until they rise to the surface.
5. Meanwhile, in a large, heavy sauté pan, melt the butter and add the sage leaves and chicken stock. Turn the heat to high and bring the mixture to a simmer.
6. Pull the pasta with some of the water and add it into the sauté pan. Coat the pasta very gently with the butter mixture. Garnish and serve immediately.

Form and fill the agnolotti. Cut 2" wide pasta sheets. Put the filling into a pastry bag and distribute it onto the dough strips. A Ziplock bag with a small hole cut in the corner also works.

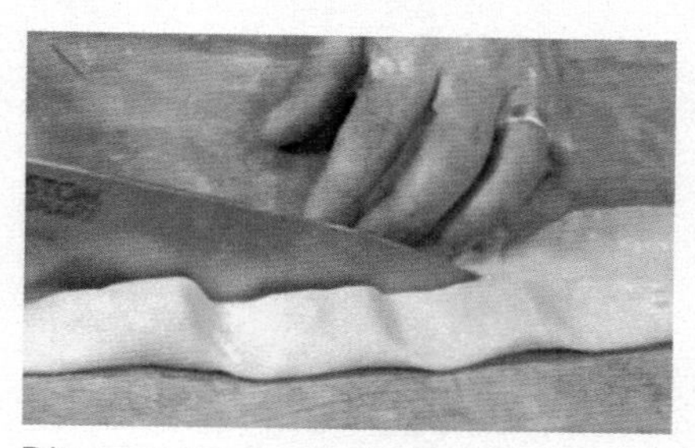

Dip a pastry brush in water, shake off the excess and paint a strip of water along the long side of the dough strip to create a sticky glue. Fold the dough over the filling strips, pinch the dough to make 2" pillows making sure you pinch out any excess air. If there is air in the pasta pillow, it will explode in the boiling water. Cut off any excess dough and re-pinch the strips to secure the dough around the filling.

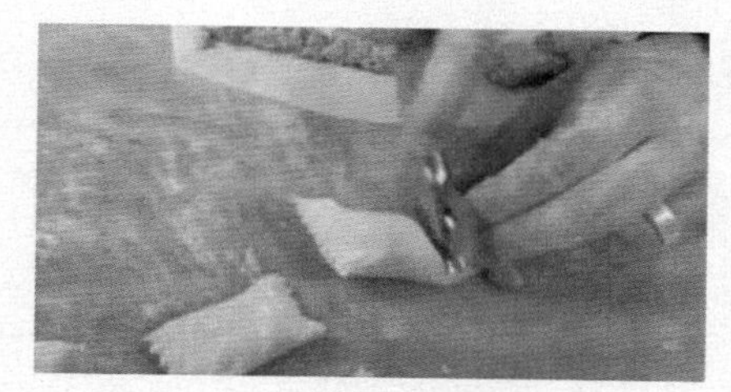

Use your pastry cutter to cut the shapes in the middle of each pinch and secure the dough again.

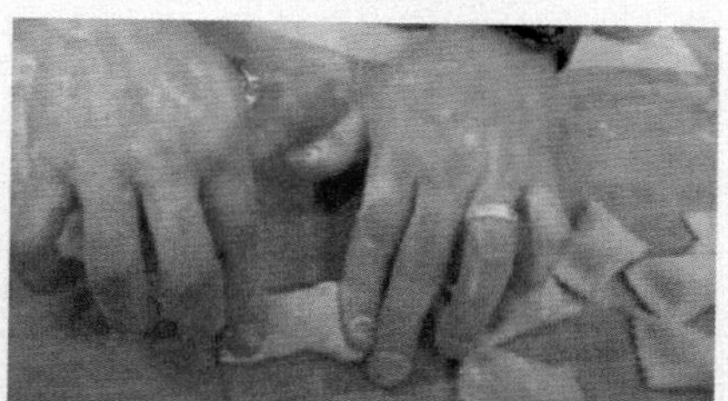

BRASATO AL BAROLO CON POLENTA

I like to make this hearty stew with beef short ribs because bones and their marrow add flavor. Allow three days to make this dish. Marinate the beef overnight. Make the stew the next day and chill overnight. Finish the dish and serve on the third day.

INGREDIENTS
6 SERVINGS

For the beef:

- 3 lbs. beef short ribs
- 1 bottle Barolo wine or other hearty red wine
- Sprig of fresh rosemary, 4 fresh sage leaves, 1 bay leaf
- 1 clove of garlic, minced

For the stew:

- 4 tbs. unsalted butter and 2 tbs. olive oil
- Chopped: 1/4 pound pancetta, 2 carrots, 2 medium onions, 1 stalk celery
- 2 tbs. caramelized tomato paste

For the polenta:

- 4 cups water and 1 tsp. salt
- 1 cup of Sclafani Instant Polenta
- 2 tbs. unsalted butter, 1/2 cup Parmigiano-Reggiano, grated
- Garnish: chopped fresh parsley

DIRECTIONS

1 Marinate the meat in the whole bottle of wine, rosemary, sage, bay leaf and garlic for a minimum of 6 hours or up to 24 hours.

2 In a large heavy pot, heat the butter and oil over medium heat. Remove the meat from the marinade and pat it completely dry. Save the marinade. Brown the meat well on all sides, remove from the pot and set aside.

3 Sauté the pancetta in the drippings until crispy and add the carrots, onions, celery until soft. Add the caramelized tomato paste and mix well. Return the beef to the pot, add back the wine marinade and slow cook for 2 hours. Taste and season with salt and pepper, then slow cook for another 2 hours until very tender. Cool overnight.

4 Remove any fat from the cooled stew before you reheat it. When it's warm, remove the ribs from the gravy, pull the meat and any visible marrow from the bones and shred. Skim any additional grease from the cooking juices and then blend with an immersion blender to make a smooth gravy. Return the shredded meat to the gravy and cook down until thickened.

5 Make the polenta. Bring 4 cups of water and 1 tsp. salt to a boil in a large saucepan. Pour polenta slowly into the boiling water, whisking constantly until there are no lumps. Gently stir in 2 tbs. butter and the Parmigiano-Reggiano cheese. Cover and let stand 5 minutes to thicken. Season to taste.

After you marinate the meat overnight in the wine, it's important to pat it completely dry before you brown it.

Get a good char on all sides of the meat to seal in the juices.

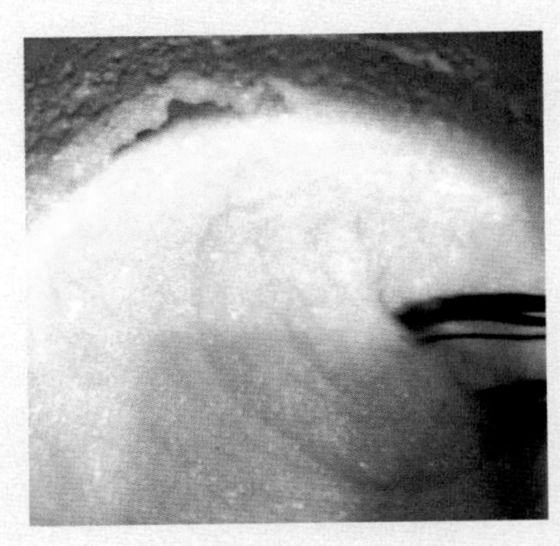

Instant polenta is a good choice to more easily get a nice, smooth paste with no lumps.

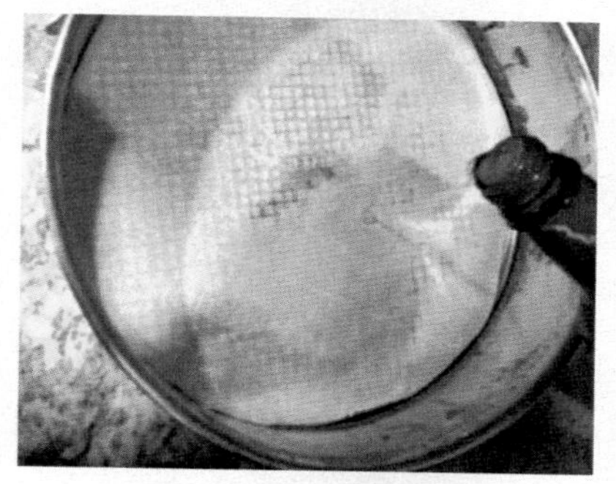

Cut a piece of parchment paper to match the circle of your springform pan to more easily release the cake. Oil the parchment paper on both sides.

Do not overbeat the egg whites. Gently fold the egg whites into the batter. Don't overmix.

Let the cake cook slightly before you remove it from the springform pan. Cool on a cake rack.

TORTA GIANDUIA

Chocolate. Hazelnuts. Who doesn't love Nutella? The famous hazelnut chocolate cream was invented by a pastry maker in Alba, Piedmont. Today, you can find it in this flourless cake in every patisserie in the region. Make a Torta Gianduia (pronouced zahn-DOO-yah) to celebrate World Nutella Day on February 5.

INGREDIENTS

For the cake:

- 1 stick unsalted butter
- 4 oz. bittersweet chocolate, chopped
- 3/4 cup skinned hazelnuts, lightly chopped and toasted
- 4 large eggs, separated
- 1, 13-oz. jar Nutella
- Pinch of Kosher salt
- 1 tbs. brandy or cognac

For the ganache:

- 1/2 cup heavy cream and 3/4 cup Nutella
- Garnish: coarsely chopped hazelnuts.

DIRECTIONS

1. Preheat the oven to 350˚F. Prepare a 9-inch spring form pan by cutting a piece of parchment paper to fit the bottom circle. Butter or oil both sides of the parchment, which will help the cake slide off easily after baking.
2. Melt the chocolate in the top of a double boiler or a metal bowl set over a saucepan of simmering water. You can also microwave the chocolate in a glass bowl on medium power, in 30 second intervals, stirring in between, until the chocolate is completely melted. Let it cool slightly.
3. Grind the hazelnuts until they are fine, but not pasty.
4. Beat the egg whites until they are foamy. Add the sugar and beat until the whites form stiff peaks, about 2 minutes.
5. In a clean bowl, with the paddle attachment, beat the butter and Nutella, about 2 minutes. Add the yolks, salt and brandy. Mix until smooth. Add the melted chocolate and ground hazelnuts. Mix until smooth. Gently fold the egg whites into the batter. Don't over-mix. Pour into the baking pan.
6. Bake about 45 to 50 minutes, or when a toothpick comes out clean. Let the cake cool for about 10 minutes and remove the side ring. Flip the cake onto a cooling rack and gently peel off the parchment paper. Cool completely.
7. The ganache. In a small saucepan warm the heavy cream until it begins to simmer. You want it to just start to bubble up around the edges of the pot. Add the Nutella into the heated heavy cream and whisk until smooth and thick. Pour the ganache over the cake. Garnish with coarsely chopped hazelnuts.

COTOLETTA ALLA MILANESE

Lombardy

LOMBARDY IS A RICH, WEALTHY REGION OF ITALY. MEAT, CHEESE AND BUTTER FEATURE PROMINENTLY IN THIS CUISINE, OFTEN TURNED INTO RICH, HEARTY STEWS. MUCH OF THE REGION ALONG THE PO VALLEY IS COVERED BY RICE PADDIES, SO THEY ARE MASTERS IN THE ART OF MAKING RISOTTO.

PAIR THESE WINES WITH THE RECIPES FROM THE REGION: NEBBIOLO, PINOT NOIR, BAROLO OR BARBARESCO FROM NEARBY PIEDMONT.

OSSO BUCCO

RISOTTO ALLA MILANESE

OSSO BUCCO

I've been serving this classic veal shank stew recipe since 1981, after I visited friends in Milan and learned how to make it. The secret? Patience. The thick veal shanks with their decadent bone marrow are served over classic Risotto alla Milanese and topped with lemon-garlic gremolada. Sublime!

INGREDIENTS
8 SERVINGS

For the stew:

- 1 cup unbleached, all-purpose flour
- 8 sections of veal shank, 2" thick
- 1/2 cup olive oil
- 1 stick unsalted butter
- 1 large yellow onion and 1 large shallot, coarsely chopped
- 6 large garlic cloves, peeled and chopped
- 1 tbs. dried basil, 1 tbs. dried oregano
- 28 oz. canned Italian whole plum tomatoes, drained and crushed with your hand. I like the Cento brand.
- 2 cups dry white wine
- 2 cups beef stock

For the gremolada:

- Combine 3/4 cups chopped Italian parsley, the grated zest of 2 lemons and 2 cloves of finely chopped garlic.

DIRECTIONS

1. Preheat the oven to 350°F.
2. Pat the shanks dry with a paper towel. Dredge well in the flour that has been seasoned with salt and pepper. Heat the oil and butter in a large Dutch oven or InstaPot and sear the shanks, browning well on all sides. Transfer the shanks to paper towels.
3. Reduce the heat to medium. Add the onion to the cooking fat, and cook for 8 to 12 minutes, until just softened and a light brown in color. Add the basil and oregano and cook for another 2 minutes to open up the flavor of the dried herbs.
4. Add the tomatoes, a bit of salt and pepper and cook for another 10 minutes. Skim the excess fat.
5. Add the wine and bring to a boil. Reduce the heat and simmer for another 5 minutes to boil off the alcohol.
6. Return the veal shanks to the casserole and add beef stock just to cover. Bring to a low boil, reduce the heat and cover the casserole. Follow the directions for slow cooking stew in your InstaPot or in the oven at 350°F for 2 hours. Remove the lid and continue to cook uncovered for another 30 minutes. Just before serving, fold in the gremolada.

RISOTTO ALLA MILANESE

This saffron based rice has a delightfully creamy texture and is the classic base to Osso Bucco. Have leftovers? Use the risotto to make Arancini.

INGREDIENTS
8 SERVINGS

- 5 1/2 cups chicken stock
- 2 tbs. extra-virgin olive oil
- 1 small onion, 1 small shallot, finely chopped
- Pinch of saffron threads
- 1/2 cup dry white wine
- 1 1/2 cups arborio or carnaroli rice.
- 2 tbs. unsalted frozen butter
- 1/2 cup freshly grated Parmigiano-Reggiano cheese

DIRECTIONS

1. Simmer your stock and have at the ready.
2. Heat the olive oil. Add the onion and shallot, season with salt and pepper and cook over moderate heat, stirring until softened, about 5 minutes.
3. Add the rice to the olive oil and vegetables and cook for 5 minutes, stirring to make sure it doesn't burn.
4. Crumble the saffron into the wine and add it to the rice. Cook, stirring, until the wine is absorbed.
5. Add 1 cup of the warm stock and cook over moderate heat. Continue adding the stock 1/2 cup at a time, pausing between additions until each portion of the liquid has been absorbed before adding more.
6. Stir. Stir. Stir. The risotto is done when the rice is thick and creamy. Take the pot off the stove to cool for about 5 minutes.
7. Cut the frozen butter into small pieces. Gently fold the butter and cheese into the rice, moving the rice back and forth, never overworking it.
8. Salt and pepper to taste. Serve immediately.

TIPS FOR MAKING PERFECT OSSO BUCCO WITH RISOTTO

- **Veal shank comes in two forms: fore shank and hind shank. Ask your butcher for the hind shank. The bone on the rear leg hind shank is larger, which yields more meat and more marrow, one of the greatest pleasures known to the culinary world. Osso Bucco is often served with a small demitasse spoon to extract the marrow and a side of fresh grilled bread to spread it on. Do not tell your cardiologist about this.**
- **Risotto is a method, not a dish. It requires constant attention and can be a tough dish to do, so it will take a little practice to get it right.**
- **Use either arborio or carnaroli, which are starchy, medium grained rices that make a creamy dish.**
- **Wine is important in the risotto-making process. Have it measured out ahead of time for the dish and the rest at the ready to put into your glass. This is key to keeping your interest at the stove and maintaining a smooth and slow stir.**
- **The key to great risotto is keeping your stock at a gentle simmer, not boiling.**
- **Because risotto can get sticky, it's best to use a large, heavy pot. I also use a wooden spoon called a *girariso*. It doubles the stirring power to help release the starch that gives the dish that extra creaminess. Don't over-stir, however, as over-stirring can ruin a risotto's texture. It's much better to stir once every 30 seconds and trust the cooking process to do its thing.**

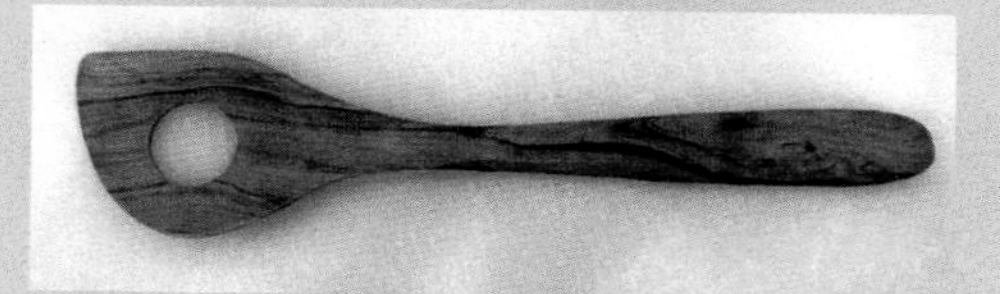

- **• The citrus and parsley in the gremolada cut the richness of the veal marrow. It's also a great garnish for any Italian dish.**

COTOLETTA ALLA MILANESE

This simple veal chop is found on every menu in Lombardy. Again, it's perfect served with Risotto Milanese.

INGREDIENTS
4 SERVINGS

- 4 veal chops bone-in, about 1" thick, with loin attached
- 2 medium eggs, lightly beaten
- 1 cup homemade bread crumbs seasoned with a bit of dried rosemary
- 1/2 tsp each salt and pepper
- Olive oil for frying
- Garnish: sprigs of fresh rosemary

DIRECTIONS

1. Remove the small bones and excess fat from the edges of the chops and cut the edges in 2 or 3 places so that the meat does not bend during cooking. Salt and pepper the meat lightly.
2. Dip the chops into the beaten eggs and then the breadcrumbs, pressing them into the meat so they don't come off during the frying process.
3. Fry the chops. The secret of the perfect Cotoletta alla Milanese is to fry the meat at high temperatures so that it turns out crunchy on the outside but stays tender and pink in the inside.

HOMEMADE BREADCRUMBS

Don't let leftover bread go to waste! Allow it to dry out and harden for a few days at room temperature. You can use any bread, but I like artisan sourdough, or a crusty loaf.

Grind down the dried bread in a food processor. Spread the crumbs in a single layer on a baking sheet and bake at 300°F for 10 minutes. Stir and continue to bake until the crumbs are lightly toasted and dry. You'll need to watch the oven carefully so they don't burn.

Store in an airtight container at room temperature for up to a month.

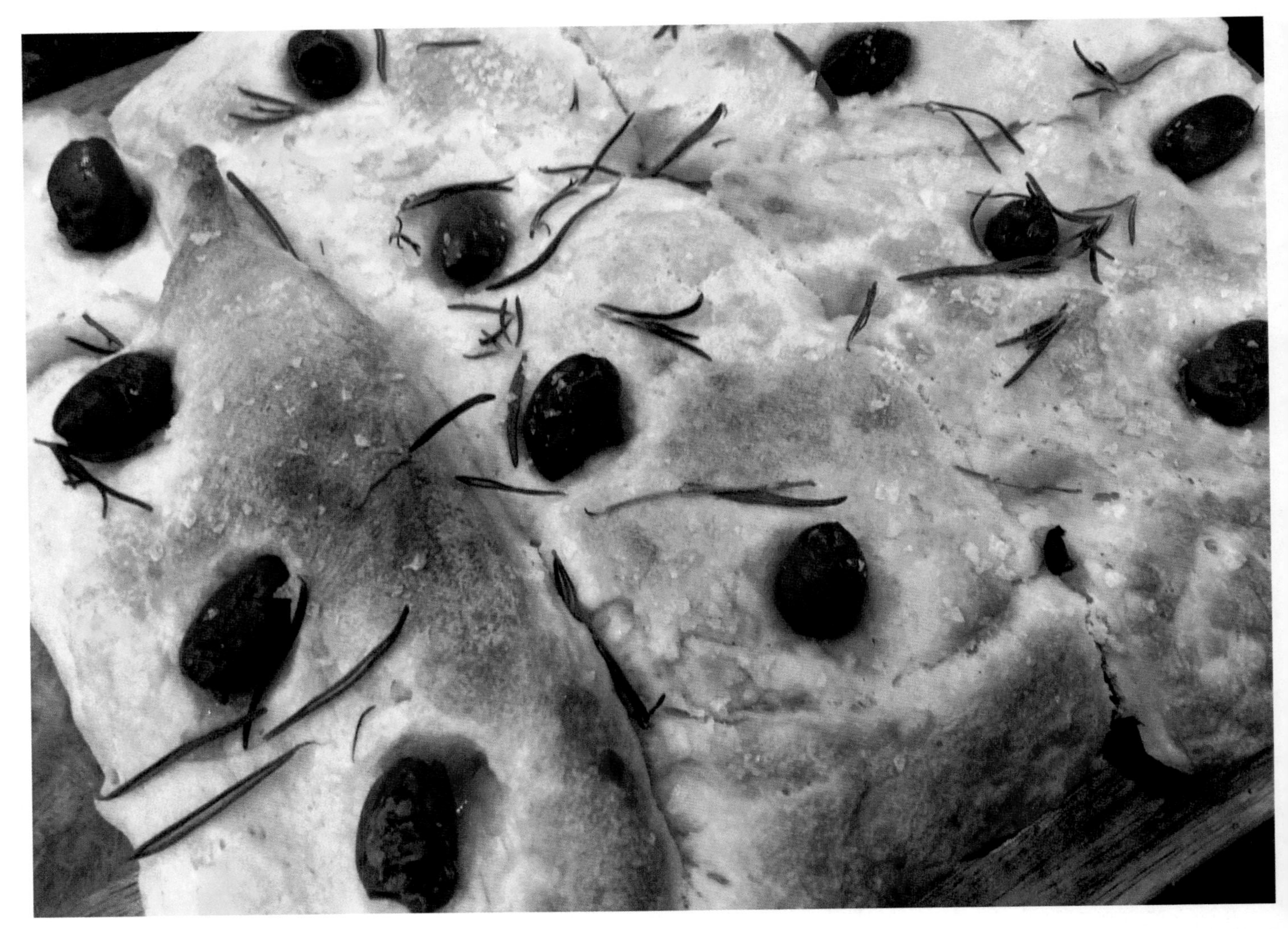

FOCACCIA

Liguria

LIGURIA'S MIX OF SEA, MOUNTAINS AND WOODS GIVES THE CUISINE FLAVORS THAT ARE DELICATE, BUT INTENSE. THE TERRAIN IS STEEP, THE SOIL THIN AND UNDER IT ... ROCK. ALONG THE MEDITERRANEAN, THE CATCH OF THE SEA ADORNS THE TABLES OF THIS REGION.

PAIR THESE WINES WITH THE RECIPES FROM THE REGION: ROSÉ, ORMEASCO, PIGATO AND SCHIACCETRA.

TROFIE CON PESTO

FOCACCIA

On our tours, our Ligurian breakfast table is always laid out with focaccia. They are crispy and salty on the outside and soft and sweet on the inside. It's a simple recipe of flour, yeast, honey, salt flakes and of course, Ligurian olive oil.

INGREDIENTS

FOR AN 8" X 13" PAN

- 2 cups lukewarm water, 105°F to 115°F, this temperature is important to get the yeast to activate correctly
- 3/4 tsp. active fast-rising dry yeast
- 2 tsp. honey
- 4 cups all-purpose flour
- 2 1/2 tbs. olive oil, plus more for the pan and finishing
- 2 tbs. Malden sea salt flakes
- 1/4 cup extra-virgin olive oil
- Fresh rosemary or sage leaves and olives

For the brine:

- 1 tsp. sea salt and 1/3 cup lukewarm water
- Sea salt flakes for finishing

DIRECTIONS

1. In a small bowl, mix together the lukewarm water, honey and yeast. Stir until dissolved. Let sit 5 minutes. Combine the flour and 1 tbs. of the salt to your KitchenAid bowl. Using a pastry hook, add the yeast mixture and olive oil, mixing it in a bit at a time. Mix until there are no bumps and it's completely smooth. It should be a soft, stretchy dough, not crumbly. If you need to, add a little more water. Scrape the side of the bowl clean and cover with plastic wrap. Leave the dough out at room temperature to ferment for one hour until it doubles in volume.
2. Oil a work surface with a little extra virgin olive oil. Gently stretch the dough by placing your hands underneath and pulling outward. Then fold it in thirds and then in half again. Rotate the dough, stretch it out and fold in thirds again. Fold in half and return it to the bowl. Cover with plastic wrap and let rest at room temperature again for 2 more hours.
3. When it has doubled in size again, you are ready to prepare the dough for baking. Spread 2 to 3 tbs. oil evenly onto the pan. Prepare your workspace with a dash of flour and pull the dough from the bowl. Knead gently as you fold in the other tablespoon of salt, and then the rosemary, sage or the chopped up olives.
4. Lay the dough out onto the pan. Gently spread more oil all over the dough. The oil lends a rich flavor and creates a crisp, but tender crust. Gently stretch the dough to the edge of the sheet by placing your hands underneath and pulling outward. Don't worry if it doesn't fully stretch to fit. Set aside for 30 minutes.
5. Make the brine. Dimple the dough by pressing with the pads of your fingers. Pour the brine over the dough to fill dimples. It will look wet. The brine adds a delicious saltiness and crunch.
6. Proofing is the final rise a mass of bread dough must make before it is baked, but after it has been shaped into a loaf. Proof the formed focaccia in the oven by placing a glass baking dish on the bottom rack and fill it with boiling water. Put the dough on the middle rack and shut the door. The steam and heat from the boiling water will create a warm and steamy environment. It will take about 35 minutes to proof and become puffy.
7. After 35 minutes, remove the glass baking dish and turn on the oven to 450°F. Pull out the foccaccia and sprinkle it generously with the sea salt flakes. Bake at 450°F for 30 minutes on the center rack. Then move the pan to the upper rack and bake for another 5 to 7 minutes until the top is golden brown.
8. Remove from the oven and immediately put the focaccia onto a wire rack. Finish by brushing the top with extra virgin olive oil. Don't worry if it pools in the dimples, the oil will gradually soak into the bread.
9. Serve warm or at room temperature.

Gently stretch the dough by placing your hands underneath and pulling outward. Then fold it in thirds and then in half. Rotate the dough, stretch it out and fold in thirds and then in half again. Return it to the bowl.

Dimple the dough by pressing it with the pads of your thumbs.

Pour the brine over the dough to fill dimples. It will look wet. The brine adds a delicious saltiness and with the flake salt, a wonderful crunch.

TROFIE CON PESTO

"Pesto" can refer to any paste of herbs that is mashed up with a mortar and pestle. When I bring my guests to the Cinque Terre, we enjoy platters of trofie, a small twisted pasta, liberally dressed with traditional pesto made of fresh basil, pine nuts, parmesan cheese, coarse salt and of course, plenty of extra virgin olive oil. Making pesto is all about tasting and adjusting the ingredients.

INGREDIENTS
4 - 6 SERVINGS

- 1 lb. of pasta dough. Do not roll the dough into sheets.
- 1/2 clove garlic, chopped
- 3 good handfuls fresh basil leaves, picked and chopped
- 1 handful pine nuts, very lightly toasted
- 1 good handful Parmigiano-Reggiano cheese, freshly grated
- 1 good handful Pecorino Romano cheese, freshly grated
- 1/2 cup extra virgin olive oil, plus more as needed
- 1 small squeeze of lemon juice

DIRECTIONS

1 Form the trofie. Making trofie is like playing with PlayDough. With your hands, roll portions of the dough into tubes about 1/2-inch around. Keep the dough lightly floured to prevent sticking. Cut these tubes into 1/4-inch nuggets. Rub each nugget back and forth between the palms of your floured hands to create a thinner tube with tapered ends. Keep the tubes on a floured surface until you are ready to use.

2 Make the pesto. You can use a food processor, but the Italian nonnas only use a morter and pestle so as not to bruise the basil. Gently grind the garlic with a pinch of salt. Add the basil a bit at a time and then the pine nuts to form the paste. Turn out into a bowl and make it your own.

3 Add some of the cheese. Stir gently and add some olive oil – you will need just enough to bind the sauce to an oozy consistency. Keep adding a bit more of the cheese and oil until you are happy with the taste and consistency. Season to taste.

4 Cook the trofie in a large pot of boiling salted water unti *al dente***.** Drain and mix with the pesto.

5 Pesto freezes well or will last a few weeks in a sealed container in the refrigerator.

LASAGNE VERDE AL RAGÙ

Emilia-Romagna

IF ITALY IS FOOD AND FOOD IS ITALY, THE EMILIA-ROMAGNA IS ITS CULINARY CAPITOL. BOLOGNA HAS BEEN NICKNAMED “LA GRASSA” OR “THE FAT.” THE REGION IS HOME TO THE MOST FAMOUS CURED PORK MEATS OF ITALY, BALSAMIC VINEGAR AND THE MOST RENOWNED AGED CHEESE ON THE PLANET, PARMIGIANO-REGGIANO.

PAIR THESE WINES WITH THE RECIPES FROM THE REGION: MALVESIA, BARBERA, LAMBRUSCO AND PIGNOLETTO.

RAGÙ ALLA BOLOGNESE

RAVIOLI DI PERE CON BALSAMICO

TORTELLINI EN BRODO

PANNA COTTA

RAGÙ ALLA BOLOGNESE CON TAGLIATELLI

Bologna is one of Italy's wealthiest cities, and this richness is reflected in its ragù. Ragú is a thick, chunky sauce usually made by slow-cooking several kinds of meats in a tomato sauce. Beyond a dash of nutmeg, there are no herbs in this dish. Nor is there garlic. It is this surprise ingredient that gives the body to the sauce and makes the meat so tender: whole milk. Meaty but surprisingly delicate, aromatic and creamy, this ragù takes time to create the layers of flavor.

INGREDIENTS
6 - 8 SERVINGS

For the tagliatelli: Make 1 lb. pasta dough and roll out the sheets. Cut the thinned pasta sheets to fit the diameter of the pasta machine and dust with flour. Cut the tagliatelli ribbons immediately.

- Soffritto: 1 1/3 cups each: onion, celery, carrots and 1 large shallot, all chopped fine
- 4 oz. chopped pancetta
- 1/2 lb. each: ground chuck, ground pork, ground veal
- 2 cups dry white wine
- 2 cups whole milk
- 1/8 tsp. freshly grated nutmeg
- 3 1/2 cups tomato purée
- 4 tbs. tomato paste, caramelized
- 1 small Parmigiano-Reggiano rind

DIRECTIONS

1. In a large heavy pot, heat the pan to smoking then melt the olive oil and butter. To make the soffritto, add the onions, celery and carrots and cook until very soft. Add the pancetta. When the vegetables and pancetta have caramelized, add the ground meats to the pan and brown. Drain off the fat. Over medium heat, pour the white wine into the sauce pan and reduce for about 15 minutes.
2. Heat the milk in a separate pan, then add it to the pot, stir it into the meat mixture and simmer until the milk has cooked into the meat. Note: the milk will take about an hour to totally cook into the meat mixture. When it is done, it should just be moist around the edges of the meat, not soupy.
3. Add the tomato paste and puree to the meat mixture and stir well. Add the Parmesean cheese rind. Bring to a simmer. Reduce heat to low, add the grated nutmeg, and cook uncovered for at least 3 hours in a low oven for 2 hours. Add water or beef broth if the ragù thickens too much. Season to taste.
4. Serve with tagliatelle or Lasagne Verde al Ragù.

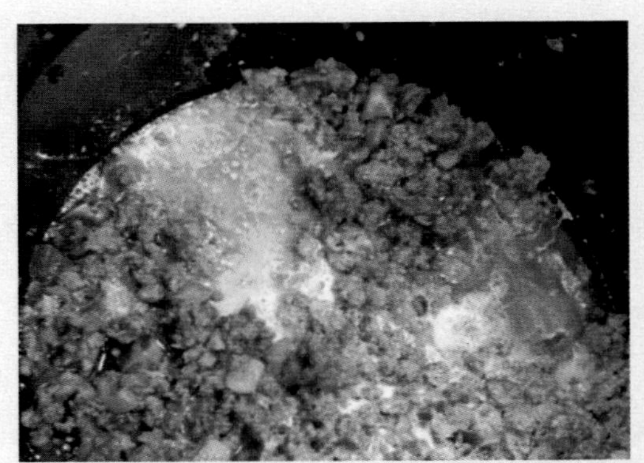

Whole milk gives rich body to the sauce and makes the meat tender. Cook it down until it is completely absorbed into the meat.

To make tagliatelle. The dough should be room temperature before you cut the ribbons. Crank the sheets through the cutter smoothly as you support the ribbons with your other hand. Do not reverse the crank or the machine will clog.

Lay the cut pasta on a baking sheet dusted with flour. Pasta can be cooked immediately or allowed to air dry, uncovered, for up to 2 hours. You can also freeze the pasta ribbons for future use.

Making spinach pasta can be a challenge, so feel free to skip the spinach and use the plain white pasta dough, or even use store-bought lasagne sheets. If you do make the spinach pasta, it will take a few more times through the pasta machine rollers to get the spinach and dough to meld.

Use a knife or a bicicletta to cut the thinned pasta sheets to fit the pan.

Have the pasta sheets ready for assembly. You can place them on floured parchment paper.

LASAGNE VERDE AL RAGÙ

All Italians know that an heirloom family recipe is sure to vary in its preparation, depending on who is in the kitchen. Here is the classic recipe from Bologna. Layers and layers of spinach-green pasta sheets, rich red ragù and white bechamel sauce make this delicious — and beautiful — dish. Making spinach pasta can be a challenge, so feel free to skip the spinach and make plain white pasta dough, or even use store-bought lasagne sheets. This makes a large lasagne.

INGREDIENTS
10 - 12 SERVINGS
9" X 13" EXTRA-DEEP LASAGNE PAN

The pasta: Make 2 lbs. pasta dough blended with 12 oz. fresh or frozen spinach.

The ragù: See the recipe on the previous page or use the *Sugu Pomodoro Classico* recipe found in the Campania section of this cookbook.

- 2 cups Parmigiano-Reggiano, grated
- Shredded mozzarella for a bubbly, crusty top

The bechamel sauce: 6 tbs. butter, 6 tbs. all-purpose flour, 4 1/2 cups whole milk, 1 egg and 1 tsp. nutmeg. Salt and pepper to taste.

DIRECTIONS

1. Make the pasta sheets. Steam the cleaned spinach and squeeze out all of the liquid using a clean kitchen towel. Puree the spinach in a food processor. You should have about 1 cup of puree. Add the puree to the basic dough recipe and follow the steps to make the pasta sheets. Cut the pasta sheets to fit the pan and have ready for assembly.
2. Make the bechamel sauce. Melt the butter in a sauce pan over medium heat. Add the flour slowly and stir until a smooth paste is formed. Slowly add the milk and bring the mixture to a simmer. Continue to stir until the sauce is very thick (about 8 to 10 minutes). Add the egg and nutmeg, and salt and pepper to taste.
3. To build up the layers of your lasagne, have your ingredients laid out and ready. Coat the lasagne pan with the olive oil.
4. Start by spreading a layer of ragù and sprinkle with some of the Parmigiano-Reggiano. Next, add a single layer of pasta sheets. Then, add a layer of the bechamel followed by another single layer of pasta sheets. Top that with more ragù and Parmigiano-Reggiano. Carry on alternating the ragù, pasta sheets and bechamel until you get to the top of the dish, leaving room for a final layer of the ragù, mozzarella and Parmigiano-Reggiano cheese.
5. Bake at 375˚F covered with tin foil for 30 minutes. Remove the foil and bake for another 20 to 30 minutes, or until the sauce is bubbling. Finish with a quick broil to make the top golden and crispy. Allow the lasagne to set for 10 minutes before serving.

TORTELLINI EN BRODO

Legend has it the creation of tortellini was inspired by the navel of Venus. The classic Bolognese pasta is served in a rich broth or *brodo*. It's simple and perfect, but allow a few days to put it together.

INGREDIENTS
4 - 6 SERVINGS

Pasta dough. Make 1 lb. of pasta dough.

For the tortellini filling:

- 1/2 lb. each, veal loin and pork loin
- 1 tsp. each salt, pepper, rosemary and garlic
- 4 tbs. unsalted butter and a glug of olive oil
- 4 oz. prosciutto and 4 oz. mortadella, chopped finely
- 1/2 cup Parmigiano-Reggiano, grated
- 1 egg, beaten and 1/4 tsp. grated nutmeg

For the brodo (broth)

- 1 frying chicken, cut into pieces, and 5 chicken wings to add more flavor and thickness
- 1/2 lb. each: veal bones and beef bones with marrow
- 1 large carrot, 1 medium onion, 1 stalk celery, halved
- 1 bay leaf, 4 black peppercorns, 1 tsp. salt
- 8 cups chicken stock

DIRECTIONS

1 Make the tortellini filling. Create a dry rub for the veal and pork loins with the salt, pepper, rosemary and garlic. Rub onto the meat, wrap and marinate in the refrigerator for 2 days.

2 Melt 2 tbs. butter with a splash of the oil and cook the meat on low heat until fully cooked. Cool and shred. Add the shredded meat to a food processor with the prosciutto and mortadella and pulse until finely chopped, but not puréed. Mix in the egg, cheese and nutmeg. Refrigerate overnight.

3 Make the brodo. Sauté the chicken in 2 tbs. butter and a splash of olive oil until browned. Add the soup bones, chicken stock, vegetables, bay leaf, peppercorns and salt. Bring to a boil.

4 Reduce the heat and skim off any foam that has risen to the surface. Simmer gently for at least 4 hours. Remove the chicken and bones from the broth. Pour the broth through a fine strainer to catch any last pieces of meat or bone. Chill the broth and skim the fat solids.

5 Fill and form the tortellini. See the directions to the right.

6 Bring the broth to a boil in a large pot over medium heat. Gently drop the tortellini into the pot. Cook until they rise to the surface and are tender but still firm to the bite, about 2 to 3 minutes. Serve immediately with a sprinkle of grated Parmigiano-Reggiano and parsley.

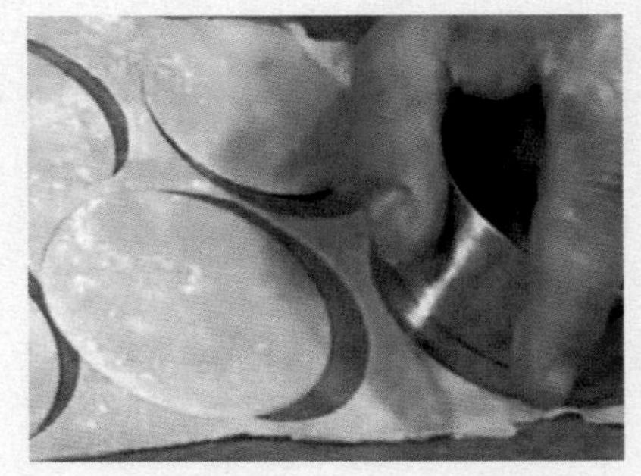

Roll the dough to the finest setting on your pasta machine. It should be almost translucent. Cut 3" rounds.

Fill a pastry bag with the filling and dot it on to the dough rounds. Wet the dough with the pastry brush to create a glue.

Fold the rounds in half and press together to seal tightly around the filling, making sure you squeeze out all of the air. Wet the dough again on the ends of the semi-circle. Press the ends together to form the tortellini.

RAVIOLI DI PERE CON BALSAMICO

Fresh pear and good balsamic add a contrasting sweetness to the savory pecorino and marscapone filling of these delicate ravioli. Come to Modena with me to get the real stuff!

INGREDIENTS
4 - 6 SERVINGS

- 1 lb. pasta dough

For the filling:

- 1/2 cup pecorino cheese, grated, plus more for serving
- 8 oz. container of mascarpone cheese
- 2 bartlett pears, RIPE BUT FIRM, peeled, cored, and shredded on the largest holes of a grater. Then put the shredded pears into a strainer. Gently press out any excess liquid.
- 1/4 tsp. each of nutmeg and sugar

For the sauce:

- 12 tbs. unsalted butter
- Balsamico di Modena to drizzle

DIRECTIONS

1. Make the dough and roll out into sheets.
2. Make the filling. Stir the pecorino, mascarpone and pears in a bowl. Chill until ready to use.
3. **See the Gnudi pasta recipe on how to form and fill the ravioli.**
4. Bring a large pot of salted water to a boil. Cook ravioli until *al dente*, 3 to 4 minutes. Meanwhile, melt butter in a 12" skillet over medium-high heat. Using a slotted spoon, transfer ravioli to skillet, along with 1 cup cooking water, salt, and pepper. Toss to combine.
5. Transfer ravioli to a serving platter and drizzle with balsamic. Sprinkle pecorino and pepper to taste. Serve immediately.

PANNA COTTA

This chilled custard is served with chocolate sauce, caramel or berries. I like it best with berries, which brings out its light and fresh taste. It's a popular, colorful dessert served all over Italy.

INGREDIENTS
8 SERVINGS

For the custard:

- 1 tbs. unflavored gelatin
- 2 tbs. cold water
- 2 cups heavy cream
- 1 cup half and half
- 1/3 cup sugar
- 1 vanilla bean, split lengthwise, seeds scooped out

For the coulis:

- 1/2 cup sugar
- 3 tbs. orange juice
- 12 oz. frozen raspberries or blackberries, thawed
- 1 tbs. Chambord Framboise or Grand Marnier (optional)
- Garnish: fresh berries and mint

DIRECTIONS

1. Make the custard. In a small saucepan sprinkle gelatin over the water and let it stand about 1 minute to soften. Mix together and heat until gelatin is dissolved. Remove the pan from the heat.
2. In a large saucepan bring the cream, half and half, vanilla bean seeds and sugar just to a boil over a moderately high heat, stirring. Remove this pan from heat and stir in the gelatin mixture. Divide among 8 dessert cups and cool to room temperature. When it is cooled, cover and chill at least 4 hours or overnight.
3. Make the coulis. Combing the sugar and orange juice. Heat on low until the sugar crystals are dissolved.
4. Combine this hot syrup with the berries and blend until the mixture is smooth and puréed. Strain the seeds. Add the liqueur, if using, and chill.
5. Garnish the custard with the coulis, assorted fresh berries and sprigs of fresh mint.

FAGIOLI ALLA TOSCANA

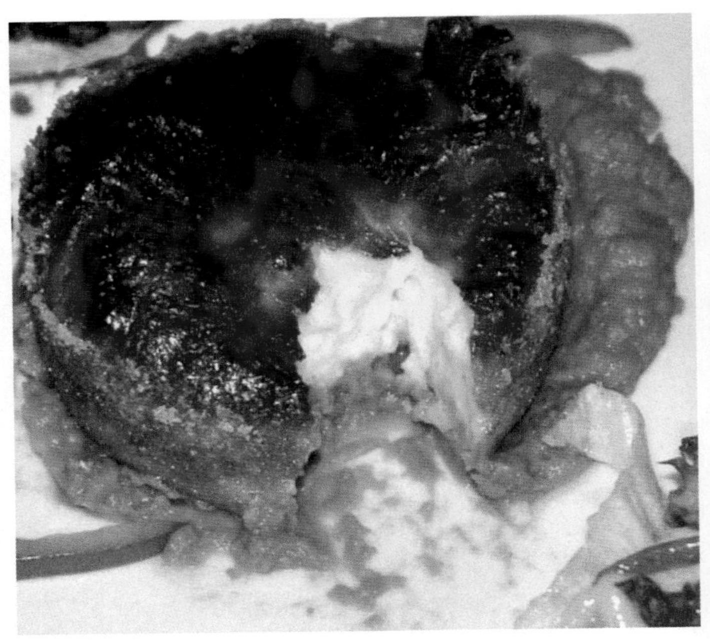

BUDINO AL FORMAGGIO

CROSTINI FEGATINI

Toscano

TUSCAN FOOD IS BASED ON THE ITALIAN IDEA OF CUCINA POVERA OR "POOR COOKING." HEARTY WITH SIMPLE INGREDIENTS, TUSCAN DISHES ARE BASED UPON WHAT IS FRESH AT THE MARKET AND DRESSED WITH SOME OF THE FINEST OLIVE OIL IN ITALY.

PAIR THESE WINES WITH THE RECIPES FROM THE REGION: CHIANTI, BRUNELLO DI MONTALCINO, VINO NOBILE DI MONTEPULCIANO AND SUPER TUSCANS.

RIBOLLITA

VITELLO CON PORCINI

GNUDI AL FORNO

RAVIOLI DI GNUDI

FAGIOLI ALLA TOSCANA

Humble white beans are infused with the flavors of garlic, fresh herbs and spices, then topped off by a drizzle of the high-quality extra virgin olive oil.

INGREDIENTS

6 - 8 SERVINGS

- 3 cups dried cannellini or white beans, rinsed, picked over, soaked and cook. Canned cannellini beans work well in a pinch, but drain and rinse them well.
- 2 tbs. olive oil
- 6-8 cloves garlic, peeled and smashed
- 2 bay leaves
- 10-12 large fresh sage leaves
- 2 large sprigs fresh thyme
- 2 large sprigs fresh rosemary
- 20 whole black peppercorns
- Salt and pepper to taste
- 2 tbs. extra virgin olive oil
- Pecorino-Romano

DIRECTIONS

- Rinse and clean the beans well. Place in a large bowl and cover with cold water. Cover and set aside for at least 8 hours or overnight.
- Drain and rinse the beans again and transfer them to a large, heavy pot. Cover with 2"-3" inches of cold water and add the olive oil, garlic, bay leaves, fresh herbs and black peppercorns. Bring to a low boil for 1 minute over medium-high heat, then reduce heat to medium-low. Remove and discard any foam that collects on the surface while boiling.
- Cover and simmer, stirring occasionally, for 1 to 1 1/2 hours or until beans are tender. Remove from heat and let beans cool in the pot with the cooking liquid for 15-20 minutes.
- Carefully drain the beans. Remove and discard the herbs.
- Season with salt and black pepper. Drizzle with high-quality olive oil and sprinkle with Pecorino-Romano.

BUDINO AL FORMAGGIO

This is always a guest favorite when we are eating at one of my "go to" restaurants in Florence. It is a specialty of the chef, so not found anywhere else in Italy, but I have included his recipe in the cookbook because it is just so yummy.

INGREDIENTS

8 SERVINGS

For the bechamel:

- 3/4 cup bechamel sauce made with 2 tbs. unsalted butter, 2 tbs. flour, 1 cup of whole milk (heated), a pinch of nutmeg, salt and pepper

For the flan:

- 1 cup of assorted cheeses, shredded and mixed: Gruyure, Emmental, Parmigiano-Reggiano and fresh Pecorino Romano
- 2 eggs, beaten
- 1/2 cup unseasoned breadcrumbs

For the pea sauce:

- 1 clove garlic, chopped fine, and 2 tbs. olive oil
- 1 cup fresh peas

DIRECTIONS

1. Bechamel Sauce: The foolproof way to attain a perfectly smooth sauce is to have the milk hot when added to the butter and flour. Melt the butter in a saucepan over low to medium heat. Using a whisk, stir in the flour and mix well. Continuing stirring over low heat for 2 minutes. Begin adding the milk in small quantities — about 2 tbs. at a time — fully incorporating the liquid before adding more. After you have added half the milk, pour in the rest and give the mixture a good whisking. Continue to heat the sauce on low to medium heat until the mixture thickens. Whisk in the nutmeg, salt and pepper and lower the heat.
2. Fold in the grated cheeses until melted. Remove from the heat and fold in the beaten eggs.
3. Generously butter a flan mould or large muffin tin and sprinkle it with the bread crumbs. Fill halfway with the cheese mixture. Bake at 350˚F for about 15 minutes and then turn on the broiler to brown the top.
4. The Pea Sauce: Sauté the garlic in the olive oil, add the peas and cook for about 10 minutes until soft. Blend into a smooth sauce.
5. Place a few spoonfuls of the pea sauce on a small plate and top with the flan. Serve immediately.

CROSTINI FEGATINI

While staying at a friend's country house outside of Arezzo, I had the opportunity to learn this recipe from a pro. I happened upon the local butcher making fegatini and he asked me if I would like to help. Of course I did! Here's our recipe. (The secret is the Vin Santo).

INGREDIENTS
6 - 8 SERVINGS

- 1 tbs. olive oil and 2 tbs. butter
- 12 chicken livers, roughly chopped
- 4 oz. pancetta, chopped
- 1/2 red onion chopped finely
- 1 shallot, chopped finely
- A handful of chopped parsley
- 3 dried porcini mushrooms, soaked in warm water and finely chopped
- 2 fresh sage leaves
- 1 tbs. salted capers
- 5 tbs. Vin Santo or other sweet dessert wine such as sweet Marsala or Madiera
- 1 tbs. salted butter
- Salt and pepper to taste

DIRECTIONS

1. Wash the salted capers with cold water and then leave them 15 minutes in a bowl with cold water. Pat dry and set aside.
2. In a pan, sauté the shallot, onion and parsley gently in the the butter and a splash of olive oil. When the vegetables are soft, add the chopped pancetta and the chicken livers to the pan and sauté until browned, about 3 minutes.
3. Remove the mixture from the pan and place on a chopping board together with the softened porcini mushrooms and chop everything into a rustic paste.
4. Return the chopped mixture to the pan and add the capers, sage leaves and Vin Santo. Mix well and simmer on low temperature about 10 minutes.
5. Remove from the heat and discard the sage leaves. With an immersion hand blender, blend in the butter and make a smooth, soft paste. Season to taste and chill overnight.
6. Bring the pate to room tempurature before serving on grilled Italian bread slices.

VITELLO CON PORCINI

Veal medallions are served in a variety of ways in Tuscany: with lemon sauce, with capers, with wine sauce and of course, with porcini mushrooms. Mixing dried porcinis with fresh portabellos gives you a rich, mushroom taste.

INGREDIENTS
4 - 6 SERVINGS

- 2 lbs. veal scallopine
- 3/4 oz. dried porcini and 8 baby portabello mushrooms
- 1 cup chicken stock
- Flour seasoned with salt and pepper
- 2 tbs. olive oil
- 4 tbs. unsalted butter
- 2 shallots minced
- 2 cloves garlic minced
- 1/2 cup Marsala or Madeira wine
- 3/4 cup heavy cream
- Juice of 1/2 fresh lemon plus the zest

DIRECTIONS

1. In a saucepan, combine the dried porcinis with the chicken stock and bring to a boil. Reduce the heat to low and cook 2 minutes. Remove the pan from the heat and let steep for 30 minutes. Remove the porcinis from the liquid, chop finely and set aside. Chop the portabellos to the same size.
2. Lay the veal slices between 2 pieces of parchment paper and pound them with a meat mallet or small pot until they are very thin.
3. Season the veal with salt and pepper; dredge in the seasoned flour. In a skillet over medium high heat, add 1 tablespoon of oil and 2 tablespoons of butter. Add in the veal and cook quickly until golden brown and crispy. Set veal aside on a warm plate and repeat until the veal is cooked, wiping the pan in between batches if necessary.
4. After the last batch, don't wipe the skillet. Add the mushrooms, shallots and garlic. De-glaze the pan with the Madeira. When the wine has reduced by about half, add in the reserved porcini broth and cook a few minutes. Add in the heavy cream, and the juice of the lemon. Season with salt and pepper to taste and add the veal back into the cream sauce to heat through. Serve Immediately with a little zest of lemon on top.

GNUDI AL FORNO

RAVIOLI DI GNUDI

Gnudi means naked or undressed. These yummy dumplings are made with ricotta cheese and spinach, poached and served with fresh cherry tomatoes. They are great when you are watching your carbs, but still need an Italian food fix. If you're going for the carbs, this is also the perfect filling for ravioli.

INGREDIENTS
4 - 6 SERVINGS

For the gnudi:

- 1 lb. fresh or chopped frozen spinach
- 2 cloves of garlic, peeled and lightly crushed
- 2 tbs. olive oil
- 1 lb. ricotta cheese, well drained
- 1/2 cup grated Parmigiano-Reggiano cheese
- 1 egg
- 1 tbs. dried oregano and a pinch of nutmeg
- Unbleached white flour

For the gnudi sauce: A carton of fresh cherry tomatoes, handful of fresh sage and Parmigiano-Reggiano

DIRECTIONS

1. Trim the stems off the fresh spinach, rinse well to remove any grit. Drop the leaves into boiling, salted water and remove just as soon as they have wilted. Drain, squeeze them *very* dry and chop finely. If you are using frozen chopped spinach, thaw and squeeze out all of the water, using a cotton tea towel.
2. Sauté the garlic cloves in olive oil. When they are lightly browned, remove them and sauté the spinach leaves. Cool.
3. Mix together the spinach, ricotta, Parmigiano-Reggiano, eggs and nutmeg. Season to taste. Add a heaping spoonful of flour and mix again. The mixture should be quite moist but hold together. If not, add another spoonful or two of flour.
4. With well-floured hands, form the dumpling balls. Roll each in flour to cover and set them out on a well-floured baking sheet.
5. Poach the dumplings in simmering (not boiling) salted water by gently immersing them with a large slotted spoon. When they rise to the top, gently pull them out. You are ready to assemble.
6. In a large pan, quickly sauté the fresh cherry tomatoes in olive oil. Add the gnudi and garnish with sage and cheese.

For the ravioli: Make 1 lb. of pasta dough and follow the directions to the right to make the pasta pillows. Fill with the gnudi mixture. Melt 8 oz. butter in a large pan. Add a handful of fresh sage. Place the ravioli in boiling salted water and cook until they rise to the top. Drain and transfer to the butter/sage sauce and garnish with Parmigiano-Reggiano.

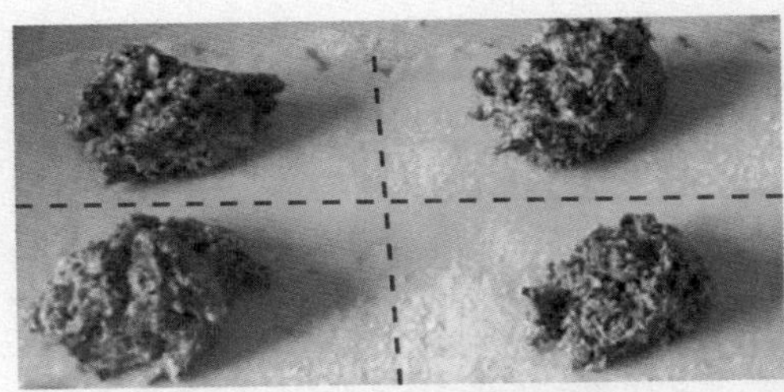

To form the ravioli pillows. Use your square or round ravioli cutter to measure out the squares. Indent the dough so you know where to place the filling, making sure there is enough dough to seal around the filling. Wet the dough with the pastry brush to create a glue.

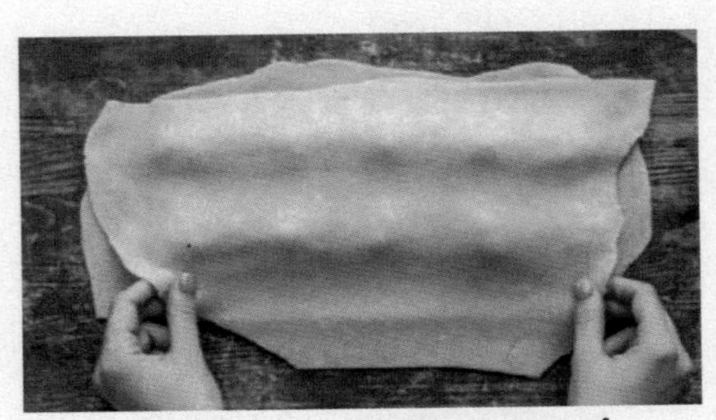

Place another pasta sheet on top of the filling. Press the 2 sheets together to seal, using your fingers gently to mould the dough tightly around the filling while pressing out all of the air.

Cut out the raviolis. Seal the sheets together again with your fingers or a fork to make sure the pasta pillows are completely sealed. If there is air in the pillow, it will explode in the boiling water.

Start with a basic minestrone.

Dry and chop the bread.

In a deep baking dish, layer the minestrone with the dried bread. Drizzle generously with olive oil and Parmigiano-Reggiano and bake until bubbling.

RIBOLLITA

Ribollita means re-boiled. This classic recipe is an industrious way to use yesterday's minestrone soup and leftover bread. I discovered this dish early in my tour directing days at a lovely family-run restaurant in Cortona. Paula ran the show from a tiny kitchen located on a back street, far from the main square. After a long day enjoying the Tuscan countryside, steaming bowls of Ribollita are the perfect primo. Here is her recipe.

INGREDIENTS
4 - 6 SERVINGS

For the minestrone:

- 4 tbs. olive oil
- 4 oz. pancetta, chopped
- Soffritto: 1 red onion, 4 carrots, 3 stalks celery, 1 leek (white part only) and 1 garlic clove, all finely chopped
- 1/2 tsp. each dried chili flakes, rosemary and oregano and 1 bay leaf
- 16-oz. can crushed tomatoes
- 2 cups cabbage, 1 cup spinach, shredded
- 4 zucchini, sliced into 1/2" rounds
- 2 cups canned white cannellini beans, rinsed well and drained
- 8 cups chicken stock
- 1 Parmigiano-Reggiano rind

For the ribollita:

- 1 loaf dried, day-old Italian bread, chopped
- Garnish: Parmigiano-Reggiano, fresh parsley and olive oil

DIRECTIONS

1. Make the minestrone. In a large, heavy pot, sauté the pancetta for a minute in the oil and add the chopped onion, carrot, celery, leek and garlic, stirring often until the onion has turned translucent.
2. Add the tomatoes, cabbage, spinach, zucchini, chili peppers, rosemary, oregano, bay leaf, beans, chicken stock and the Parmigiano-Reggiano rind.
3. Bring to a very slow simmer and cook, uncovered, for about 2 hours.
4. Discard the rind. The soup should not be too soupy, but rather the consistency of a stew. Season to taste.
5. Cover, cool and refrigerate overnight.
6. Make the ribollita. Re-heat the soup and layer it in a deep baking dish with the chopped dry bread. Drizzle with a generous amount of olive oil and Parmigiano-Reggiano and bake until bubbling.
7. Garnish with more olive oil, Parmigiano-Reggiano cheese and fresh parsley.

OLIVE ALL'ASCOLANA

Umbria and Le Marche

THESE REGIONS REMAIN BLISSFULLY UNSCATHED BY THE EFFECTS OF MASS TOURISM. THEIR DISHES ARE INSPIRED BY MOUNTAINS, FERTILE VALLEYS AND THE WARM ADRIATIC SEA. THE RESTAURANTS DON'T ALWAYS CATER TO FOREIGNERS, SO I HAVE HAD TO CHARM MYSELF INTO THEIR KITCHENS FOR A PEAK AT THE RECIPES.

PAIR THESE WINES WITH THE RECIPES FROM THE REGION: ROSSO CORNERO, MONTEFALCO, TREBBIANO AND SANGIOVESE.

BRODETTO ALL'ANCONETANA

BACI MOUSSE AL CIOCCOLATO

OLIVE ALL'ASCOLANA

These stuffed olives are a popular street food, served in paper cones, or as part of an *antipasti frito misto*. Traditionally they are made with the large, green Ascolana Tenera variety of olive, but you can use any large, mild, brine-cured pitted green olive.

INGREDIENTS

- 1 lb. of pitted green olives, drained and rinsed

For the olive stuffing:

- 3 tbs. olive oil
- 1/2 onion, 1 carrot, 1 stalk celery, very finely diced
- 1/2 cup of dry white wine
- 1/2 lb. ground veal
- 1/2 lb. of ground pork
- 2 egg yolks, slightly beaten
- 1 cup Parmigiano-Reggiano
- Freshly grated zest of 1 lemon
- Pinch of nutmeg, black pepper

For the olive coating:

- 1 1/2 cups all-purpose flour
- 2 eggs, slightly beaten
- 2 1/2 cups bread crumbs
- 2-3 cups frying oil, peanut or other high-smoke point oil

DIRECTIONS

1. In a large skillet, heat the olive oil. Add the diced onion, carrot and celery and sauté until onion is translucent and vegetables are softened, 6 to 8 minutes.
2. Add the white wine and cook for 1 minute. Add the diced meats and salt continue to cook, stirring with a wooden spoon until meat is cooked, about 10 to 15 minutes.
3. Pulse the mixture in A food processor, then transfer to a large mixing bowl. Add the egg yolks, Parmigiano-Reggiano, lemon zest, nutmeg, and pepper. Stir to combine all ingredients well.
4. Stuffing the olives. Gently butterfly the olives and spread out. Stuff each olive with the meat puree, reforming it to its olive shape, pressing slightly to make sure it holds all together. Don't overstuff, or they won't hold together.
5. Roll each olive in the flour, dip into the beaten egg, and then roll in the breadcrumbs. Heat the frying oil in a large heavy-bottomed pot until hot, but not smoking, and fry the breaded olives in batches. Do not try to fry too many olives at a time, or it will lower the temperature of the cooking oil and they will not brown evenly or cook properly.
6. Serve immediately with lemon wedges.

Gently butterfly the olives and spread out.

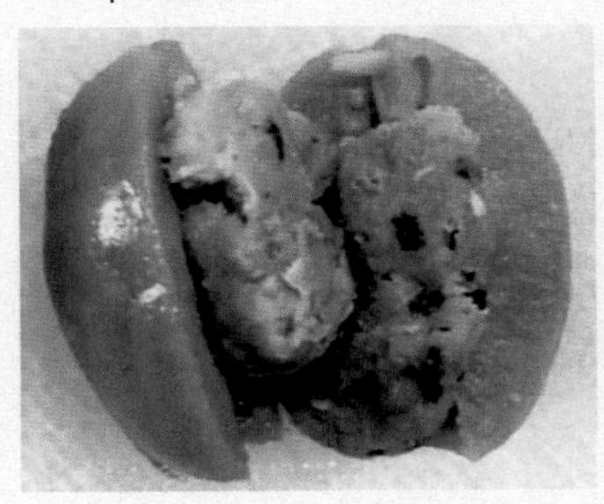

Stuff each olive with the meat puree, reforming it to its olive shape, pressing slightly to make sure it holds all together. Don't overstuff, or they won't hold together.

Roll each in flour and dip in the beaten egg.

Roll each in the breadcrumbs and fry.

BRODETTO ALL'ANCONETANA

In the Tuscan town of Livorno, they call it *cacciucco*, in France, *bouillabaisse*, in Portugal *cataplana*, in Spain *zuppa peche*, in Italy *cioppino*. But, in Le Marche, the regional name is *brodetto*. The Adriatic Sea is bursting with an abundance fish and seaside restaurants serving this local dish. Traditionally, 13 different varieties of fish are used to make *brodetto*, but you can use whatever you have available at your local fish market.

INGREDIENTS
8 SERVINGS

- 4 tbs. extra virgin olive oil
- 1 onion, chopped
- 2 garlic cloves, chopped
- 1/4 tsp. chili flakes
- 1/2 fresh fennel, chopped
- 1/2 cup white or red wine vinegar
- 28 oz. canned tomatoes, strained and coarsely chopped
- 2 cups fish or clam stock
- 1/2 tsp. fennel seeds, 1/2 tsp. coriander seeds
- 2 lbs. mixed fish such as swordfish, red snapper, squid, large prawns, clams, mussels, scallops, crabs or lobster
- Salt and pepper to taste
- Garnish: fresh Italian parsley and lemon wedges
- Crusty Italian bread

DIRECTIONS

1. Put the oil in a very large pan, add the onion, fennel, chili flakes and garlic. Fry over medium heat for 10 minutes or until soft. Gradually add the vinegar to de-glaze the pan, stirring constantly, until the sharp vinegar smell has disappeared.
2. Add the strained tomatoes, fennel and coriander seeds, stir and simmer for 10 minutes. Add the stock and bring to a simmer. Gradually add the fish, one at a time. Cooking times may vary and you'll need to watch this carefully so as not to overcook. Start with the lobster and clams and cook for 5 minutes, covered. Add mussels and cook for 3 minutes, covered. Add the chunks of cod, red snapper and other fleshy fish, cook until they are white, covered. Add scallops and cook for five minutes, covered. Just before serving, add the shrimp. As soon as the pink emerges, remove them from the heat.
3. Salt and pepper to taste, garnish with chopped fresh parsley and lemon wedges. Serve with crusty bread.

BACI MOUSSE AL CIOCCOLATO

My very favorite candy is made into a luscious mousse at one of my favorite restaurants in Perugia.

INGREDIENTS
4 - 6 SERVINGS

- 3 eggs, yolks and whites separated
- 3 tbs. water
- 1/4 cup white sugar, divided
- 5 Baci Perugina chocolates, chopped
- 3/4 cup whipping cream

DIRECTIONS

1. In a double boiler, bring water to a boil, then reduce heat to a gentle simmer.
2. In the top pot, combine 3 egg yolks, 3 tbs. sugar and 3 tbs. water. Beat with a whisk until thickened, increased in volume and lightened in color, about 4 min. Keep the water simmering.
3. Remove the bowl from heat. Add the chocolate until it is completely melted and smooth. If chocolate lumps remain, place bowl back over the simmering water for a few seconds, stirring all the while, until chocolate is smooth. Reserve.
4. In separate bowl, beat egg whites with hand mixer, until soft peaks form.
5. Fold half the beaten egg whites into chocolate base, taking care not to stir too much. Fold in remaining beaten egg whites, stirring gently until just incorporated.
6. Wash and dry hand mixer blades. In separate bowl, beat whipping cream and remaining 1 tbs. sugar with hand mixer until thickened, about 5 min.
7. Fold cream into chocolate mousse base, stirring gently until just combined.
8. Cover and refrigerate 12 hours or longer. Serve with a Baci on the side.

CACIO E PEPE

SPAGHETTI ALLA CARBONARA

WHEN YOU THINK OF PASTA FROM LAZIO, YOU THINK OF TWO INGREDIENTS: PECORINO ROMANO AND GUANCIALE. PECORINO ROMANO IS A SALTY, RICH, SHEEP CHEESE. GUANCIALE IS A RICH, SAVORY HOG JOWLS CURED WITH SALT, PEPPER AND HERBS. YOU CAN FIND BOTH AT GOOD ITALIAN STORES.

PAIR THESE WINES WITH THE RECIPES FROM THE REGION: MELVASIA, TREBBIANO AND PINOT GRIGIO.

BUCATINI ALL'AMATRICIANA

SALTIMBOCCA ALLA ROMANA

GIOVEDÌ DI GNOCCHI

TIRAMISU

CACIO E PEPE

Cacio e pepe is one of the most traditional dishes in Rome. The name *cacio e pepe* comes from the two ingredients of the dish: *cacio*, or Pecorino Romano D.O.P, and *pepe*, black pepper. This is a dish you make quickly and serve immediately. Pecorino Romano, when mixed with a little bit of the hot pasta water, develops into a smooth cream. The starchy cooking water is the key to a successful cheese sauce. The pecorino you get in the U.S. is not true sheep's cheese, and is very salty. Make the effort to order imported Pecorino Romano D.O.P for these recipes.

INGREDIENTS
4 - 6 SERVINGS

- 1 lb. dried spaghetti, bucatini or I also like a long fusilli which adds a fun twirl to the pasta
- 1 3/4 cup imported Pecorino Romano D.O.P., very finely grated to almost a powder, leave out to room temperature
- 6 tsp. black peppercorns, crushed
- 2 tsp. salt for the water

DIRECTIONS

1. This pasta requires a low water-to-pasta ratio to maximize the starch, so instead of our usual 4 quart (16 cups) ratio, use only 3 quarts (12 cups) of water per pound of pasta. When it is at a rolling boil, add the salt and pasta and cook to very *al dente*.
2. While the pasta is almost finished cooking, crush your peppercorns and toss them into a dry pan. Turn the heat on and let them roast for about a minute. Pour a little of the pasta cooking water onto the pepper: the water will sizzle, which is exactly what you want it to do. Then add another cup of the pasta water. Take it off of the burner and let sit for 3 minutes, stirring a bit to help cool.
3. Pour the cheese, a little at a time, into the pepper/water mixture. Mix well with a whisk until the cheese becomes a smooth cream. Keep whisking until it gets creamy. Have patience, this dish will take a few times to perfect.
4. Pull the pasta from the water with pasta tongs and add to the pan, tossing until evenly coated. You can add additional pasta water if needed to loosen the pasta or cook it down a bit if you want it to thicken. Garnish with a bit more cracked pepper and a sprinkle of cheese.
5. Serve immediately.

Pecorino Romano D.O.P. is made with sheep's milk and can be made only in certain parts of Italy. American cheesemakers make Romano cheese with cow's milk. There is a difference in taste, so it's worth getting the imported. D.O.P. indicates a protected designation of origin and an important step to assuring the heritage and quality of the product. You can buy Pecorino Romano D.O.P. at fine Italian stores or online.

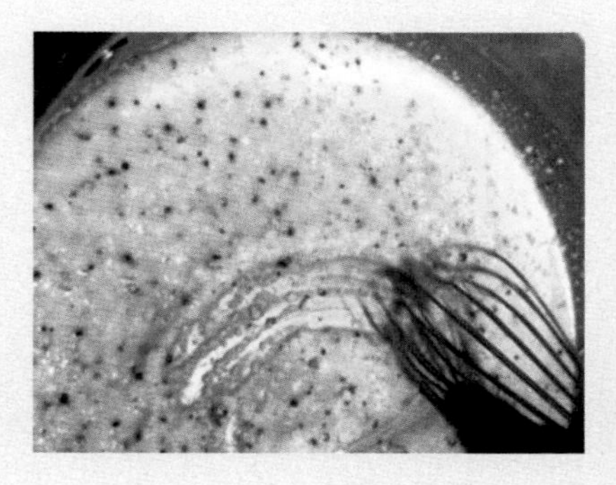

Guanciale (gwaan - *chaa* - lay) comes from the jowl of the pig and is typically cured with salt, pepper, sage, rosemary and garlic. It is very fatty and less meaty than bacon or pancetta. I highly recommend using the guanciale for these authentic recipes, but if you can't find it, use pancetta, which is pork belly cured in salt and pepper.

SPAGHETTI ALLA CARBONARA

The key to preparing real carbonara is timing and using good ingredients to create a smooth creamy sauce. When making carbonara, the raw egg mixture is added to the hot pasta, which pasteurizes the eggs without cooking them fully and turning them into scrambled eggs.

INGREDIENTS
4 - 6 SERVINGS

- 1 lb. dried spaghetti
- 2 tbs. olive oil
- 1 lb. guanciale, diced in short strips. Pancetta is a good substitute if you can't get the guanciale.
- 3 eggs
- 10 tbs. Pecorino Romano D.O.P., grated
- Salt and pepper to taste
- A dash of dried oregano

DIRECTIONS

1. Bring a large pot of salted water to a boil.
2. Cook the spaghetti in the boiling water, stirring occasionally until *al dente*.
3. While the pasta is cooking, heat olive oil in a large skillet over medium heat; add the guanciale, turning occasionally, until lightly browned and crispy, 5 to 10 minutes. Keep warm.
4. Whisk the eggs, half of the Pecorino Romano D.O.P. cheese, the oregano and some black pepper in a bowl until smooth and creamy.
5. When the spaghetti is *al dente*, use spaghetti tongs to transfer it with a bit of the pasta water into the large pan with the warm guanciale. Mix. Then, pour the egg mixture over pasta, stirring quickly, until creamy and slightly cooled.
6. Top with remaining Pecorino Romano D.O.P. cheese and more black pepper. Salt to taste. You could also add a pat of butter for even more creaminess.
7. Serve immediately.

BUCATINI ALL'AMATRICIANA

Amatriciana comes from the town of Amatrice, near Rome, and has the guanciale we find in our other Lazio recipes. In this recipe, however, it is simmered in a sauce made with fresh tomatoes.

INGREDIENTS
4 - 6 SERVINGS

- 1 lb. dried spaghetti or bucatini
- 1 tbs. extra-virgin olive oil
- 6 oz. guanciale, cut into slices about 1/8 inch thick and then into 3/4- by 1/4-inch strips
- 1, 28-ounce can whole peeled tomatoes, drained and crushed by hand
- Salt and pepper
- 1/2 cup grated Pecorino Romano D.O.P. cheese, plus more for serving

DIRECTIONS

1. In a large skillet, heat the olive oil over medium-high heat. Add the guanciale strips, stirring, until lightly browned and crispy, about 5 minutes.
2. Add the tomatoes and bring to a simmer. Season with salt and pepper.
3. Meanwhile, boil the pasta in salted water until just shy of *al dente*, about 1 minute less than package recommends. Transfer the pasta to sauce along with about a 1/4 cup of the pasta cooking water. Cook over high heat, stirring and tossing rapidly, until the pasta is *al dente* and the sauce has thickened and coated the pasta.
4. Remove from the heat, add cheese, and stir rapidly to incorporate it into the sauce. Season to taste with salt and pepper.
5. Serve immediately, garnished with more Pecorino Romano D.O.P. and some red pepper flakes as a garnish.

SALTIMBOCCA ALLA ROMANA

Saltimbocca means "to jump into the mouth" in Italian. Pounded veal cutlets, prosciutto, and sage are cooked in white wine and butter. Perfect and simple, served over a bed of pasta or sautéed spinach.

INGREDIENTS
8 SERVINGS

- 16 slices of veal cutlets
- 16 slices of prosciutto
- Fresh sage leaves
- Flour for dredging
- 4 tbs. unsalted butter and 1/4 cup olive oil
- 1/2 cup dry white wine
- Salt and pepper to taste

DIRECTIONS

1. Lay the veal cutlets between two pieces of parchment paper and pound them with a meat mallet or small pot until they are very thin.
2. Place one slice of prosciutto on each slice of meat and cover with 2 sage leaves on top. Secure with a toothpick.
3. Season the veal with salt and pepper; dredge in the seasoned flour. In a skillet over medium high heat, add the oil and 2 tablespoons of butter. Cook the cutlets until golden brown and crispy. Do not overcrowd the pan.
4. To make the sauce, de-glaze the pan with the white wine, add 2 tbs. butter to the pan, stir to combine.
5. Place the slices of meat on a plate, sage side up. Top with the sauce and serve immediately.

GIOVEDÌ DI GNOCCHI GNOCCHI ON THURSDAY

Giovedì DI gnocchi is an old Catholic tradition, and many Roman restaurants still feature this potato gnocchi dish on Thursdays. Gnocchi (*nyow*-kee) literally means 'lump,' and is traditionally served with a salsa pomodoro classico or ragú.

INGREDIENTS
4 - 6 SERVINGS

- 4 large russet potatoes, skins on
- 2 eggs
- 1 to 2 cups of flour
- 1 tsp. salt
- Gnocchi board
- Pomodoro Classico or Ragú

DIRECTIONS

1. In a large pot, boil the whole potatoes until tender. Let them cool and gently remove the skin.
2. Mash the potatoes and mix in the egg and salt.
3. Put 1 cup of the flour on your workspace. With your fingers, work in the mashed potatoes, adding more flour as you go to create a soft dough.
4. Cut the dough into 4 sections and with the palm of your hands, gently roll the sections into 3/4" tubes. Cut the tubes into 3/4" squares. Dust the gnocchi with flour to prevent them from sticking.
5. Place each square of dough onto the gnocchi board and press slightly to imprint it. Then, roll it along the ridges with a gentle pressure to imprint the entire circumference. The ridges add a texture that holds more sauce.
6. Let the gnocchi rest about 20 minutes and then boil them in a large pot of salted water until they rise to the top. Pull them out with a little of the pasta water and add them to the sauce. Serve immediately so they don't get gummy.

TIRAMISU

Tiramisu means pick me up because of the caffeine in the recipe's espresso and chocolate. This classic dessert is a velvety mélange of Savoiardi ladyfingers dipped in espresso, layered with delicately sweetened mascarpone cheese and topped with a dusting of cocoa powder.

INGREDIENTS
10 - 12 SERVINGS

- 8 large eggs, separated
- 1 lb. mascarpone
- 1 cup granulated sugar
- 1 1/2 cups brewed espresso, cooled
- 3 tbs. coffee liqueur, such as Kahlua
- 10.5 oz. package of Italian Savoiardi ladyfingers
- 1 1/2 cups heavy cream
- 1 tbs. powdered sugar
- 1 tsp. vanilla extract
- Garnish: Unsweetened cocoa powder

DIRECTIONS

1. Whisk together the egg yolks and mascarpone in a large bowl until smooth. Add the sugar and whisk until dissolved and set aside.
2. With your whisk attachment, beat the egg whites until they form soft peaks. Fold the egg whites into the mascarpone mixture and set aside.
3. Combine the brewed espresso and liqueur in a medium bowl. Dip the ladyfingers quickly into the coffee. Cookies should not absorb too much of the coffee, otherwise your tiramisu will turn out soggy. Line them in a 12" x 8" glass pan.
4. Evenly spread half the mascarpone mixture over the ladyfingers. Do another layer of dipped ladyfingers and cover with the rest of the mascarpone mixture.
5. In a large bowl, whisk together heavy cream, confectioners' sugar and vanilla until soft peaks form. Spread the whipped cream evenly over tiramisu. Chill at least 2 hours and preferably overnight before serving.
6. Garnish with the unsweetened cocoa powder.

SALSA POMODORO CLASSICO

CARCIOFI RIPIENI

Campagna

MOZZARELLA, LEMONS AND TOMATOES ARE THE BASIS FOR THE CULINARY DELIGHTS OF SOUTHERN ITALY. THE SEA BREEZE COMING INLAND IS TRAPPED IN THE STEEP MOUNTAIN VALLEYS, WHERE IT SETTLES AND CREATES A UNIQUE MICROCLIMATE THAT IS PERFECT FOR GROWING THE FRUITS THAT MAKE THE DISHES SO RICH.

PAIR THESE WINES WITH THE RECIPES FROM THE REGION: AGLIANICO, GRECO DI TUFO AND FIANO.

MELANZANE ALLA PARMIGIANA

LINGUINE VONGOLE

ITALIAN SAUCES DE-CONSTRUCTED

Here a few of the types of sauces you'll find on Italian menus. They will vary regionally.

Sauce comes from the Italian word "*salsa*," meaning "a topping" and it is usually liquid or semi-liquid. "Sauce" can mean your standard tomato sauce, or it can also refer to a pesto sauce, carbonara or any other cream-based sauce.

Marinara is a loose, chunky tomato-based sauce consisting of fresh tomatoes, garlic, herbs and onions that are quickly cooked in a pan and used immediately. Marinara was originally used to top seafood. It comes from the word "mariners" on the sea coasts of Italy.

Pomodoro is smoother and thicker than marinara because it is slow-cooked for hours, resulting in a darker red color. Pomodoro sauce is often used as pizza sauce or as a base to add seafood or vegetables for pasta.

Sugo in Italian directly translates to 'sauce.' In culinary terms, however, it derives from the word *succo* (juices) and refers to pan drippings from the cooking of meats. So "sugo" is used to describe rich, meat-based sauces.

Ragú is a thick, chunky sauce usually made by slow-cooking several kinds of meats in a tomato sauce. That said, a ragú can also made with seafood, vegetables or a combination of these.

Gravy is the word many American-Italians use when they talk about their meat sauce or ragú.

SALSA POMODORO CLASSICO

Start from here to make a basic red sauce. Keep it chunkier for a marinara, blend with an immersion blender for a pomodoro sauce, or add meat and the drippings for a sugo, ragú or gravy.

INGREDIENTS
6 - 8 SERVINGS

- 48 oz. (about 6 to 7 cups) crushed tomatoes. Use 2, 28-ounce cans San Marzano crushed tomatoes, or a combination of the canned tomatoes and roasted fresh roma tomatoes. Sliced the romas in half and slow-roast about an hour with salt, pepper and some garlic cloves. Discard cloves after roasting and crush by hand.
- 1 small can of tomato paste, caramelized
- 1/4 cup extra-virgin olive oil and 4 tbs. unsalted butter
- Soffritto: 1 medium onion, 1 carrot and 1 celery stalk, minced
- 4 cloves garlic, minced
- 1 tsp. red pepper flakes and 1 tbs. dried oregano
- 1 large stem fresh basil, *do not chop*
- 1 1/2 cups dry red wine
- 1 cup beef stock, plus more to thin out the sauce if necessary
- Parmigiano-Reggiano rind
- A pinch of sugar
- A squeeze of anchovy paste
- 2 tbs. butter
- 1/2 cup minced fresh parsley and basil for garnish

DIRECTIONS

1. Heat the olive oil and butter over medium heat in a large, heavy pot until the butter is melted. Sauté the soffritto until soft. Add the garlic and cook until softened and fragrant but not browned, about 2 minutes. Add the pepper flakes and oregano and cook until fragrant, about 1 minute. Add the crushed tomatoes and caramelized tomato paste. Mix well. Add the Parmigiano-Reggiano rind, basil stalk, pinch of sugar, red wine and beef stock.
2. Bring to a simmer for about 1/2 hour, stirring occasionally. Remove the cheese rind and basil stalk.
3. Finish the sauce just before serving with a squeeze of anchovy paste and a generous hunk of butter and then — only at the end — salt and pepper to taste.
4. Serve over pasta, Gnudi al Forno, with the Braciole al Sugo Pugliese, Melanzane alla Parmeseana or Il Timpano. You can also thin this sauce with some water and olive oil and puree it well for a great pizza sauce.

Slice fresh, ripe Roma tomatoes in half and slow-roast with salt, pepper and garlic cloves. Discard the cloves after roasting.

You can make a combination of fresh and canned tomatoes. Add the tomatoes and caramelized tomato paste to the soffritto to create the base of your salsa pomodoro.

THE BATTLE OF THE SAUCES: SUNDAY SAUCE, RAGÙ, GRAVY OR SUGO DELLA NONNA

Virtually all Italian Americans are split along the Sunday sauce/sugu/ragú vs gravy line. Our family calls it gravy. I learned this recipe by watching my great grandmother, Nonna DelBello, in the same way she taught my grandmother and my mother. Among my four siblings, the real recipe is a constant source of discussion. We're all good cooks and have developed our own variations. When my mom thought your gravy was up to par, she awarded you with a gravy pot. My sibs all have a good gravy, a solid gravy, a fine gravy. However, mine is the best. Just ask anyone.

INGREDIENTS
6 - 8 SERVINGS

- Salsa Pomodoro Classico
- 2 lbs. pork neck bones or country ribs
- 1 lb. Italian sausage links
- 1 lb. ground chuck
- 2 tbs. butter and a splash of olive oil
- 1 generous pinch of red pepper flakes
- Garnish: Parmigiano-Reggiano and chopped parsley

DIRECTIONS

1. Start with a batch of Salsa Pomodoro Classico.
2. Dust the neck bones or ribs with salt and pepper and spread them out with the Italian sausage links on to a large sheet pan lined with parchment paper. The parchment helps for easy clean up. Roast for about 1 hour at 350°F.
3. Sauté the ground chuck in 2 tbs. butter and a splash of olive oil.
4. Bring the pomodoro sauce to a simmer and add the roasted meats and browned ground chuck.
5. Bake uncovered in the oven for a few hours at 325°F. Skim the grease and stir as you go, season to taste.
6. Remove the meats from the sauce and serve in a separate bowl. Finish the sauce off just before serving with a squeeze of anchovy paste and a generous hunk of butter.
7. Pour over pasta that is cooked *al dente* and garnish with Parmigiano-Reggiano cheese and chopped parsley.

CARCIOFI RIPIENI

Italians always eat fresh foods, especially seasonal fruits and vegetables when they are at their peak and plentiful. Throughout winter and into spring, artichokes are one of my favorites. This is one of my personal specialties.

INGREDIENTS
SERVES 4

- 2 large artichokes. If the artichoke feels heavy and squeaks when squeezed, you have found a fresh artichoke. If its spongy, put it back.
- 1 tbs. extra virgin olive oil
- 1 cup Italian bread crumbs
- 4 slices prosciutto, chopped very fine
- 1/4 tsp. crushed red pepper flakes
- 1 tsp. minced garlic
- 1/4 cup grated Parmigiano-Reggiano cheese
- 1/2 cup chicken stock
- 1 fresh lemon
- A glug of olive oil
- Garnish: fresh parsley

DIRECTIONS

1. Clean the artichokes and steam in the microwave for about 5-7 minutes to soften the leaves. Let cool.
2. Mix the bread crumbs with the prosciutto, red pepper flakes, cheese and garlic. Fan out the leaves, and with a small spoon, stuff the breadcrumb mixture between each leaf starting at the outermost leaves and working your way toward the center.
3. Place the stuffed artichokes in a heavy pot. Pour water over the chokes until it reaches 3 inches; add the stock. Drizzle the chokes generously with extra virgin olive oil, a squeeze of lemon and then slip in a few small slices of the lemon rind into the leaves. Cover and bake at 350˚F for 30 minutes. Remove the lid and cook for another 45 minutes.
4. Throughout the cooking process, periodically baste the chokes. Use a turkey baster with the cooking water. The water will cook off as the leaves bake brown. Pull off a leaf to test if they are done. You should be able to easily scrape off the artichoke meat and breadcrumb mixture with your teeth. Add more water and time if the meat is not soft.
5. Let sit for 5 minutes before you serve.

With a sertated knife, cut the top off of the artichoke.

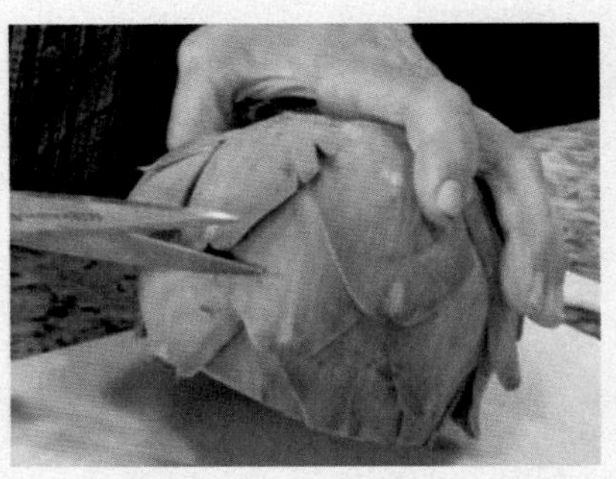

Cut the spikey tips off of each leaf.

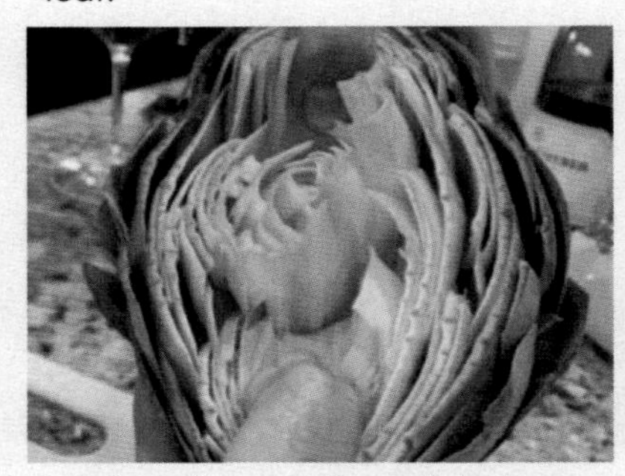

Gently pull apart the artichoke leaves and pull out the light inner leaves to expose the choke, or heart of the artichoke.

Scrape out all of the fuzzy hairs from the choke with a spoon. You are now ready to steam and stuff the artichokes.

MELANZANE ALLA PARMIGIANA

The Italian-American version of this classic dish is usually heavily breaded before frying. The traditional Italian version is not breaded. This makes for a lighter and healthier dish. Make the Salsa Pomodoro Classico ahead of time.

INGREDIENTS
SERVES 8

- Salsa Pomodoro Classico
- 3 medium eggplants
- 2 small eggs
- 1/2 cup Parmigiano-Reggiano, grated
- 9 oz. ball mozzarella (fresh, soft; preferably buffalo mozzarella)
- Parsley chopped for garnish
- Salt and pepper to taste

DIRECTIONS

1. Start with a batch of Salsa Pomodoro Classico.
2. Sweat the eggplant: Slice the eggplant into 1/2" thick long slices and line them up on paper towels. Sprinkle with coarse kosher salt. Let sit for about a 1/2 hr. You will see that the salt causes the eggplant to sweat out extra moisture. Use plenty of dry paper towels to wipe off the salt and moisture. Then salt the other side and let them sit for another 1/2 hr. Wipe and dry the slices well.
3. Fry the eggplant slices, 2 or 3 at a time, in the hot oil until well browned on each side, about 3 to 5 minutes. Drain them on paper towels.
4. Preheat the oven to 350°F. Transfer one-third of the tomato sauce to a small mixing bowl and the remainder to a large mixing bowl. Add the eggs to the larger bowl of sauce and mix well to combine.
5. Cover the bottom of a well-oiled rectangular baking dish with a thin layer of the *eggless* tomato sauce, top with a layer of eggplant.
6. Layer the egg-tomato sauce, then a generous sprinkling of grated Parmigiano-Reggiano, then pieces of mozzarella distributed evenly.
7. Repeat until the ingredients are used up. The top layer should be a layer of the *eggless* tomato sauce, topped with a final sprinkling of mozzarella and grated Parmigiano
8. Bake for 30 minutes, until the cheese on top is bubbly and golden brown. For the best results, let it sit for 1/2 an hour. Serve and enjoy!

LINGUINE A VONGOLE

Sitting at my favorite beachside restaurant in Positano is the ideal way to enjoy a day on the Amalfi Coast. Simple and perfect, linguine with clam sauce is always my go-to order. Here's the recipe from the restaurant.

INGREDIENTS
SERVES 4-6

- 1 lb. linguine
- 2 dozen littleneck clams, scrubbed well under running water
- 1 small can of cherrystone clams
- 1/2 cup olive oil
- 1/4 cup water
- 1/2 cup white wine
- 4 cloves garlic, peeled. Cut 3 cloves into thin slivers, keep one garlic clove whole.
- 1/8 tsp. red pepper flakes or to taste
- 12 cherry tomatoes, cut in half
- Salt & pepper to taste
- Garnish: Fresh parsley and a few quarters of fresh lemon

DIRECTIONS

1. Place the well-washed littleneck clams in a large size pot with the water, wine and the whole garlic clove. Cover and turn the heat up to high and cook the clams until they just open. Turn the flame off. Remove the clams from pot and reserve the cooking liquid. Discard any clams that did not open completely.
2. Cook the pasta in salted water.
3. Sauté the 3 peeled and sliced garlic cloves in the olive oil in a large sauté pan over medium until garlic just starts to brown, lower the heat and add the red pepper flakes. Cook 1 minute. Add the cherry tomatoes and cook over medium heat for 2 minutes.
4. Add both the littleneck clams, drained canned clams and the clam cooking liquid. Cover and heat thoroughly on high.
5. When the pasta is *al dente*, pull it into the pan with a bit of the pasta water. Gently mix.
6. Garnish with a drizzle of olive oil, fresh parsley and lemon wedges. And remember, NO CHEESE.

ORECCHIETTE CON CIMA DI RAPA

Puglia

THERE IS A SAYING IN PUGLIA, "THERE IS NO ONE WHO IS HAPPIER THAN US." THE FOOD OF PUGLIA IS AN EXAMPLE OF *CUCINA POVERA*, OR CUISINE OF THE POOR. THE SIMPLE DISHES ALLOW THE QUALITY OF THEIR LOCAL, SEASONAL INGREDIENTS TO TAKE CENTER STAGE. IF SOMETHING GROWS WELL AND NATURALLY, YOU DON'T NEED ANYTHING ELSE.

PAIR THESE WINES WITH THE RECIPES FROM THE REGION: PRIMATIVO, UVA DI TROIA AND BOMBINO BIANO.

BRACIOLE AL SUGO PUGLIESI

ORECCHIETTE CON CIMA DI RAPA

This simple recipe is made with only a few ingredients: pasta, broccoli rabe and herbs. *Orecchiette* [oh-reh-KEYetay] means little ears.

INGREDIENTS
SERVES 4-6

- 1 lb. dried orecchiette pasta
- 1 bunch broccoli rabe fresh, trimmed and cut into 2-inch pieces (stems and leaves)
- 4 cloves garlic minced
- 4 anchovy fillets with oil
- 1/2 tsp. red chili flakes
- 4 tbs. unsalted butter
- 3 tbs. olive oil
- Garnish: browned breadcrumbs, grated Pecorino Romano cheese and fresh lemon wedges.

DIRECTIONS

- Heat up a heavy skillet until it's smoking and add the olive oil and butter; then add minced garlic and sauté on medium heat for 1 minute. Add the anchovy fillets with some of the oil that the fillets were packed in. Sauté for 2 minutes, or until the anchovies have melted down. Add the red chili flakes. Stir and keep warm on low.
- Brown the breadcrumbs in a separate frying pan with a little olive oil.
- In the meantime, bring your salted water to a boil. Boil the broccoli rabe for 5 minutes, remove, strain and mix it into the garlic and anchovy mixture.
- Add the orchiette to the boiling water and cook until it is *al dente*.
- When the pasta is finished cooking, add it to your warm anchovy broccoli mixture, making sure you bring some of the pasta water with you to the pan. Stir gently to mix all of the ingredients.
- Add salt and pepper to taste.
- Serve immediately with a sprinkling of breadcrumbs and grated pecorino. A wedge of lemon is also a nice garnish.

La Strada Delle Orecchiette

In the city of Bari there is a section of town called *Bari Vecchia* which means old city. This part of the city is a maze of twisting and turning streets. It is within these charming walls, on the Via Arco Basso, where you find local women sitting on their front stoops making authentic orecchiette pasta. Unofficially, it's known as the Strada Delle Orecchiette. Up and down the little alleyway, the orecchiette ladies sit at their rustic wooden work tables, dusted in semolina, rolling out dough, cutting, twisting and shaping it into orecchiette shapes. The pasta shapes are left to dry in the sun in big wooden-framed trays, and then scooped into little plastic bags to sell to people passing by.

Breadcrumbs are used to garnish pasta. Since many items like cream, cheese and succulent meats were considered a luxury in the poorer south, meals were adapted to make use of what was accessible and affordable. Bread, vegetables and pasta are the staples in Puglia, so bread crumbs were often used to garnish a dish instead of cheese.

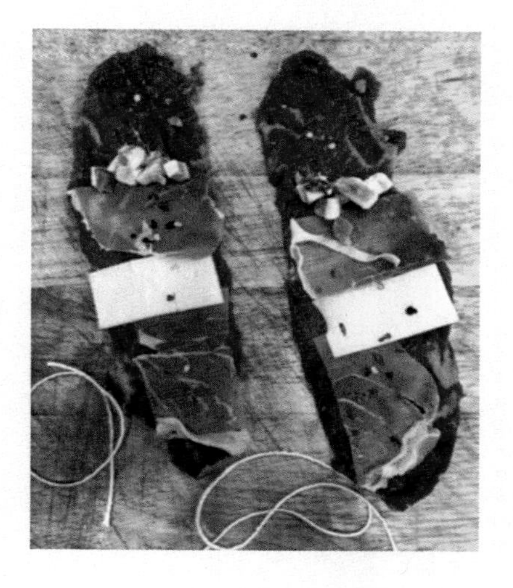

BRACIOLE AL SUGO PUGLIESI

Braciole are little stuffed meat pockets cooked in Salsa Pomodoro Classico and served over Puglia's classic pasta, orchiette. As many say, "It's so good it will make you cry!"

INGREDIENTS

SERVES 6

- Salsa Pomodoro Classico.
- 12 slices of top sirloin sliced thinly into sheets. Unless you have mad knife skills, ask your butcher to slice the beef into very thin sheets. You should still pound it a bit yourself so they are as thin as you can get them.
- 12 slices provolone cheese
- 12 slices of pancetta
- 1/4 cup freshly grated Pecorino Romano cheese
- 1/2 cup chopped Italian parsley
- Hot pepper flakes to taste
- Cotton butcher's string to tie the braciole
- 2 tbs. olive oil and 4 tbs. butter
- Gremolada: Mix the zest of 2 lemons with 4 cloves of garlic and 1/4 cup of Italian parsley, chopped fine.

DIRECTIONS

1. Start with a batch of Salsa Pomodoro Classico.
2. On each slice of beef, lay out a slice of provolone, a slice of pancetta and a sprinkle of Pecorino. If you like it spicy, add a sprinkle of hot pepper flakes to taste.
3. Roll up the sheet of beef to form a roll and tie it securely with butcher's twine.
4. Heat the olive oil and butter in a skillet and brown the braciole on all sides until nicely caramelized.
5. Simmer the braciole in the Salsa Pomodoro until tender.
6. Serve over orecchiette pasta and garnish with gremolada.

CAPONATA

IL TIMPANO

Sicily

THE FOOD OF SICILY IS THE CUISINE OF THE SUN AND SEA. THE LAND IS EXTREMELY FERTILE, THANKS TO THE REGION'S HOT DRY CLIMATE. THE MEDITERRANEAN SEA THAT SURROUNDS THE ISLAND PROVIDES THE BOUNTY OF THE SEA. RECIPES ARE INSPIRED BY THE MANY DIFFERENT CONQUERORS WHO RULED OVER THE ISLAND AND LEFT A DISH OR TWO — THE GREEKS, ARABS, NORMANS, SPANISH AND EVEN THE ENGLISH.

PAIR THESE WINES WITH THE RECIPES FROM THE REGION: NERO D'AVOLA, FRAPPATO AND PERRICONE.

ARANCINI

CANNOLI

CAPONATA

Caponata is a Sicilian sweet and sour version of ratatouille. Some people add raisins to this recipe to add pops of juicy sweetness, but I like mine more savory. It's traditionally served as an appetizer, spread on grilled bread, but it also makes a great veggie pasta sauce or served with fish.

INGREDIENTS
SERVES 4-6

- 2 large eggplants, sliced 3/4" thick, sweated with kosher salt and cut into cubes, skin left on.
- 3 tbs. salt
- 1/4 cup olive oil
- 4 celery stalks, chopped
- 2 medium-size zucchini, chopped
- 1 onion, chopped
- 14 oz. canned tomatoes, chopped
- 1 tbs. sugar
- 1/2 cup red wine vinegar
- 1/2 cup capers, rinsed
- 1/4 cup green olives, sliced
- Salt and pepper to taste

DIRECTIONS

1. Sweat the eggplant: Slice the eggplant into 3/4" thick slices and line them up on paper towels. Sprinkle with coarse Kosher salt. Let sit for 1/2 hr. You will see that the salt causes the eggplant to sweat out extra moisture. Use plenty of dry paper towels to wipe off the salt and moisture. Then salt the other side and let them sit for another 1/2 hr. Wipe and dry the slices well and cube.
2. Heat the oil in a skillet until hot but not smoking, and sauté the eggplant cubes until golden brown; remove and drain on paper towels. Put the celery in the skillet and sauté in the same oil until it is golden brown, remove and drain.
3. Add the onion and the zucchini to the cooking oil, sauté until they are soft, then add the tomato to the skillet. Cook the onion-zucchini-tomato mixture for 10 minutes, stirring frequently until very soft.
4. In a saucepan, combine the sugar and vinegar and heat. Add the capers and olives and simmer 10 minutes. Add the eggplant, celery and onion-zucchini-tomato mixture. Simmer about 5 minutes. Remove from the heat and allow the caponata to stand in room temperature for about an hour before serving. It's even better if you serve it the next day.
5. Serve on toasted bread, on pasta or on the side of fish.

ARANCINI

Arancini means "little oranges" in Italian. They are stuffed rice balls — crispy on the outside and soft and moist on the inside. In Catania, the rice ball is formed into a conical shape, inspired by Mount Etna. Make the risotto and ragú a ahead of time or use leftovers. I use two classic stuffings: mozzarella cheese with prosciutto and peas with ragú and mozzarella, but feel free to be creative and stuff them with anything you'd like.

INGREDIENTS
ABOUT 18 ARANCINI

Make a batch of **Risotto alla Milanese** and chill. Make the **Ragú**.

For the rice balls:
- 4 tbs. Parmigiano-Reggiano cheese, grated
- 4 tbs. unsalted butter, frozen
- 1 egg
- 2 tbs. fresh or dried parsley

For the two fillings:
- 9, 1/2" mozzarella squares, 18 large frozen peas and a few cups of ragú
- 9, 1/2" mozzarella squares and 4 slices of prosciutto, chopped.

For the batter:
- 2 1/2 cups water
- 2 1/3 cups all-purpose flour
- 1 pinch salt

For the breading and frying:
- 3 cups breadcrumbs
- Corn oil

DIRECTIONS

1. **Make the risotto.** Make the risotto as directed on page 236. Then fold in the frozen butter, grated cheese, herbs and beaten egg. Chill well.
2. **Shape the rice balls:** Use an ice cream scoop to form uniform balls. Wet your hands in some water to shape and seal the rice ball starch. Place them on a tray lined with parchment and leave them to rest for half an hour so that the rice becomes compact, making the filling process easier.

3 **Fill the rice balls:** Again, wet your hands. Hold the rice ball with one hand. With the thumb of the other, create large indent and begin to enlarge it by gently pushing the rice both downward and to the sides.

4 Fill half of the rice balls with a cheese square, a bit of ragú and 2 peas.

5 Fill half of the rice balls with a cheese square and a bit of the chopped prosciutto.

6 Close the rice around the fillings and gently re-shape them into a ball, working it so the surface is smooth and compact, without any holes or small cracks. Line the balls up on a sheet pan lined with parchment paper.

7 Whisk the water, flour and salt together for the batter. The batter serves to seal the rice and help the breading become brown, thick and crunchy. Line it up next to a bowl of breadcrumbs and the pot of hot oil. Have a sheet pan lined with paper towels.

8 **Fry the rice balls:** Again, wet your hands in water and Immerse the rice ball into the batter. Let the excess drip off, then cover thickly with the breadcrumbs, pressing them into the batter with your hands to ensure they stick. Continue to press and re-form the rice ball until it's tight.

9 When all of the rice balls are formed, heat the oil and deep fry each until lightly golden. Set on the paper towels.

10 Garnish with ragú or a simple sprinkling of Parmigiano-Reggiano cheese. Serve immediately or reheat them in the oven just before serving.

CANNOLI

Cannoli are the most famous dessert in Sicily. Here is the classic recipe, but you can of course, make it your own. There is only one rule: cannoli must be filled just before serving to enjoy all their crunchiness!

INGREDIENTS
12 - 14 SERVINGS

For the shells:

- 1 cup all-purpose flour
- 1/4 cup sugar, 1/2 tsp. cinnamon powder and 1 tsp. salt
- 4 tbs. very cold unsalted butter, chunked into small pieces
- 1 egg for the dough + 1 egg white to glue the shells
- 3 tbs. of Marsala wine
- Plenty of peanut oil (for frying)
- **Cannoli tubes**

For the filling:

- 1.5 cups whole milk ricotta, drained overnight in a thin sieve sitting over a bowl. Make sure it is dry before you use it.
- 1/4 cup mascarpone cheese, 1/4 cup heavy cream
- 1/4 powdered sugar, plus more for garnish
- 2 tsp. pure vanilla extract, zest of 1 fresh lemon, 1/4 tsp. salt

Garnish: Mini dark chocolate chips, chopped pistachios, candied fruit or powdered sugar

DIRECTIONS

1 Make the shells. In a large bowl, combine flour, sugar, cinnamon and salt in a KitchenAid. Using the pastry hook, fold in the chunks of cold butter and mix until the flour starts to clump. Add the egg and Marsala wine and mix together until the dough forms into a ball.

2 Knead the dough for 2 minutes and reform into a ball, wrap well in plastic. Let it rest for 1 hour in the refrigerator.

3 Gently roll out the dough on a floured board until it is at least 1/8" thin. Cut out 5" circles with a pastry ring or the rim of a jar.

4 Gently remove each circle from the work surface and wrap it around the cannoli tube. Wet the ends of the disk with a bit of the egg white and press well to seal. Make sure you create a good seal. This will prevent the cannoli from opening during cooking.

5 Fry for 2 or 3 minutes in plenty of peanut oil until golden. The oil should be deep enough to submerge the pastry roll. Do not crowd the oil with the rolls and don't move the rolls around during frying. Drain on paper towels, and let cool before sliding the shells off of the tubes.

6 Make the filling. Combine all of the ingredients and mix well. Just before serving, put the cheese mixture into a pastry bag and fill the shells. Garnish and serve immediately.

IL TIMPANO

In the movie, *Big Night*, Stanley Tucci and Tony Shalub play Italian immigrant brothers who lovingly prepare a dish called the *Timpano di Pasta* for a special event in their restaurant. It is meticulously sculpted during the day, carefully unmolded in the kitchen, and finally wheeled out to be sliced, dramatically unveiling the luscious layers inside. Their guests take their first bite and swoon.

I watch the movie every New Year's Eve and make the timpano. *Timpano* means drum. It's a deep dish pie filled to the brim with Italian yumminess. It takes a bit of effort, but the presentation is beautiful and the taste, divine. You'll need to prepare a few things beforehand, so make sure you review this recipe before you plan to cook. These are the ingredients we like to use, but please feel free to make it your own.

INGREDIENTS
SERVES 8

For the drum: 2 lbs. pasta dough.

Salsa Pomodoro Classico

Italian Sausage links. 1 lb. baked, sliced into 1" thick rounds

Meatballs. Combine the ingredients with your hands, form into small meatballs and fry.

- 1/4 pound each: ground veal, pork and beef
- 1/2 cup bread crumbs softened with 2 tbs. milk
- 1/2 cup Parmigiano-Reggiano cheese
- 2 large eggs
- Season with 1 tbs. chopped parsley, 1 clove minced garlic, 1 tbs. salt and 1 tbs. pepper.

For the filling layers: You'll need a 6-quart, heavy enamel casserole pot or Dutch oven to assemble and bake the timpano.

- 6-7 cups of Salsa Pomodoro Classico
- 1 lb. dried bucatini pasta, cooked to very *al dente*. Some people use ziti pasta, but I like the bucatini because it holds all of the ingredients together, so you get cleaner slices.
- 4 large eggs, beaten
- 2 cups Genoa salami cut into bite-sized cubes
- 2 cups provolone cheese cut into bite-sized cubes
- 3 hard boiled eggs, halved, room temperature
- Meatballs and sausage chunks, room temperature
- 1 cup finely grated Parmeseano-Reggiano cheese

DIRECTIONS

1. Prepare the Salsa Pomodoro Classico, meatballs, sausage and fresh dough ahead of time.
2. When you are ready to make the timpano, bring the salted water to a boil. Partially cook the bucatini until it is very al dente. About 7 minutes. Pull it out with a little pasta water and cool in a bowl for a few minutes before you add 3 cups of the room temperature tomato sauce and the beaten eggs. Mix and set aside.
3. Roll out the fresh pasta dough to create the drum. Generously grease the baking pot and follow the directions pictured on the next page to line the pot with the dough.
4. Cut a circle of parchment paper to diameter of the pot. You will use this to gently push down the layers to help them meld in the baking process.
5. Layer the ingredients in the drum. Begin by covering the bottom of the pot with at least 1" of the plain tomato sauce. Top with 1/3 of the pasta, tomato/egg sauce mix.
6. Layer in the boiled egg halves, salami and provolone cubes. Dust with a little of the parmesean cheese. Top with another 1/3 of the pasta, tomato/egg sauce mix. Press down lightly with the parchment to condense the layers.
7. Layer in the meatballs and Italian sausage. Dust with a little of the parmesean cheese. Top with the last 1/3 of the pasta, tomato/egg sauce mix. Press down lightly with the parchment to condense the layers.
8. Finish with a very thick layer of plain tomato sauce. Sprinkle with the Parmesean. Stretch the dough over the drum and seal with water. Press down on the drum gently one more time to condense the ingredients.
9. Bake at 350°F for about an hour until the dough is lightly browned. Cover with tin foil and continue baking about 30 to 45 minutes until the timpano is cooked through and the inside temperature is 125°F. Use a cooking thermometer and monitor carefully.
10. Remove from the oven and allow to cool, uncovered, in the pot for at least 30 minutes. This will allow the timpano to cool and contract away from the sides of the pot so you can slide it out more easily without it cracking. Use a spatula or knife to gently separate any part of the dough that is still attached.
11. Invert a large serving platter or cutting board over the top of the timpano. Hold the platter and pot tightly together and flip gently. The timpano should slide out easily. Allow it to cool for 20 more minutes.
12. Using a long, serrated knife, slice the timpano like you would a layer cake into thick, individual slices. What you'll find is a cross-section of all of the ingredients that look beautiful on a plate. You can garnish with more tomato sauce, parsley and cheese.

1. Roll out the dough so it is about 1/16" thick and a in a circle that measures long enough in diameter to cover the bottom, sides and top of the pot.

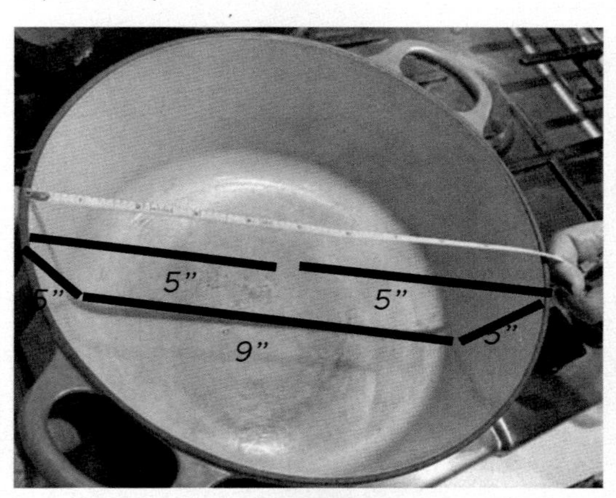

2. A 6-quart casserole needs a pasta drum dough circle that measures about 29" in diameter. Measure the 5" top flap + 5" deep side + 9" bottom + 5" deep side + 5" top flap = 29"

3. Fold the dough circle in half and then in half again, forming a triangle. Place the dough sheet in the pot and unfold it so it comes up the sides of the pot.

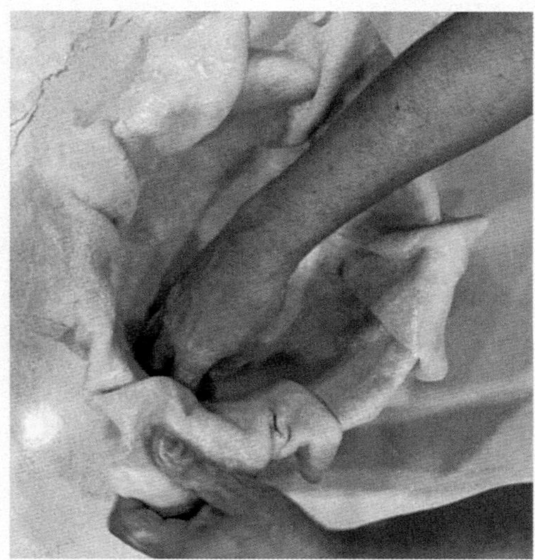

4. Use your hands to secure the dough snugly to the bottom and sides of the pot. Let the excess dough fall over the top rim of the pot.

5. Layer the meats and cheeses with the pasta/sauce/egg mixture, which will help bind all of the ingredients together.

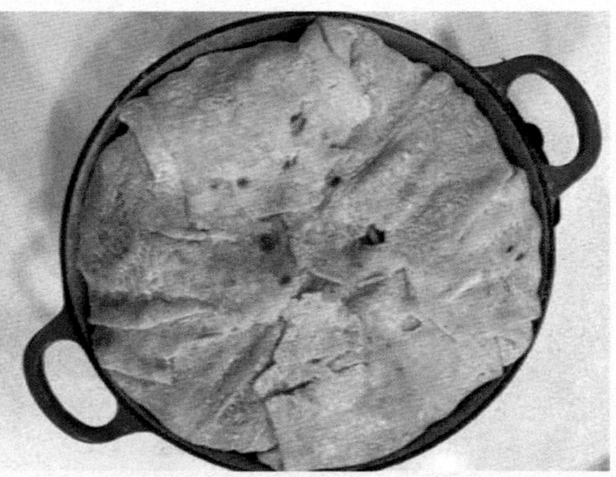

6. Bring the excess dough over and top off the drum. You can cut off any excess dough and seal the flaps together with a pastry brush and a little water.

MAKING MEMORIES

BY CHRIS SERIO MARTIN

It's time to go. After reading Sandy's book, I bet you are no longer overwhelmed by your dream to travel to Italy.

Sandy, my sister, influenced my own inner adventuress, and I hope she inspires yours as well. Travelers — people who move way beyond "taking a vacation" and approach new ports of call with curiosity and adventure — know that when they travel somewhere, something changes inside and they return, well, different.

On the piano in my home are a collection of family photos from our travels. The most cherished are from the time Sandy took our large Italian family to Italy. My young son's chocolate gelato melting all over his grinning face as he sits in front of the Colosseum. My brother, Danny, smiling contently and listening to family stories in a Firenze ristorante. And my favorite, us four Serio siblings with my dad sharing a moment of laughter in a villa in Umbria, a glass of vino nobile in our hands. Sandy inspired those memories and took us on the most glorious, memorable trip for our family.

When Sandy invites you to come along with her on an adventure, know that it will create memories you cannot even anticipate. You will return changed and more full of the beauty, history and friendships the world has to offer. You will look through your travel memories and be grateful to have had such an extraordinary experience. And dare I say, you will be hungry for the next opportunity to pack your bag for the next adventure.

Andiamo!

Left *Our family's 2004 villa at Lake Trasimeno in Umbria with dad, Mike Serio, and siblings Mike Danny, Chris and Sandy.*

Below *Sibs in Assisi*

Photos by Todd Martin

Contributors

JANETTE TEPAS IMAGES

Janette became a Certified International Tour manager in 2010. Since then, she has worked and traveled with me extensively, leading tours throughout Europe. Janette is also is an artist and professional photographer, and has contributed some of her amazing photographs of Italy to this book. There is a thrill that comes with being surrounded by the beautiful landscapes, art and history of the Old World, and she gets great joy from sharing amazing photography moments with her guests. If you are interested in more of her work, contact her at *janettetepasimages.com*.

ALESSANDRO CECCHI
ITALY OPERATIONS

Ales lives in Siena and has worked with Che Bella Tour since 2010. He has his finger on the pulse of everything happening throughout Italy and keeps abreast of new, exciting and off-the-beaten-path experiences. We work closely together, creating rich travel itineraries. Whether I'm on tour with my guests, or they are traveling independently with our Concierge Travel Services, Ales keeps a watchful eye on all.

CINZIA TREVISAN
ITALY OPERATIONS

Cinzia belongs to a proud Venetian family, and has worked with Che Bella Tours in Venice and The Veneto Region since 2009. She has contributed some great insights into this book and made sure my sometimes "creative" Italian phrases are correct.

Cinzia earned a master's degree in The Economics and Management of Arts and Cultural Activities, focusing on international law, the protection of cultural heritage, UNESCO and sustainable tourism. She has dedicated herself to the dissemination of Venetian culture, the restoration of Venetian art and is the local expert for Che Bella Tour's guests who travel to Venice.

VICCI RODGERS
CONTENT EDITOR

Vicci's youth was spent relocating whenever her Naval Captain Dad was reassigned. She spent part of her 18th year as an exchange student with AFS Intercultural Programs in the Philippines. Her J-School training from UW Madison helped guide her career, as did family roots that lead back to Edgar Allen Poe. Vicci's time with Borg-Warner Corp. brought her to Chicago where she met and started The Rodgers Group, LTD., a marketing consulting firm, where she began many years of collaboration with Sandy's design firm, Serio Design. Vicci's keen eye has always been part of Sandy's projects ... the rest of the story continues to be written.

CHRIS SERIO MARTIN
MAKING MEMORIES

Chris Serio Martin is a published journalist, emerging artist and women's rights advocate with UN Women USA. She loves living in Sarasota, Florida, but her passport is always at the ready. Like her sister, Sandy, she is an adventuress who loves to learn and explore this marvelous world. She is a graduate of Northwestern University and earned her master's degree from the University of Illinois. She considers travel, curiosity and engagement with the world her continuing education. Check out Chris' Spirit on Fire artwork, writing projects and UN Women engagement at *csmartindesign.com*.

CHEF DANNY SERIO
COOKBOOK

When Danny was happy, he cooked. When Danny was sad, he cooked. So after studying at Northern Illinois University, he attended Kendall Culinary College. His career has taken him all over the U.S., including positions in Sonoma, West Palm Beach, Atlanta, Alabama, Chicago and Denver. He has also has run a catering company and opened two restaurants. Danny used that experience to redirect and become a food broker and restaurant consultant in 2002. Today, he is the Corporate Sales Trainer and Dairy Sales Trainer for Key Impact Sales. He continues to do cooking demonstrations and catering and is the head chef at the "Che Bella Tours Test Kitchen."

GINGER WHEELER
COPY EDITOR

Ginger is a marketing communications specialist based in Chicago. A graduate of the University of Illinois, she has a background in a variety of disciplines including development, copywriting, editing, and the management of print, video and social media. An avid traveler, Ginger worked closely with Sandy on this book, not just dotting the i's and crossing the it's, but providing invaluable input and insights.

DAVID BRYANT
WINE

After a successful 30-year career as an attorney, David traded his briefcase for a wine glass and began a path which has led him to pass various levels of examination from the Court of Master Sommeliers and the Wine and Spirit Education Trust. A frequent and avid traveler, David now teaches and writes about wine.

Acknowledgements

The travel industry was hit particularly hard during the COVID-19 pandemic. The blessing of time during this period, however, allowed me to write this book. I couldn't have done it without the people below.

Grazie a tutti!

The people of Italy hold a very special place in my heart. This book would not have been possible without the support and insight of my in-country partners, guides, concierges, restaurateurs, chefs, drivers and friends, who welcomed me into their country and homes, taught me about their culture and kept an eye on me. I've been listening!

A heartfelt thank you to **my cherished guests** who have traveled with me all these years. I appreciate your continued support and friendship and look forward to creating new memories together again.

Special thanks to **my contributors** Janette Tepas, Cinzia Trivisan, Alessandro Cecchi, Vicci Rodgers, Chris Serio Martin, Ginger Wheeler, Danny Serio and David Bryant, as well as my graphics editor, Don Zegler, for your talent and expertise.

I am so grateful for **my friends**, whose time, insights and encouragement helped me tighten up this book to create not just an entertaining memoir, but also a useful tool, especially Kristi Kreamer, Michelle Friedman, Catherine Pagone, Tina Kelly and Mary Lynn Veatch.

Sending out big "*Ciao!*" to **my fellow road warriors.** What a ride it has been! Thank you for your companionship, input, hard work, bright faces and good humor. I look forward to our continued collaboration.

To my family. Thank you to my husband, Odell Isaac, who kept the home fires burning, enabling me to focus on this writing effort while the world — and my business — was at a stand still during the COVID-19 pandemic. Thank you, love, for holding me up. To my very best work, Jackson Gregory and Joe Gregory. Thank you for your unconditional support of my life, my work and my travels. To everyone in my crazy loud, close-knit family: thanks for being my sounding boards, recipe consultants, sous chefs, kitchen clean-up crew, taste testers and all around fan club. Wherever we gather as a family is home, and my memories are wrapped tightly around all of you. To "The Unit," my Board of Directors Chris Serio Martin, Mike Serio and Danny Serio. Chris, thank you for the not-so-gentle-at-all urging to start this project and the encouragement to keep on going. Mike, for ski breaks and fresh, mountain air. And Danny, for being three doors down, working out the recipe details and hanging out with me every step of the way to make sure I finished this thing.

To **my service pup in training, Frisco**. This big, black beast is the fifth dog I have trained for Canine Partners of the Rockies. During the early days of quarantine, I was cancelling tours, refunding trip money and scared out of my mind. You came into my life and gave me joy. Thanks for hanging on every word I read aloud and assuring me that my book was genius. By the time this book is out in the world, I hope we both will be as well, doing what we were built to do.

Want to be notified when Sandy has a new release?

Go to ***chebellatours.com*** to sign up for our newsletter, ***The Bella Buzz***, and be the first to know.

The Bella Buzz is our quick-read newsletter chock full of concise articles that are both informative and entertaining, with equal parts creative inspiration, travel news, tips and tricks, and recipes, as well as tour itineraries and special promotions.

Consider traveling with Che Bella Tours.

Go to ***chebellatours.com*** for details on our exciting, worldwide tour itineraries.

There are a few ways you can travel with Che Bella Tours:

1. Small Group Tour. Join a Che Bella Tours small group tour, and enjoy their in-depth knowledge of food and wine, art and style, history and culture — all surrounded with breathtaking views. Consider our many trip offerings, and see what we have on our Tour Calendar. If you don't find what you're looking for, let's get something started!

2. Concierge Travel Services. Do you have a personal travel dream? Want to take your significant other or your family on a trip of a lifetime tailored just for you? We take the time to ask the right questions and then craft custom itineraries into a high-quality, worry-free travel experience. Whether you travel with a Che Bella Tour Director or independently, you will feel cared for the entire way ... even when travel realities throw you a curve ball.

3. Trailblazer Tours. It is a big world and we want to see as much of it as we can. In the spirit of adventure, Che Bella Tours offers our guests a special discount when we create tours to new places. While new, these trips are sound in their preparation and detail, as well as in the care of local expert guides and drivers. We're up for new adventures. Let's blaze the trail together!

Andiamo! Let's go!

Sandy Gregory

Founder, Che Bella Tours

chebellatours.com

sandy@chebellatours.com

If you liked my book, would you mind taking a moment to **write a review** on Amazon? Even a short review helps, and it would mean the world to me. Go to **Your Orders,** click **write a customer review** in the Customer Reviews section, select a star rating. Add text, photos or videos and click **Submit**. A green check mark shows for successfully submitted ratings. Grazie!

TRAVEL CHEAT SHEETS

IMPORTANT CONTACTS IN ITALY

PACKING CHECKLISTS

ITALIAN LANGUAGE CHEAT SHEETS

Scan this code to go to the Che Bella Tours Marketplace for direct links to products, books and films listed in this book.

IMPORTANT CONTACTS AND EMERGENCY NUMBERS

U.S. Department of State Warnings and Advisories
state.gov/travelers/

U.S. Embassy Rome
via Vittorio Veneto 121
(+39) 06.46741

U.S. Consulate General Florence
Lungarno Vespucci, 38
(+39) 055.266.951

U.S. Consulate General Milan
via Principe Amedeo, 2/10
(+39) 02.290351

U.S. Consulate General Naples
Piazza della Repubblica
(+39) 081.583.8111

Pan-European Emergencies
(+39) 112

Police Emergencies
(+39) 113

Medical Emergencies and Ambulance
(+39) 118

PERSONAL CONTACT NUMBERS WHILE TRAVELING

- ☐ ______________________________
- ☐ ______________________________
- ☐ ______________________________
- ☐ ______________________________
- ☐ ______________________________
- ☐ ______________________________
- ☐ ______________________________
- ☐ ______________________________
- ☐ ______________________________
- ☐ ______________________________
- ☐ ______________________________

Carry-On Checklist

Money and Documents

- ❑ Passport
- ❑ Travel and tour documents
- ❑ Copy of prescriptions
- ❑ Travel purse or daypack
- ❑ Money belt and your cash
- ❑ Pacsafe Portable Safe

Electronics

- ❑ Mobile phone and/or tablet
- ❑ Pre-downloaded movies and books
- ❑ Earbuds or headphones
- ❑ Mobile phone wrist band
- ❑ Multiple charging cords
- ❑ Portable charger
- ❑ UPWADE mini power strip
- ❑ Converter/adaptor
- ❑ Memory cards
- ❑ BAGSMART travel cable organizer

For the plane

- ❑ An extra set of clothes
- ❑ Large pashmina scarf
- ❑ Disinfectant and deodorant wipes
- ❑ Eye mask
- ❑ Compression knee socks
- ❑ Flip flops or light slippers to wear on the plane and in your hotel room
- ❑ Slipper-type anklet socks
- ❑ Silk eye mask
- ❑ Collapsible water bottle
- ❑ Inflatable neck pillow
- ❑ Macks Silicone earplugs

Medications and Sundries

- ❑ Prescription medication
- ❑ Any other personal medications
- ❑ Sundown Naturals Melatonin
- ❑ Zzz-Quil with Melatonin
- ❑ Toothbrush, toothpaste and mouthwash
- ❑ Aquafor
- ❑ Neutrogena face wipes in travel packets
- ❑ The Inkey List Hyaluronic Acid serum
- ❑ Face and hand moisturizer
- ❑ Saline nasal spray
- ❑ Afrin nasal spray
- ❑ Compeed Blister Bandages
- ❑ Travel pack of tissues
- ❑ Sunscreen
- ❑ Ziplock bags
- ❑ Cosmetics
- ❑ Non-perishable snacks such as Baby Bell cheese and nuts

Personal Notes

- ❑ ____________________
- ❑ ____________________
- ❑ ____________________
- ❑ ____________________
- ❑ ____________________
- ❑ ____________________

Checked-Bag Checklist

Recommended for a ten-day to two-week trip:

- ❑ LugLoc GPS luggage tracker
- ❑ Spacesaver compression packing bags
- ❑ Rolled-up nylon duffel bag
- ❑ Toiletry bag with travel size bottles
- ❑ Styling tools, check the voltages
- ❑ Bathing suit, if applicable
- ❑ Ziplock bags
- ❑ Wine Skin travel bags
- ❑ Dryer sheets
- ❑ Tide pods or Sink Suds
- ❑ Downy Wrinkle Release
- ❑ Travel Smart Digital Luggage Scale
- ❑ Kolumbo "Unbreakable" travel umbrella and disposable rain ponchos
- ❑ Door stop wedge for hotel safety
- ❑ Portable humidifier
- ❑ Safety whistle
- ❑ Tactical flashlight

Men

- ❑ 3 shirts, made of quick dry material
- ❑ 2 golf or collared shirts
- ❑ 2 basic t-shirts (No sports teams)
- ❑ 2 pairs slacks
- ❑ 1 pair jeans
- ❑ 1 pair dress shorts (to the knees)
- ❑ 2 lightweight sweaters
- ❑ A dinner jacket (optional)
- ❑ 5 pairs underwear
- ❑ 5 pairs socks
- ❑ 1 lightweight jacket, waterproof
- ❑ 1 sun hat

Footwear

- ❑ 1 pair walking shoes or sandals such as the Jungle Moc slip-on shoe
- ❑ 1 pair black or neutral-colored athletic shoes
- ❑ 1 pair casual dress shoes
- ❑ 1 pair flip flops for the hotel floor
- ❑ Rubz Ball and Yoga Toes

Women

- ❑ 3 basic tank tops or camisoles for layering
- ❑ 3 basic nicely fitting t-shirts
- ❑ 3 nice blouses
- ❑ 1-2 skirts (skorts from Athleta or Title 9 are a nice option for daytime touring)
- ❑ 2 dresses
- ❑ 3 pairs pants and/or capris: 1 black, 1 tan or light color and 1 pair of crisp jeans
- ❑ 2 lightweight sweaters
- ❑ 1 pair yoga pants
- ❑ 5 pairs socks
- ❑ 5 pairs underwear
- ❑ 1 lightweight jacket, waterproof
- ❑ 1 sun hat
- ❑ Scarves to dress up an outfit and cover shoulders and knees, or wait and buy a few in Italy

Footwear

The streets of Europe are lined with cobblestones, so keep your spike or kitten heels at home.

Think about bringing:

- ❑ 2 pairs walking shoes and/or sandals to switch out every day. Bjorn, Clarks and Sketchers Walkers are good brands
- ❑ A low-rise wedge sandal for the evening
- ❑ 1 pair comfortable flat boots in cooler weather
- ❑ 1 pair flip flops for the hotel floor
- ❑ Rubz Ball and Yoga Toes

Learn a Little Italian

With languages, you are at home anywhere.

Edward De Waal

GREETINGS

Hello

Ciao (informal) (Chow!)

Salve (formal) (*Saal*-vay)

What is your name?

Come si chiama?

(*Koh*-meh see *kyah*-mah?)

My name is _______.

Mi chiamo _______.

(Mee *kyah*-moh)

Glad to meet you.

Piacere

(Pyah-*cheh*-reh)

How are you?

Come sta?

(*Koh*-meh stah?)

Good, thank you.

Bene grazie.

(*Beh*-neh *grah*-tsee-eh)

And you?

E tu? (informal) (Ay *too*?)

E lei? (formal) (Ay *lay*?)

Goodbye

Ciao (informal) (Chow!)

Arrivederci (formal)

(Ahr-*ree*-veh-*dehr*-chee)

GREETINGS

See you later.

A dopo.

(Ah *doe* - poe)

See you soon.

A presto.

(Ah *pres*-toe)

Good morning .

Buongiorno.

(Bwohn *johr*-noh)

Good evening.

Buonasera.

(*Bwoh*-nah *seh*-rah)

Goodnight

Buonanotte.

(Bwoh–nah *noh*–teh)

Please

Per favore

(Pehr fah-*voh*-reh)

Thank you

Grazie

(gra-*zee*-ay)

You're welcome.

Prego.

(*Preh*-goh)

Like many first-generation immigrants, my great-grandparents and grandparents wanted to integrate into American culture. So they made it a point not to teach their native language to children or grandchildren. The only way to prepare myself for living and working in Italy was through classroom Italian. I became a competent Italian speaker when I lived in Florence. Years later, I built on that working as a tour director.

Language, however, remains one of the most challenging parts of my job. I am a work in progress, persevering and enduring kind corrections and giggles from my Italian colleagues. While most of them speak English, communicating with them in Italian is a sign of respect. Here are a few of my cheat sheets. They are the size of a Euro bill, so will fit nicely into your wallet. Cut them out and keep them handy when you travel.

SPEAK ENGLISH?

Excuse me. (to get attention)

Scusi. (*skooh*–zee)

Do you speak English?

Parla Inglese?

(*Parh*-la een-*glay*-zeh)

Yes Sì (See) **No** (Noh)

Please speak slowly.

Parla lentamente per favore.

(*Parh*-la len-*ta*-men-tay *pehr* fah-voh-reh)

I didn't understand. Could you repeat?

Non ho capito. Può ripetere?

(Non oh ka-*pee*-tow. Pwoe ri-*peh*-teh-ray)

I don't understand.

Non capisco.

(Non kah-*pee*-skoh)

I'm sorry.

Mi dispiace.
(Mee dees-*pyah*-cheh)

DIRECTIONS

Entrance

Entrata (En-trah-tah)

Exit

Uscita (Ooh-shee-tah)

Excuse me.

Permesso.

(Pehr-mehs-soh)

Where is... ?

Dov'è...?

(Doh-veh)

To the left.

Giri a sinistra.

(Gee-ree a see–nee-stra)

To the right.

Giri a destra.
(Gee-ree a deh-stra)

Go straight ahead.

Vada dritto.

(Vada dree-toh)

THE AIRPORT

Welcome!

Benvenuto!

(Ben-ven-*ooo*-tow)

Customs

Controllo Passaporti

Departures

Partenze

Arrivals

Arrivi

Baggage Claim

Area Ritiro Bagagli

Lost and Found

Oggetti Smarriti

I'm missing a suitcase.

Mi manca una valigia.

(Mee *man*-ka oon-a va-*lee*-ja)

I need a porter.

Ho bisogno di un portiere.

(Oh *bee*-zon-yo un *port*-tee-*air*-ee)

This is for you.

Questo è per lei.

(*Kwest*-o ay *pear* lay)

TAXIS

Where can I get a taxi?

Dove posso prendere i taxi? (*Doh*-veh *poe*-so *pren*-dar-aye ee tahk-zee)

Can you take me to this address please?

Può portarmi a questo indirizzo, per favore?

(Pw-*oh* poor-*tahr*-mee ah *kwest*-oh een-*dee*-reets-zo pehr *fah*-voh-*reh*)

How much will it cost?

Quanto costerà?

(*Kwan*-toh kohst-eh-*rah*)

Please slow down!

Per favore, può andare più piano?

(*pehr* fah-voh-reh, *peew*-piaano)

Stop here.

Si fermi qui.

(See *fer*-mee kwee)

How much?

Quanto? (*Kwan*-toe)

Note: Tip a taxi driver by rounding up. For example, if your fare is 12 Euro, give him 15. If your fare is 28 Euro, give him 30.

THE TRAIN STATION

One ticket to ____, please.

Un biglietto di ____, per favore.

(Oon beel-yet-to di ______, pehr fah-voh-reh)

One way

Sola andata

(So-la an-da-ta)

Round trip

Andata e ritorno

(Ahn–dah-tah eh ree-torn-oh)

First class

Di prima classe

(Dee pree-ma kla-see)

Second class

Di seconda classe

(Dee se-kon-da kla-see)

How much?

Quanta costa?

(Kwahn-toh kohs-tah)

Which platform?

Da quale binario?

(Dah kwal-eh bee-nar-ee-oh)

ON THE TRAIN

Does this train go to ____?

Questro treno va a _____?

(kwe-stoh tre-noh vah ah _____)

Is this an express train?

È questo un treno rapido?

(Aye kwe-stoh oon tre-noh ra-pee-doh)

How many more stops?

Quante fermata ancora?

(Kwan-te fair-ma-tah an-kor-ah)

The next stop

La prossima fermata

(Lah pro-see-mah fair-ma-tah)

Where should I get off?

Dove devo scendere?

(Do-veh deh-voh shen-der-eh)

Do I have to change trains?

Devo cambiare treno?

(Deh-voh kam-bee-are-eh tre-noh)

We have these seats.

Abbiamo questi posti.

(Ah-bee-ah-moh kwes-tee pos-tee)

HOTEL CHECK IN

Hotel Albergo (Al-*bair*-go)

I have a reservation.

Ho una prenotazione.

(O *oo*-na *pre*-noh-*tatz-ee*-o-neh)

A room ...

Una camera ...

(Oona *cam*-mair-eh)

... with a king size bed

un letto matrimoniale

(oon *let*-toe ma-*tree*-mo-*nee*-a)

... with twin beds

due letti (*doo*-eh *let*-tee)

Please keep the air conditioning on all night.

Si prega di tenere l'aria condizionata accesa tutta la notte.

(See *pray*-ga dee *ten*-er-ay l'a-ria con-dit-*zeeo*-na-ta *too*-tee la *no*-tee.)

Tip: Some hotels turn the air conditioning off at midnight to save electricity, so inquire when you check in and ask them to keep it on through the night.

What floor is it on?

A che piano è?

(Ah keh *pya*-noh eh)

Is there an elevator?

C'e l'ascensore?

(Che *la*-shen-*sor*-eh)

What time is breakfast?

A che ora si fa la colazione di mattina?

(Ah keh *o*-rah see fa ko-*lat*-syo-neh)

What is the WiFi password?

Qual è la password Wi-Fi?

(*Kwal*-eh la password wee-fee)

I need more/another ...

Ho bisogno di un altro (a) ...

(Oh *bee*-zon-yo di un *al*-troh)

key chiave (*key-a*-veh)

bed letto (*let*-toh)

pillow cuscino (koo-*shee*-noh)

towel asciugamano (ah-*shug*-a-ma-noh)

soap sapone (sa-*pone*-eh)

blanket coperta (ko-*pear*-tah)

toilet paper carta igienica (*kar*-tah ee-*gen-ee*-kah)

May I have a quieter room?

Posso avere una stanza più tranquilla?

(*Po*-so ah-*ver*-eh oo-na *stan*-zah pyu tran-*kwee*-lah)

RESTAURANTS

We have a reservation for (time) for (how many) people.

Noi abbiamo una prenotazione per __ per __ persone.

(Noy ah-*biam*-oh oo-na *pren*-oh-*tatz*-io-nee)

Waiter Cameriere (ka-*mair*-*yair*-eh)

A menu please.

Il menu, per favore.

(Eel *men*-oo, *pehr* fah-voh-*reh*)

What do you recommend?

Che cosa mi consiglia?

(Kay *koh*-za mee kon-*seel*-yah)

I'd like ______.

Vorrei ______. (Vor-*ray*)

Excuse me, could you bring me

Scusi, potrei avere un __

knife cotello (koh-*tel*-loh)

fork forchetta (for-*ket*-ah)

spoon cucchiaio (koo-*chai*-oh)

napkin tovagliolo.

A glass of

Un bicchiere di

(OO-n beek-*kyeh*-reh)

A bottle of

Una bottiglia

(Una boht-*tee*-lyah)

red wine

vino rosso (*vee*-no *ro*-so)

white wine

vino bianco (*vee*-no be-*an*-co)

Where's the bathroom?

Dov'è il bagno?

(*Do*-vey eel *ban*-yo)

The check please.

Il conto, per favore.

(Eel *con*-to *pehr* fah-voh-*reh*)

Separate checks, please.

I conti separati, per favore.

(Ee *con*-tee sep-a-*ra*-tee, *pehr* fah-voh-*reh*)

Is the service included?

È incluso il servizio?

(Ey in-*kloo*-so eel ser-*vi*-zio)

This is for you.

Questo è per lei.

(*Kwest*-o ay pear lay)

Thank you. Everything was delicious.

Grazie, Tutto era delizioso.

(Gra-zee-ay, *too*-toe era dee-*liz*-*eeo*-so)

SHOPPING

Excuse me.

Mi scusi.

(Mee *skoo*-zee)

I just want to look around.

Vorrei solo dare un'occhiata in giro.

(Vor-*ray* solo *dar*-eh oon-ok-*kya*-ta een jee-ro)

Where can I find ... ?

Dove posso trovare ... ?

(*Do*-vay *poe*-so tro-*var*-eh)

Can you help me?

Puo aiutarmi?

(Pwo *I*-you-*tar*-me)

beautiful: Bello/Bella

cash register la cassa

on sale saldi

the same lo stesso

What size is this?

Di che taglia?

(Dee key *ta*-li-ah)

What? Che cosa?

Which? Quale?

How much? Quanto?

Can I taste please?

Posso assaggiare, per favore?

(*Poe*-so as-sa-*giar*-eh, pehr fah-voh-reh)

Is it a local product?

È un prodotto locale?

(Ay oon pro-*do*-toh lo-*ca*-leh)

I would like to buy it.

Lo vorrei comprare.

(Lo vor-*ray* com-*pra*-reh)

It is a bit too expensive.

È un po' troppo caro.

(Aye oon poe *troe*-poe *ka*-roh)

It's a good price.

È un buon prezzo.

(Aye oon bu-on *pre*-tzo)

Can you give me a better price?

Mi può fare un prezzo migliore?

(Mee pwo *fa*-ray oon *pre*-tzo mee-*lyo*-re)

I'll take it.

Lo prenderò. (Low pren-der-oh)

I want to pay with a credit card/cash.

Lo voglio pagare con carta di credito/in contanti.

(Low *vo*-lio pa-*gar*-eh con *kar*-ta dee kre-*di*-toh/een con-*tan*-tee)

THE PHARMACY

Help!

Aiuto! (Ay-*oo*-toh!)

I need a doctor.

Ho bisogno di un dottore.

(Oh *bee*-zon-yo dee oon dot-*or*-eh)

Do you have something for ...

Ha qualcosa contro il mal di ...

(Ha *kwal*-koza *con*-troh eel maal dee ...)

headache testa

stomach ache il mal di stomaco

fever la febbre

cough la tosse

insect bite la puntura d'insetto

cramps i crampi

a cut il taglio/la ferita

Can you make up this prescription for me?

Mi puo preparare questa ricetta, per favore?

(Mee pwo *pre*-atr-ar-eh *kwes*-ta ree-*chet*-ta, *pehr* fah-voh-*reh*)

Can you suggest something for ...

Mi puo indicare qualcosa contro ...

(Mee pwo ee-dee-*kar*-eh kwal-ko-za kon-tro)

back la schiena

chest il petto

eye l'occhio

ear l'orecchio

hand/wrist la mano/il polso

foot il piede

heart il cuore

legla gamba

lungs i polmoni

knee il ginocchio

mouth la bocca

neck il collo

shoulder la spalla

How much?

Quanto costa?

Made in the USA
Monee, IL
20 January 2023